Aurelia

Aurelia

Art and Literature Through the Mouth of the Fairy Tale

CAROL MAVOR

REAKTION BOOKS

For Marina Warner
and her beguiling magic (sombre and sweet), which feeds me

Published by Reaktion Books Ltd
Unit 32, Waterside
44–48 Wharf Road
London N1 7UX, UK
www.reaktionbooks.co.uk

First published 2017

Printed and bound in China by 1010 Printing International Ltd

A catalogue record for this book is available from the British Library

ISBN 978 1 78023 717 6

Contents

A book on fairy tales could not be written without the help of the great fairy-tale scholar Jack Zipes, who is also the key translator of the Grimms' tales. When citing one of their stories, I have tried to consistently use Zipes's translation of *The Original Folk and Fairy Tales of the Brothers Grimm: The Complete First Edition* (Princeton, NJ, and Oxford, 2014). However, I could not help borrowing quite a bit of sugar from Philip Pullman's delightful new English version of the tales (*Grimm Tales for Young and Old*, London, 2012), as well as a few pinches of salt from Zipes's translation of later versions of the stories (found in his *The Complete Fairy Tales*, London, 2007).

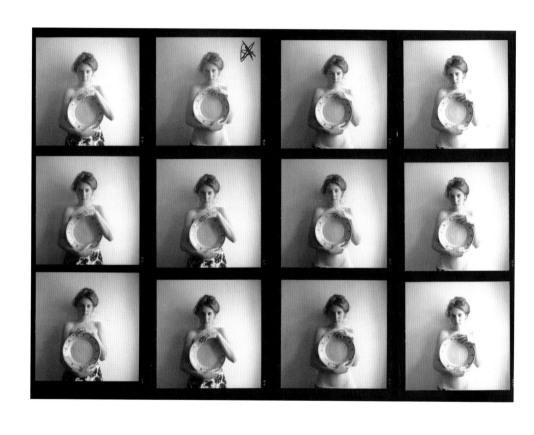

Preface: O

The opening of a tale . . . All we need is the word 'Once . . .' and we're off.

Philip Pullman, *Grimm Tales for Young and Old*

Your mouth opens clean as a cat's.

Sylvia Plath, 'Morning Song'

O, she says (because she loves to say O) . . .

Hailey Leithauser, 'O, She Says'

'A tone licked clean'

When we were children, our first fairy tales were aural, were oral. Many of the best stories came to us from the Brothers Grimm. The Grimms' tales are short, like the tail of a Manx cat. Their pared-down stories are to the point. They are an 'unseasoned telling'.[1] Baby food. 'A tone licked clean'.[2] 'No psychology . . . little interior life . . . if people are good, they are good, and if they're bad, they're bad.'[3] The Grimms' Once-upon-a-time O 'opens clean as a cat's'.[4] Once upon a time . . .[5] and we fall . . . into sleep.

Not unlike Alice, who after falling asleep, fell down the big O of the rabbit hole, where she would meet a cat who was all mouth. '"Well! I've often seen a cat without a grin," thought Alice; "but a grin without a cat! It's the most curious thing I ever saw in my life!"'[6]

An O is the mouth from which the fairy tale emerges. 'The mouth is always full, abundance itself.'[7] Yet, the letter O, full and abundant, looks like a numerical 0. Empty, not full.

Full and empty, an O is a zero is a doughnut hole. In the spirit of *The Wonderful Wizard of Oz*, the name of the popular doughnut holes sold at the American franchise Dunkin' Donuts is Munchkins (who in L. Frank Baum's story are little people full of business doing empty tasks).[8] As a child, I considered these little balls of cake glazed in sugar all around – the salvaged holes, the Munchkins – to be superior to the whole doughnut.

'The mouth
is always full,
abundance itself.'

The origin of the name of Oz may have come from Baum's eye landing on a filing cabinet labelled 'A–N' and 'O–Z'. With its circular iris and pupil hole, the eye (like the mouth) is an O. An O is the eye from which the fairy tale emerges.

We also know that Baum liked stories that caused him to exclaim 'Ohs' and 'Ahs' of wonder. The word Oz can be pronounced either way.[9]

Oh.

Ah.

We're off . . .

———

Introduction: I Am an Aurelian

An 'aurelia' is the pupa of an insect, which can reflect a brilliant golden colour, as the chrysalises of some butterflies do. Vladimir Nabokov, author and lepidopterist, was beguiled by 'those butterflies that have carved golden pupa, called also chrysalis, which hang from some surface in the open air . . . with golden knobs and plate-armor wingcases'.[1]

The origin of the word 'butterfly' is obscure, but it is possible that it has to do with golden butter. One thought is that the emergence of insects in warm weather coincided with butter-producing time. Another is that throngs of yellow Brimstones, one of the first butterflies to appear in the European summer, reminded people of the colour of butter. In folklore butterflies, or witches in the shape of butterflies, stole milk and butter.[2]

Aurelia is a feminine name, derived from the Latin *aureus* meaning golden. (Sylvia Plath's mother was named Aurelia. Gérard de Nerval wrote a short story about an ideal woman whose name was Aurélia.[3]) I think of a huge medieval manuscript, Nicholas of Lyra's Commentary on the Bible, *c.* 1270–1349, even bigger than a child's luxury picture book, with its fairy-tale gold leaf, marginalia of butterflies, strange metamorphoses and big ornamental letters. Note the 'D' of Deuteronomy that opens up the text like a gold-trimmed door unto another world. Note the multi-metamorphoses of the gold-spotted caterpillar-lion-man, with bird-feet made of coral, an aurelian-amphibian tail, who poses atop a flesh-coloured vegetal mushroom-jellyfish with blue tentacles. All this painted on parchment made from animal skin: the very making of a fabulous magical metamorphosis, thereby changing animal into book.

Like a doll, like the piece of wood before it was made into Pinocchio, the pupa is inert. Pupa means doll in Latin, hence the French *poupée.*

like a gold-trimmed door unto another world

Play and imagination magically animate the doll, just as biological life 'magically' animates (metamorphoses) the pupa into a butterfly.

Tales by the Brothers Grimm, Hans Christian Andersen, Lewis Carroll, Carlo Collodi and the 'huge narrative wheel of the *Arabian Nights*'[4] all turn round and round on magic; fairies may or may not be present. As Marina Warner (proclaimed queen of the fairy tale) writes:

ci tmb) die
ypto ñse.
ūi. x·c· 7 eo
p̄ane v̄nd
pico quib;
er sezr en̄
·die qb;
reclusa ñ
cm̄ · ex hr
s isit q̄li-
nssioms
ozatouz
ptū · 7 io
s̄ hāt ex
·uiz ad
zeb i seyr.
o dieb; fe
k̄ resiou
i expuit
uz isit de
sit ssūc
icissetis
des 7 pez
etu filiu

Fairies do not need to appear to stamp a story a fairy tale: standard favourites ('Red Riding Hood', 'Puss-in-Boots', 'Rapunzel') do not feature them . . . Magic, however, needs to be implied and present in a fairy tale, and it conjures the presence of another world, a sense that the story has casements thrown open on a view of fairyland.[5]

In the world of fairy tales, the world transforms. Humans fly. Things talk. In fairy tales, as in cuisine, materiality transforms. Like turning water, salt, yeast and flour into delectable bread. Like turning your son into a hearty soup.

In the Brothers Grimms' 'The Juniper Tree', the stepmother of the little boy decapitates him, chops him into pieces and makes him into a stew, seasoned with his sister's salty tears. When the biological father of the boy sits down to eat the stew, he exclaims: 'Oh wife, the food tastes great! Give me some more!'[6] (To which the writer Alissa Nutting has remarked: 'As a child, what fascinated me most about the Grimms' tale of "The Juniper Tree" was that the father could not detect that he was eating his son; it seemed that such a bond would somehow be – dare I say – tasteable.'[7])

In Charles Perrault's 'Sleeping Beauty in the Wood', the Queen Mother has a strong desire to eat children. She cannot help it. It is in her blood. She 'came from a family of ogres'.[8] In fact, when 'she saw small children going by she found it almost impossible to prevent herself from jumping on them'.[9] When she eats lamb in a lovely sauce Robert,[10] she finds it particularly delicious, because she believes she is eating her grand-daughter L'Aurore. My aurelian ears prick.

Aurore is French for 'Aurora', the Roman goddess of dawn, who flies across the sky every morning announcing the arrival of the golden sun.[11] Julia Margaret Cameron photographed Aurora (1864–75), with her hair lit by the brilliant sunshine magically derived from a vine of buttercup-yellow black-eyed susans. I close my eyes and see her shawl as made of saffron. My aurelian mouth opens.

Mixed-up imaginative eating is the milky *eatingmagination* of the mixed-media artist Samantha Sweeting,[12] whose own name has a

fairy-tale ring. In Sweeting's *In Came the Lamb* (2009) the artist, wearing a white cotton dress, sits bare-legged on the barn's scratchy hay as she guides the routing lips of a piebald lamb to her nipple for a feed. Blending erotic Surrealism with fairy-tale surprise, the photograph quotes images of the Virgin and Christ Child (as sacrificial lamb), as in the saccharine-sweet paintings by William-Adolphe Bouguereau. One thinks also of images of Christ in the manger. In English, a 'manger' is an open box in which food for farm animals is placed; in French, *manger* means to eat. In Sweeting's 2008 video *His Fleece was White as Snow*, the artist perverts the famous nursery rhyme 'Mary had a little lamb' by kneeling on all fours in a barn made of stone, so as to offer her exposed breast to a lamb to nurse. Here Sweeting becomes all at once 'Mary', sheep, and Georges Bataille's milk-inflected Simone (from his disturbing *Story of the Eye*, 1928). At the time of making *In Came the Lamb* and *His Fleece was White as Snow,* Sweeting was living with a menagerie of abandoned animals between rural England and a derelict farmhouse in the French Pyrenees.

'Mary', sheep, and Georges
Bataille's milk-inflected
Simone

With my open fairy-tale mouth, I remember how the Duchess of Wonderland flung her sneezing, howling baby at Alice, saying: '"Here! You may nurse it a bit, if you like!"'[13] But as soon as Alice 'had made out the proper way of nursing it (which was to twist it up into a sort of knot [...] so as to prevent its undoing itself' – the baby began grunting and 'there could be no mistake about it [...] it was neither more nor less than a pig.'[14] For his illustrations of this passage, John Tenniel 'interprets the word *nurse* in a general way and depicts Alice simply holding the pig-child. Nevertheless, she is holding it in the typical nursing position, which very subtly reinforces a grotesque maternal relationship.'[15] Or, perhaps, not so subtly, in keeping with Carroll's own dictum: 'I hate babies!'[16]

Eatingmagination: The Goat

Goats are known for trying to eat anything; while this reputation is cartoonish, our impression of their uninhibited dining is based on some fact. Goats like to take advantage of temporary food sources and are known as 'browsers', rather than grazers. Like a goat, who is characterized as willing to try to eat anything, both the fairy tale and aurelia want it all. 'In Italian, the phrase *capra e cavoli* ("goat and cabbage") is the equivalent of the English phrase "to have your cake and eat it"'.[17]

In her film *Ulysse* (1954), Agnès Varda films a goat eating a black-and-white photograph of itself. With this strange image playing before us, a goat eating a photograph of a goat, with an effect that is tragic and comic, Varda, the narrator of the film, says this: 'How does she see her own goat image? Without making animals talk, like in American cartoons, or defining memory as a rumination of mental images, may I suggest that there is an animal "eatingmagination," a self-predatory imagination?'[18]

Varda's 'eatingmagination' is a pun in French that is impossible to translate. She is making a portmanteau word out of *manger*, to eat, and *imaginaire*, imaginary, make-believe. Together they make a new word, a new dish: *imanginaire*. Only in a fairy-tale-like *imaginaire* place can you have your cake and eat it too.

'there could be no mistake about it . . . it was neither more nor less than a pig.'

I Am an Oralian

The fairy tale is a big feast. Discovering the origins of a tale is as fascinating and as impossible as the fairy tale itself. Fairy tales come from an oral tradition, revelling in the mouth. The Brothers Grimm invited storytellers to their home and had them 'tell the tales aloud', which the two then 'noted down on first hearing or after a couple of hearings'.[19]

The first volume of the Grimms' *Children and Household Tales* was published in 1812, with the second volume published in 1815. 'Little did the Grimms realize at that time that their tales would become the most famous "fairy tales" in the world.'[20] There were many editorial changes that would

Bêêee   Agnès

take place between the first edition of 1812–15 (with six more in between) and the final edition of 1857, comprised of 'polished artistic "gems"'.[21] Jack Zipes has recently translated the first edition, which he argues is:

just as important, if not more important than the final seventh edition of 1857, especially if one wants to grasp the original intentions of the Grimms and the overall significance of their accomplishments. In fact, many of the tales in the first edition are more fabulous and baffling than those refined versions in the final edition, for they retain the pungent and naïve flavor of the oral tradition.[22]

Aurelia favours the 'pungent and naïve flavor of the oral tradition' and, when turning to the Grimms, will more often than not use Zipes's translation of these first tales: 'not yet "vaccinated" or censored . . . with their puritanical ideology'.[23]

Every fairy tale has endless variations that cross cultures and time.[24] The recipes have been shared. As Angela Carter notes: 'A fairy tale is a story where one king goes to another king to borrow a cup of sugar.'[25] For example, the story of 'Yeh-hsien', narrated by Li Shih-yüan and recorded by Tuan Ch'eng-shih around AD 850, and then finally translated by Arthur Waley in 1947, is only one of many Chinese Cinderellas.[26] While we may know the names of people who tell a particular story, because the collector noted the name down, 'we can never know the name of the person who invented that story in the first place.'[27]

Defeating origin stories along their long and sordid paths, fairy tales are wandering pilgrims in search of a better life and a full belly. For them, the 'inspired creator of unique one-offs' is not sacred.[28]

Fairy tales are best understood as a domestic art, a kind of cooking. As Carter quips: 'Who invented meatballs? In what country? Is there a definitive recipe for potato soup?'[29] 'Rapunzel' is a kind of lettuce. The windows of the witch's house in 'Hansel and Gretel' are made of sugar. From the bottle marked 'DRINK ME', Alice swallows a strange elixir, with a 'very nice' taste: 'a sort of mixed flavour of cherry-tart, custard, pineapple, roast turkey, toffy, and hot buttered toast.'[30]

I am an oralian. I am an aurelian.

'Aurelia' is a homonym of 'oralia', a word coined by the literary scholar Michael Moon, which is suggestive of both the oral tale and eating.[31] My *Aurelia* speaks in gold and has much to do with eating.

I Am an Orwellian

Aurelian and oralian tales also sound *Orwellian*, for the fairy tale is not only magical: it is political. It is for good reason that George Orwell's *Animal Farm* is subtitled *A Fairy Story*. After all, the fairy tale gives even the little guy hope, insisting that one deserves to be happy and free. This concept has been celebrated by Ernst Bloch and Jack Zipes, Marxist philosophers intrigued by the fairy tale. In a mirroring gesture of Ovid's original 'Golden Age', Thomas More's *Utopia* provides his own 'Golden Age': not of the past, but of the future. The long, original title of More's book in Latin reads: *A Truly Golden [Aureus] Little Book, No Less Beneficial than Entertaining, of a Republic's Best State and of the New Island 'Utopia'.*

I Am an Auralian

Aurelia also sounds like *auralia*, as in aural for hearing. Homonyms, homographs and homophones give me great joy. They open up what Jean-Luc Nancy calls 'listening to the beyond-meaning'.[32] In Simone Martini and Lippo Memmi's *The Annunciation* (1333), the golden words of the angel Gabriel travel from his mouth to the Virgin's ear: 'Greetings, favoured one! The Lord is with you!' (Luke 1:28). His words are foreplay for the conception soon to come. Listening is erotic. Through the striking words she is impregnated with aurelia, oralia and auralia, built up three-dimensionally, like piped sugar icing made of real gold. In Kelly McCallum's disturbing *Do You Hear What I Hear?* (2007) a taxidermied fox has (aural) ears crawling with cast gold-plated (aurelian) maggots.

More Gold Bugs

like piped sugar icing made of real gold

In collaboration with a group of insects called caddisflies (closely related to the butterfly, they like to live near streams and ponds), the French artist Hubert Duprat has made his own gold bugs.[33] It is the habit of the aquatic larvae of the caddisfly to protect their tender developing bodies with cases by spinning silk incorporated with substances for protection, such as grains of sands or tiny bits of fishbone. Caddisfly larvae are underwater architects that use silk excreted from salivary glands near their mouths for building their protective armour. Duprat gives them the haberdashery to construct their golden chainmail with pearls and gems. When he introduced bits of gold into their environment, the Rumpelstiltskin-like *larvae* made golden jewel-like sheaths fit for a Tiffany's window display. Here spinning takes place near the mouth and tells an aurelian tale.

Do
You Hear
What I Hear?

Catching Butterflies and Fairy Tales

> Wide open on its pin (though fast asleep) . . .
> Vladimir Nabokov, 'On Discovering a Butterfly'

'The Aurelian' is Vladimir Nabokov's melancholic story of an ageing man named Paul Pilgram who had always intended to travel the world (like a pilgrim) to catch exotic butterflies. Although he was a first-class entomologist, he never made those journeys. He stayed put in Berlin, never venturing 'farther than Peacock Island on a neighboring lake'.[34] He remained in his 'old crinkly cocoon' with 'his legs too thin for his body',[35] managing his butterfly store with its fantastic specimens, which also sold school supplies, to keep things afloat. But Pilgram did tour the world in his dreams. This German shopkeeper, who 'fed mainly on *Erbswurst* and boiled potatoes',

dreamed of things that would have seemed utterly unintelligible to his wife or his neighbors; for Pilgram belonged, or rather was meant to belong (something – the place, the time, the man – had been ill-chosen), to a special breed of dreamers, such dreamers as used to be called in the old days 'Aurelians' – perhaps on account of those chrysalids, those 'jewels of nature', which they loved to find hanging on fences above the dusty nettles of country lanes.[36]

I was a small child in 1965 when my parents took me to see *The Collector*, the terrifying film directed by William Wyler, based on the John Fowles novel of the same name. The narrative turn occurs when the tiptoeing, creepy, butterfly-collecting aurelian switches prey and begins to stalk a pretty young art student: a Nymphalidae of another kind.[37] The 'collector' kidnaps and chloroforms 'Miranda' as if she were a treasured butterfly. It was probably not such a good idea for my parents to take me to this film. Yet it was my first apprenticeship as an aurelian.

London's 'Society of Aurelians' (founded *c.* 1740) was the first learned association devoted to entomology. With a suitable nod to 'the gilt decorated chrysalides of certain nymphalid butterflies', the name has 'a rather charming, boyish, mock-heroic flavour'.[38] Members of the Society of Aurelians would have put their butterflies to sleep in glass killing jars with elixirs and gases favoured by the lepidopterist (chloroform, potassium cyanide, ether, even the more romantic-sounding crushed laurel leaves), before fixing them with gold-headed pins and framing them behind glass. One thinks not only of Briar Rose and Sleeping Beauty, but also especially of Snow White, who was given a poisoned apple and then placed in a glass coffin trimmed in gold: 'With letters of gold they wrote "PRINCESS SNOW WHITE."'[39]

Nabokov began his aurelian life in childhood. He caught his first butterfly at the age of seven, a 'pale-yellow' swallowtail. The experience filled the young aurelian with a burning passion: 'As it probed the inclined [honeysuckle] flower from which it hung, its powdery body slightly bent, it kept restlessly jerking its great wings, and my desire for it was one of the most intense I have ever experienced.'[40] After its capture, the swallowtail was transferred to a wardrobe 'where domestic naphthalene' administered by Nabokov's nanny was expected 'to kill it overnight'.[41] But the following morning, when the wardrobe, in which it lay dreaming, was opened, the treasured swallowtail, 'with a mighty rustle . . . made for the open window' and quickly became nothing but a 'golden fleck dipping and dodging and soaring eastward'.[42] Like a fairy. Like a fairy tale. It was not dead; it was in a Snow White slumber.

When lecturing on 'Good Readers and Good Writers', Nabokov noted: 'Great novels are great fairy tales.'[43] Clearly with *Lolita* (1955), his most famous book, Nabokov sought to write a great novel, a great fairy tale. Like ocelli on butterfly wings, seemingly every page of *Lolita* is spotted with fairy-tale references. Humbert Humbert calls Lolita 'a fairy princess'.[44] H.H. gives a copy of *The Little Mermaid* to Lolita. Allusions are made to 'Bluebeard', 'Hansel and Gretel', 'Sleeping Beauty', Goethe's 'Erlkönig', 'The Emperor's New Clothes' and, of course, *Alice's Adventures in Wonderland*. (As connoisseurs of the girl-child know,

Dedication

To the WORTHY MEMBERS of the Aurelian Society.

GENTLEMEN,

Permit me the Honour of laying before You Twelve new DESIGNS of English BUTTERFLIES: Creatures whose Elegance and Variety of Beauty demand our Admiration. Ignorance long imagin'd them the Spontaneous Productions of Putrifying Matter and undesigning Chance; Causes as little able to form an Animal as to create a World: but your Discoveries have Rectify'd that mistake, and prov'd them to proceed from Parents like themselves; after a constant, tho' wonderful Order of Generation.

The pregnant Female, with unerring Sagacity, deposites her Eggs in some secure Concealment, where the Infant Brood may find, as soon as hatch'd, immediate and proper Sustenance. Here they feed, and thrive, and cast off several Skins, till arrived at full growth, every Species in a manner peculiar to it self, is chang'd into an AURELIA: whence in due Time a Moth or Butterfly issues forth, array'd with all the Glories of its Parent. This too partakes the Joys of Love, lays Eggs, & dies; And thus one Race succeeds another in an uniform & unalterable manner.

The Care that has been taken to render These DESIGNS Exact Representations of NATURE, may I hope recommend Them to your Favour; and excuse the Presumption of

Gentlemen,

Your most Obedient humble Servant,
BENJ: WILKES.

1. The Bee Tyger Caterpillar 2. The Great Magpye Do 3. This Caterpillar feeds on Nettles. 4. The Privet Hawk Caterpillar. 5. The Elephant Do 6 The Buff Tipt Do 7 The Small Tortoiseshell Do (with its Chrysalis) 8. The Poplar Hawk Caterpillar 9. A Looper 10. The Great Egger Caterpillar 11. The Puss Do 12. This Caterpillar feeds on Oak.

Setts Plain (or Colourd from the Real Flyes) Sold by B. Wilkes against the Horn Tavern in Fleet Street. Where any Gentleman or Lady may See His COLLECTION of INSECTS.

Published by Benjn Wilkes, June ye 15, 1742. According to Act of Parliament.

Design'd by B. Wilkes.   Engrav'd by H. Roberts.

Nabokov translated *Alice* into Russian and dreamed of filming Lewis Carroll's picnics.[45]) Nabokov charged his adored child with the oralia of *Alice in Wonderland* in a *mise en scène* of 1950s America. As H.H.'s greedy epicurean hands reveal:

She had entered my world, umber and black Humberland, with rash curiosity . . . To the wonderland I had to offer, my fool preferred the corniest movies, the most cloying fudge. To think that between a Hamburger and a Humburger, she would – invariably, with icy precision – plump for the former.'[46]

Humbert Humbert is not only imaged as a fairy-tale wolf: he is also a spider (the butterfly's enemy).[47] As a deranged lepidopterist, H.H. calls Lolita a 'nymph', which in the world of entomology is another word for 'pupa' or 'the young of an insect undergoing incomplete metamorphosis'.[48] One of Nabokov's butterfly finds is known as '"Nabokov's Wood-Nymph" . . . belonging to the family *Nymphalidae*'.[49]

H.H. catches Lolita, takes her to the Enchanted Hunters hotel and drugs her with sleeping pills. He leaves her 'imprisoned in her crystal sleep',[50] like a butterfly in a jar, and returns later with the key, like evil Bluebeard. He unlocks the door and finds Lolita lying naked, like a floppy doll. ('She was "Dolly" at School. She was Dolores on the dotted line.'[51]) Dolly's legs are relaxed, spread unawares, like the wings of a butterfly. She wears nothing more than one sock and her charm bracelet. A velvet ribbon is clenched in her hand. Her tanned body, photographed by the sun, reveals 'the white negative image of a rudimentary swimsuit'.[52] But Lolita, in the spirit of Nabokov's first catch of a pale-yellow swallowtail, has a will of her own, and awakes with every Humbert Humbert move, as she lies drowsily next to him in the same bed.

The next morning, the bloodthirsty Bluebeard notes: 'Nothing could have been more childish than . . . the purplish spot on her naked neck where a fairy tale vampire had feasted.'[53]

The souls of artists must always be woken a little from the magic in which
they lie fettered. Inside almost every artist – certainly every true one –
lies a fairy tale realm.

Robert Walser, 'Berlin and the Artist'

Aurelia: Art and Literature Through the Mouth of the Fairy Tale is told with a
butterfly tongue that celebrates, warns, swallows, chews and rebels. *Aurelia*
awakens the fairy-tale realm in a wide range of authors, artists, books and
objects which fall down its hole. Beyond the expected Brothers Grimm
and Lewis Carroll, there are more surprising inclusions, like the gold
of Ovid's Midas; the magical materiality of glass; the real and imagined
beasts of a medieval manuscript; the tragic candyland of the 1950s child-
poet Minou Drouet; the discovery of Lascaux as a fairy-tale dream of
finding our own subterranean world of enchantment; Langston Hughes's
brown fairies for America's children of 'colour'; Miwa Yanagi's photograph
of the Grandmother and Little Red Riding Hood as a disturbing image of
Hiroshima after the bombing.

With each chapter, *Aurelia* falls deeper and deeper into darkness.
With the surprisingly melancholic rhythm of the fairy tale's close cousin
the nursery rhyme, *Aurelia*'s golden cradle falls, and down comes baby,
cradle and all. Humpty Dumpty has a great fall, and all the king's horses
and all the king's men cannot put Humpty together again. With its plum-
met into racial hatred in America, *Aurelia*'s final chapter arrives full stop,
head over heels. There is no place to go, save for back out of the hole and
back to the beginning. Like the fairy tale itself, as is already evident, I
am promiscuous with my recipe-borrowing. Always a hedonist at heart.

Let the golden feast begin . . .

1 Eating Gold

Using my eyes to eat and my mouth to see, Aurelia's first chapter gives the Midas touch to an alloy of golden tales. Narrative treasures include Aesop's 'Killing the Goose that Laid the Golden Egg', the Brothers Grimm's 'The Golden Key' and Tim Krabbé's 'The Golden Egg'. My visual treasures include eighteenth-century gold cups for drinking hot chocolate, Janine Antoni's pair of nipples cast in gold and Kiki Smith's gold tongue. In all, eating gold (from metaphorically consuming it to physically swallowing it) turns sadistic. 'Sadism demands a story,' Laura Mulvey once famously wrote,[1] and the fairy tale gives it a golden touch.

Midas wished for everything that he touched to turn to gold. But the outcome was disastrous. He found that he could not eat:

When Midas hungrily touched
the bread with his fingers, Ceres' [Mother Earth's] gifts grew rigidly hard.
Or if he attempted to tear some meat in his greedy teeth,
he found he was uselessly crunching on wafers of yellowish metal.
He mixed fresh water with wine, the god who had granted his wish;
but all that entered his throat was a trickle of molten gold.
Stunned by the turn of events, now wealthy but desolate, Midas
longed to escape from his riches and loathed the thing that he'd prayed for.
Platefuls to eat, but perpetually hungry![2]

Fairy tales and related myths and fables often turn on gold. And as the Marxist theorist Ernst Bloch notes, 'fairy tales always end in gold,' even if the gold is metaphorical. In his words:

Once upon a time: this means in fairy-tale manner not only the past but a more colorful or easier somewhere else. And those who have become happier there are still happy today if they are not dead. To be sure, there is suffering in fairy tales; however, it changes, and for sure, it never returns. The maltreated, gentle Cinderella goes to the little tree at her mother's grave, little tree, shake yourself, shake yourself. A dress falls to her feet more splendid and marvelous than anything she has ever had. And the slippers are solid gold. Fairy tales always end in gold. There is enough happiness there. In particular, the little heroes and poor people are the ones who succeed here where life has become good.[3]

The Last Story

'The Golden Key' is a surprising text from the fairy tales of the Brothers Grimm. The story appeared as the closing tale of the first edition of 1812–15 of the Grimms' *Children's and Household Tales* (*Kinder-und Hausmärchen*), and it traditionally occupies the last position. In every edition of their tales, which we call fairy tales but they never did,[4] the Brothers 'began with "The Frog King" also known as "The Frog Prince", and ended with "The Golden Key".'[5] Even today, the 'The Golden Key' is traditionally the last story. Here is the very short tale, perhaps even shorter than the tail of a Manx cat, in full.

The Golden Key

One winter when the snow was very deep, a poor boy had to go outside and gather wood on a sled. After he had finally collected enough wood and had piled it on his sled, he decided not to go home right away because he was so frozen. He thought he would instead make a fire to warm himself up a bit. So he began scraping the snow away, and as he cleared the ground he discovered a small golden key. Where there's a key, he knew, there must be a lock. So he dug farther into the ground and found a little iron casket. If only the key will fit! he thought. There are bound to be precious things in the casket. He searched and he could not find a keyhole. Then, finally, he noticed one, but it was so small that he could barely see it. He tried the key, and fortunately it fit. So, he began turning it, and now we must wait until he unlocks the casket completely and lifts the cover. That's when we'll learn what wonderful things he found.[6]

An unfinished gesture long before Roland Barthes, this concluding tale without a conclusion provides the reader with a 'small golden key' and a fairy-tale treasure box to be opened with *writerly* fingertips.[7] The story demands the reader to write, to imagine, their own words that will fill the 'little iron casket' with their desires. 'The Golden Key' makes the reader not a 'consumer, but a producer of the text': allowing the reader 'access to the magic of the signifier, to the pleasure of writing'.[8] Reading the tale, 'it is as if I had words instead of fingers, or fingers at the tip of my words. My language trembles with desire'.[9]

Yet withholding the 'wonderful things' that can be found in the casket has a touch of sadism. A key is a tongue that makes the keyhole speak. I desire to turn the key. I desire to open the book. I desire to know.

When reading 'The Golden Key', a story so short that it is hardly more than a turn, we hesitate at the first letter, which is already nearly the end. In the English translation the story opens with the promising O of 'One winter when' (only for the letter to be quickly displaced by the closed 'little iron casket'). With our mouths held open in anticipation, like the story itself, we pause. We are held open, like the casket.

Transitioning from 'hesitation to action',[10] we wait to be struck by enchantment. The nutcracker comes to life. A prince pops out of a frog. The glass slipper fits. Alice shrinks to three inches tall. The Darling children fly. The apple, and everything Midas touches, turns into gold.

A letter, a word, a keyhole, a little iron casket. 'That the world of things can open itself to reveal a secret life – indeed to reveal a set of actions and hence a narrativity and history outside the given field of perception – is a constant daydream.'[11]

Making something happen (turning 'the little golden key') is generated by sadism.[12] Teresa de Lauretis explains:

'Sadism demands a story', writes Laura Mulvey . . . The proposition, with its insidious suggestion of reversibility, is vaguely threatening. (Is a story, are all stories, to be claimed by sadism?) The full statement reads: 'Sadism demands a story, depends on making something happen, forcing a change in another person, a battle of will and strength, victory/defeat, all occurring in a linear time with a beginning and an end.'[13]

    De Lauretis argues that the telling of stories (even if it is anti-narrative) can escape the structure of sadomasochism (of masculinized agency, though not necessarily male) overcoming a masochistic figure (of feminized resistance, though not necessarily female).

    According to de Lauretis, Sophocles' *Oedipus the King* is the classic narrative structure, hence perfect fodder for Freud's development of his Oedipal theory of the child's development of sexuality, in which the boy wants to sleep with his mother and murder his father. (Freud devotes little attention to the girl child: she is symptomatically absent.) Oedipus moves through the space of the narrative driven by the desire to know the story of 'life itself'.[14] The Sphinx (the feminized obstacle) asks him a riddle: 'What has four legs in the morning, two in the afternoon and three in the evening?' 'Man,' answers Oedipus. In the eyes of Freud this is the start of a heterosexualized desire, the child's 'Oedipal' stage in which he wants to kill his father and marry his mother. While Barthes notes in 'Introduction to the Structural Analysis of Narratives' that 'it *may* be significant that man's offspring should have "invented," at the same time (around the age of three), both the sentence and Oedipus' narrative,' de Lauretis argues that it is *absolutely* significant.

    By answering the riddle, Oedipus overcomes the Sphinx and the story meets its climax:

Now everything is clear – I
lived with a woman, she was my mother, I slept in my mother's bed, and I
murdered, murdered my father.
the man whose blood flows in these veins of mine,
whose blood stains these two hands red.[15]

When it is revealed to Oedipus that he has married his mother (Jocasta), he goes to her with the violent and perverse desire to cut out her womb with his own sword. But his mother-lover, who has already learned the truth, has hanged herself in the palace bedroom. When Oedipus sees the body of his mother, he lets out a cry, takes her body down, removes the gold brooches that held her dress together and plunges them into his own eyes.

That's when it happened – he
ripped off the gold
brooches she was wearing – one on each shoulder of her gown –
and raised them over his head – you could see them flashing –
and titled his face up and
brought them down into his eyes
and the long pins sank deep, all the way back into the sockets . . . [16]

And his eyes were stabbed with two brooches made out of gold, bringing the story to a close. Shutting the eyes that see, shutting the mouth that tells. Once-upon-a-time shuts its Cyclops-eye-mouth-O and goes to sleep, to be reawakened on another day.

In the middle of Sade's Once-upon-a-time *Philosophy in the Bedroom*, 'MADAME DE SAINTE-ANGE hands EUGÉNIE a huge needle with a thick, red waxen thread.'[17] What Eugénie sews are orifices. In the hands of Sade, the golden O becomes a red wound that bleeds, with an intonation of Greek tragedy, the blood of Christ and Grimm.

Although not as outrageously explicit as Sade, fairy tales are ripe with sadism's 'enthusiasm for inflicting pain, suffering, or humiliation on others'.[18] Cinderella's wicked sisters have their eyes pecked out. In an Italian oral folktale recorded by Italo Calvino entitled 'A Tale of Cats', a wicked sister is cursed to have a blood sausage hanging over her face, which she has to constantly nibble or it will get longer. Pinocchio sprouts donkey ears and grows a preposterous phallic nose of wood. (The sadism of Pinocchio's plight is synched in Jonny Briggs's *Strap-on Pinocchio Nose* (2010), where a fetishistic thick leather buckle and wooden chair-leg are combined to

In the
hands of
Sade,
the golden
O becomes
a red
wound
that bleeds

The sadism of Pinocchio's plight is synched in Jonny Briggs's Nose

make a strap-on phallus.) The Wicked Queen desires to eat Snow White's liver and lungs. The list is endless: fairy tale takes pleasure from sadism.

Gold Food

It shows shine.
Gertrude Stein, *Tender Buttons*

Janine Antoni's pair of brooches entitled *Tender Buttons* (1994) are the artist's own nipples cast in eighteen-carat rose gold. The fronts of the brooches suggest the promise of 'golden' milk – there for suckling – and the backs hide pins for attachment. To wear them is to suffer a touch of sadism. They must be pinned on.

Tender Buttons, maternal and erotic, are suggestive of the pleasures and pain of a mother's 'on demand' infant feeding.[19] Suckling on the breasts is our first form of kissing: nutritious at first, but later developing into what Adam Phillips calls non-nutritional eating.[20] Likewise, gold is non-nutritional, but has been traditionally eaten to heal the spirit or even the body. The healing properties of *aurum potabile* (drinkable gold) cordials can be found in Robert Burton's seventeenth-century *The Anatomy of Melancholy*: drinking hot gold will cure the saddened heart.[21] In 1899, Edward Eggleston wrote of the desire to drink gold in the seventeenth century: 'Almost everything precious and rare was accounted of medical virtue, and it was inferred that gold was the most precious metal and would be the most valuable remedy, if it could be taken in liquid form.'[22] Likewise, 'fragments and leaves of gold were seethed with meats and the broth to cheer the heart and raise the strength and vital spirits of invalids beyond conception.'[23] In the medieval kitchen, the 'surface of a roast or pie could be given a handsome, smooth, glistening, golden-yellow crust with the help of a saffron paste. Although not very common . . . genuine gold . . . leaf could also be used for a coating.'[24] Likewise, 'adding gold to the wine produced a potion that bolstered the heart.'[25]

It takes 150 flower heads of saffron crocus to make a gram of the golden costly spice, and 70,000 to 250,000 flower heads to make one

pound of saffron. As precious as gold, saffron has a strong pigment and turns all food that it touches golden. Saffron has a Midas touch.

The actor James Franco has eaten dessert made out of gold with the hocus-pocus spiritual queen of performance, Marina Abramović. As Franco writes:

I was recently treated to an early prototype of a dessert that Marina Abramović, the 'grandmother of performance art,' created with the pastry chef Dominique Ansel. It's a cylindrical pastry with a lychee center sprinkled over with chili powder and raw gold. I was instructed to kiss a napkin that had been printed with a square of gold powder that would transfer to my face before eating the dessert. This way the dessert would pass through a golden gateway before it was ingested.[26]

an aurelian cast from the tip of her tongue

Yet gold is not always so easy to swallow. Kiki Smith's eighteen-carat gold pin, an aurelian cast from the tip of her tongue, is as golden as it is biting: a sadistic twist on being tongue-tied.

Wet Gold Shine on His Lips

With his touch . . .
He set his lips to the cold rim,
And others, dumbfounded
By what they had already seen, were aghast
When they saw the wet gold shine on his lips,
And as he lowered the cup
Saw him mouthing gold, spitting gold mush –
That had solidified, like gold cinders.
He got up reeling
From his golden chair, as if poisoned.
Ted Hughes, 'Midas', *Tales of Ovid*

Upstairs in the British Museum, among a treasure trove of precious objects, one can find a pair of gold chocolate cups from around 1700.

These are deadly cups of solidified
pools of gold, for Midas drinking.

The 'Palmerston cups' of thin hand-raised gold appear soft, delectable, fingered and burnished, like gold leaf. Their gold seems edible, like an *aurum potabile* cordial. (Or, nostalgically for me, like those large chocolate coins wrapped in inedible gold foil that I loved as a child.)

The insides of the handles and the bases of the Palmerston cups feature inscriptions with nods to death and to the bitterness of life. Inside one scroll handle is written in Latin: DULCIA NON MERUIT QUI NON GUSTAVIT AMARA (He has not deserved sweet unless he has tasted bitter). And on the bottom: MANIBUS SACRUM (To the shades of the departed). Inside the other cup handle we find in English: THINK ON YR FRIENDS & DEATHE AS THE CHIEF. And on the bottom: MORTVIS LIBAMVR (Let us drink to the dead).[27] These are deadly cups of solidified pools of gold, for Midas drinking.

As offspring of Midas' own deathly gold beaker, it is fitting that the Palmerston cups were made from a pile of melted-down mourning rings. While wedding rings mark the date of a promise, the 'happily ever after' of the fairy tale, mourning rings mark the date of a loss. Popular in the seventeenth century, the rings often featured skulls. Inside one such ring, so as to touch the mourner's skin, is inscribed the date and initials of the loved one's death. As Barthes writes on the first page of his *Mourning Diary*:

First wedding night.
But first mourning night?[28]

instead of
finding a
horde of
golden eggs,
he found
that she was
just like
any other
Goose

The Goose and the Golden Eggs

A Man had the great good fortune to own a marvelous Goose —every day it laid a golden egg. The Man was growing rich, but the more he got, the more he wanted. Making up his mind to have the whole treasure at once, he killed the Goose. But when he killed her and cut her open, instead of finding a horde of golden eggs, he found that she was just like any other Goose.

Beware of being greedy.
It doesn't pay to be impatient.

Aesop tells a famous fable (a form of story related to the fairy tale), 'The Goose and the Golden Eggs':

A Man had the great good fortune to own a marvellous Goose – every day it laid a golden egg. The Man was growing rich, but the more he got the more he wanted. Making up his mind to have the whole treasure at once, he killed the Goose. But when he killed and cut her open, instead of finding a horde of golden eggs, he found that she was just like any other Goose.

Beware of being greedy.
It doesn't pay to be impatient.[29]

Likewise, 'Jack and the Beanstalk' is an English fairy tale in which Jack steals from the Giant a bag of gold coins, a hen that lays eggs of gold and a gold harp. Versions of these tales sometimes feature a goose rather than a hen. Pinocchio, before he becomes a 'real boy', learns a similar lesson. As a 'simpleton', a 'wooden-head', Pinocchio is convinced that burying his handful of golden coins, all the riches he has to his name, will result in sprouting a whole field of gold.

Charles Perrault uses the nonsense rhyme 'Donkey Skin' to tackle a stock trope of fairy tales: the father who wants to marry his daughter. (The Grimms told the story as 'All Fur'.) But 'Perrault braided this material with another, durable folk motif: a magic animal whose excrement is made of gold.'[30]

Nature had made the beast so pure
That what he dropped was not manure,
But sovereigns and gold crowns instead
(Imprinted with the royal head).[31]

Eating (consuming) can only result in ordure. Thomas More imagined Utopia as a place where gold is both worthless and enslaving: there, chamber pots are made of gold and slaves are shackled by gold chains. Fairy tales, myths, fables and imagined utopias hold the promise of a golden egg, a secret to freedom, while warning the readers of greed.

Another Golden Egg

The Dutch novel *The Golden Egg* (1984), written by Tim Krabbé, centres on unstoppable desire to know. Like a goose getting ready to become pâté, we (the readers) are held by the psychological, force-feeding instrument of narrative. We give in, as if being fattened with figs in order to produce hypertrophied livers for the most delicious mixture of ground meat, fat, spices, herbs and cognac.

The 1988 Dutch-French film adaptation of Krabbé's novel, directed by George Sluizer, was released under the English title *The Vanishing*. The cinematic version has an equally terrifying effect. The original Dutch title of the film is the same as the original book – *Het Gouden Ei* (*The Golden*

The coins are not made of real gold, but are golden with love and promise.

Egg) – and is more satisfyingly suggestive of those fairy tales and fables that play out the well-versed narrative structure of greedy desire and gold. Yet to translate the film title as *The Vanishing* does provide another point of interest: it evokes the tricks of the magician, whereby women (and rabbits) often disappear right before our eyes.

The main characters of *The Golden Egg* are a young couple, named Saskia and Rex, who are starting out on a bicycling holiday. They stop for a rest in a field that extends beyond a petrol station. Following Rex's promise never to abandon Saskia, the couple bury two coins, two 'tender buttons', at the base of a tree. The coins are not made of real gold, but are golden with love and promise. They will mark the spot 'forever'. Saskia goes off to the station to buy Rex a beer and herself a soda. Rex waits in the car. And he waits. And he waits. She never returns. She vanishes. She is just gone, without a trace. Terror seizes the young man. But equal to his terror is his crippling desire to know what happened to Saskia, which also seizes the reader and obsessively overrides every aspect of his life. Rex seeks Saskia in every possible way: missing person posters, interviews with each and every person that knew her or might have had contact with her. He places an advertisement in the newspaper, along with his story of Saskia's vanishing. Eventually, eight years later, we learn who the abductor was: a man with a pleasant, plumpish face, a kind family man. As the French artist Christian Boltanski has remarked: 'Klaus Barbie [the famed Nazi war criminal brought to trial in 1987] has the face of a Nobel Peace Prize winner. It would be easier if a terrible person had a terrible face.'[32]

The kidnapper develops a twisted, almost loving sympathy for Rex. An agreement is made between the criminal and the lover. Rex can learn what happened to Saskia only by allowing the kidnapper to commit the same violation upon him. Saskia's story will be inscribed physically upon Rex. He knows he will die, but the sadistic desire to know overrides his desire to live. Arrangements are made. A meeting takes place. A driving trip. Darkness. A parking lot. A field. They arrive at the tree where the two coins are buried. Rex is given a sedative in a cup of coffee from a thermos. 'It was black coffee with sugar, hot and bitter.'[33] Rex waits until he becomes sleepy. He dreams of a strange egg, a kind of golden egg with a Surrealist touch:

Rex dreamed that he was sitting in a restaurant. Across from him
was Saskia. He didn't know her, but he knew it was her. Everything
was going to begin. It was a restaurant in gray tints, without much
light. She hadn't ordered anything, but he was served a plate of
tennis balls. When he cut one open, a duck came out, unfolded its
wings and flew away.

> Rex woke up.
> He opened his eyes, but it made no difference to what he saw: black.
> He sensed he was alone. He grasped for breath: so this was it.
> This must be what had happened to Saskia. Where *was* he?
>   . . .
> He slammed his fists above and beside him and he screamed but
> heard nothing, as though the sound was swallowed by the blackness.
> Gaahd.
> He was lying in a box buried alive.[34]

> Rex now understands that Saskia was buried alive. He is trapped in
> the 'golden egg' that Saskia had dreamed of as a child:

When she was little, she'd had a dream about being locked inside
a golden egg that was flying through the universe. Everything was
black, there weren't even any stars. She'd be stuck in there forever,
and she couldn't die. There was only one hope. There was another
golden egg flying through space; if they collided, they'd both be
destroyed, and it would be over. But the universe was so big![35]

> Rex's desire to know, at all costs, is equivalent to Midas' wish for every-
> thing to turn to gold. The result is disastrous.

———

2 An Alicious Appetite: *Alice's Adventures in Wonderland* and *Through the Looking-Glass*

At meals he was very abstemious always, while he took nothing in the middle of the day except a glass of wine and a biscuit. Under these circumstances it is not very surprising that the healthy appetites of his little friends filled him with wonder, and even with alarm. When he took a certain one of them out with him to a friend's house to dinner, he used to give the host or hostess a gentle warning, to the mixed amazement and indignation of the child, 'Please be careful, because she eats a good deal too much.'
Stuart Dodgson Collingwood, writing about his uncle Charles Dodgson (aka Lewis Carroll)

My dear Agnes,
At last I've succeeded in forgetting you! It's been a very hard job, but I took 6 'lessons-in-forgetting,' at half-a-crown a lesson. After three lessons, I forgot my own name, and I forgot to go for the next lesson. So the Professor said I was getting on very well: 'but I hope,' he added, 'you won't forget to pay for the lessons!' I said that would depend on whether the other lessons were good or not: and do you know? the last of the 6 lessons was so good that I forgot everything! I forgot who I was: I forgot to eat my dinner . . .
Lewis Carroll, letter to Agnes Hull, 10 December 1877

*L*ewis Carroll's Alice's Adventures in Wonderland *and* Through the Looking-Glass, and What Alice Found There *are remarkable stories, in which 'Alice' (who is based on a real little girl named Alice Liddell) uses her body and plays with language in order to survive the obstacles that she confronts. Yet equally surprising is Carroll's focus on eating as a form of non-eating. For Alice only eats mere morsels: a bit of cake, a nibble of mushroom, a sip from a bottle not marked poison. Alice's eating (which is* *hardly eating at all) is tied to her desire (fervent and withholding), which Carroll echoes in his photographs of young girls. To remain hungry is to remain full of Alicious desire.*

Forgetting and Eating

The Alice stories are lessons in forgetting – 'And now who am I? I *will* remember if I can! I'm determined to do it! . . . L, I *know* it begins with L!'[1] – and eating – 'it had, in fact, a sort of mixed flavour of cherry-tart, custard, pine-apple, roast turkey, toffy, and hot buttered toast' (17). In both *Alice's Adventures in Wonderland* (1865) and *Through the Looking-Glass, and What Alice Found There* (1871), but especially in *Wonderland*, action turns on eating/consumption.[2] The emphasis on food in *Wonderland* and *Through the Looking-Glass* is curiously in the absence of nourishment.[3] But in contrast to Marcel Proust's famous bite of madeleine dipped in lime-blossom tea, which is now a cultural trope for profound memory – even a cliché – Alice's eating is all about forgetting.

Alice's eating, which is barely eating at all (a bit of mushroom, a crumb of cake, a swallow from a bottle not marked poison), is a withholding, an anorectic labour, reflective of Carroll's own fears of over-indulgence. Anorectic not only denotes a lack of appetite, it shares a rhyming sound with ascetic: a term also reflective of Carroll and his Alice(s). Furthermore, I use the term anorectic as an aesthetic term, which is necessarily connected to anorexia, but is not necessarily medical.

First Empty Bite: No Memory

In *Wonderland* and *Through the Looking-Glass,* Alice remembers very little about home, save for her always-hungry cat Dinah:

Dinah'll miss me very much to-night, I should think! . . . I hope
they'll remember her saucer of milk at tea-time. Dinah, my dear!
I wish you were down here with me! There are no mice in the air,

I am afraid, but you might catch a bat, and that's very like a mouse,
you know. But do cats eat bats, I wonder? (14)

Beyond her reminiscences about Dinah, it seems that there is hardly
a nostalgic (homesick, remembering) bone in Alice's fantastic, meta-
morphosing, textual, writ(h)ing, always-hungry body.[4] As we know
from *Through the Looking-Glass*, Alice had once 'really frightened her
old nurse by shouting suddenly in her ear, "Nurse! Do let's pretend that
I'm a hungry hyæna, and you're a bone!"' (141). For Alice, bones hold no
sacred memories or pasts; they're just food, and barely that. For a bone is
for chewing and gnawing and tasting and picking and licking. It's really
not much to eat. A bone feeds a hunger of a different order.

In the Alice stories, food is impossible to eat. During *Wonderland*'s
mad tea-party Alice is offered non-existent wine. For the apocalyptic
meal at the end of *Through the Looking-Glass*, 'Queen Alice' arrives having
already 'missed the soup and the fish', only to be confronted with an
animistic leg of mutton, crowned with his own paper-frill coronet, who
would be impolite to cut into, to say the least. With a little bow on the
mutton's part and one returned by Alice, they meet: 'Alice – Mutton:
Mutton – Alice' (261). But how could Alice ever slice someone she has
just met? 'It isn't etiquette to cut any one you've been introduced to,'
the Red Queen scolds (262). There's nothing to do but remove the joint
and bring out the pudding. Avoiding further conversation with edibles
to eat, Alice hastily says, 'I won't be introduced to the pudding, please
. . . or we shall get no dinner at all' (262). No sooner has Alice said this
than the pudding is removed. In a wink, things turn annihilative, with
bottles turning into birds (with plates for wings and forks for legs) and
the Red Queen's broad, good-natured face disappearing into the soup.

(Curious is the fact that Reverend Robert Kirk's late seventeenth-
century treatise on the secrets of fairies tells us that a 'joint-eater' is a kind
of fairy who sits invisibly by his victim and partakes of the latter's food,
allowing the victim to continue to be lean despite a devouring appetite.[5])

Finding Alice's anorectic labour is an easy game to win. Consider
those tarts, stolen but not eaten. Or recall when the little bits of comfits

are handed round at the Caucus-race: 'the large birds complained that they could not taste theirs, and the small ones choked and had to be patted on the back' (33). And don't forget the Mad Hatter, who complains that 'the bread-and-butter' slices are 'getting so thin' (114). As the White Queen makes as clear as pudding, 'jam to-morrow and jam yesterday – but never jam *to-day*' (196), because 'it will never be exactly time for Alice to eat the jam.'[6] The same is true for the plum-cake. 'Hand it round first and cut it afterwards' (231), orders the Unicorn to the baffled Alice. It's all about cutting up, whether it be the roast, the pudding or the fish; but it involves eating of a different order.

Alice, we learn in *Wonderland*, 'always took a great interest in questions of eating and drinking' (75). She is surprisingly willing to eat a bit of anything she finds as she moves through those two dreamy landscapes that, undisputedly, hale the unconscious. Alice is fearless in her morsel-eating: the only thing that seems to be at stake is etiquette. When Alice says, '"Nurse! Do let's pretend that I'm a hungry hyæna, and you're a bone!"' (141), I smack my lips with dangerous thoughts of naughty, risky food. With Alice's nurse-desiring, hyæna hunger on my mind, in rushes Meret Oppenheim's own 1936 feast on a nurse, her dangerously delectable *My Nurse*. Served up, like all yummy foods, on an eye-catching platter is a pair of Freudian slippers – white ladies' pumps, to be exact – bound together with sadistic, sexy string like a gift waiting to be untied (by one's teeth, of course).[7] And best of all, the most delectable parts, the devious heels, have slipped on their own little paper frills (like the mutton leg to which Alice is introduced), as if they were a pair of yummy lamb chops. But there is nothing to nourish here in any kind of nutritional way; it is about a mouth that does not nurture its body and the pleasures and dangers of surface-orientated eating. As Freud has shown us, there is no 'no' in the unconscious. This kind of eating is closer to kissing and licking; it is an eating that is about risk.

To eat in Alice's world is to turn mouths into eyes and eyes into mouths in a substitutive practice that cooks up nonsense. In the words of Carroll's Hatter (mad, perhaps with the mercury that was once used in making hats[8]): 'Why, you might just as well say that "I see what I eat" is

then we are always hungry, always wild with desire;
we are endlessly chasing the White Rabbit

the same thing as "I eat what I see"!' (71). In Alice's world, as the Hatter knows, 'it's always tea-time' (74). And if it's always tea-time, then we are always hungry, always wild with desire; we are endlessly chasing the White Rabbit, whom Hélène Cixous rudely and hilariously describes as a *pénis trottinant* ('penis on paws').[9] The White Rabbit is a carrot on a string, *always* before us 'eternally stretching forth towards the *desire for something else*', what the French psychoanalyst Jacques Lacan calls metonymy (or displacement).[10] According to Lacan, displacement is metonymy and 'desire *is* a metonymy, however funny people may find the idea.'[11] Alice falls into a deep hole, a special Carrollinian nonsense hole – 'down, down, down. Would the fall *never* come to an end?' (13) – where memory/meaning does not grow deeper but is evacuated. Metonymy (Lacan tells us – Carroll shows us) is a 'weapon . . . against nostalgia.'[12]

Carroll stuffs nonsense into the reader through not only his non-narrative style and his wild punning, but his use of portmanteau words. 'Portmanteau' is a word for two words in one, just as it is a word for those double suitcases that are two bags in one. The Jabberwocky poem is chock-a-block with portmanteaus – like *slithy* – which packs 'slimy' and 'lithe' into one word (215). Of note is the fact that Carroll is credited in the *Oxford English Dictionary* for the linguistic coining of 'portmanteau'.

In this endless chain of Carrollinian chance-meeting-on-a-dissecting-table-of-a-sewing-machine-and-an-umbrella encounters,[13] we just might find ourselves sipping from Oppenheim's *Breakfast in Fur* (1936): a portmanteau object of the Mad Hatter and the March Hare. One sip and we are already 'mad' with desire for something else, like a hare in the month of March. (March is the rutting season of the usually very shy hare, so says the *Dictionary of Phrase and Fable*.[14]) *Breakfast in Fur* suggests a revolting glug of tea brewed in a pot packed with the Dormouse. One smells the hare. Place the soft cup on the soft saucer: it makes no *auralian* noise at all. Hardly Proustian, this cup of tea is not likely to remind anyone nostalgically of his auntie, at least in any kind of nurturing sense. *Breakfast in Fur* is padded against the possibility even of an aurelian memory prompt; no chance here of a Proustian knock of 'a spoon against a plate.'[15] Even the spoon is made of soundless fur. *Breakfast in Fur*, like

One smells the hare.
Place the soft cup on the
soft saucer: it makes no
auralian noise
at all.

the Alice stories, is about forgetting the past, as well as about forgetting the future by experiencing the present in a most non-normative way.

Like Oppenheim's work, the Alice stories present us with plenty of feeding but not much nurturing. Just as the Mad Hatter 'bit a large piece out of his teacup instead of the bread-and-butter' (113), when you take a bite in Wonderland it is more about reading than eating. Eating-as-reading makes possible all the forgetting.

Today, perhaps with our own touch of Aliciousness, we might drown our sorrows in a large bag of crisps, a pot of ice cream, a box of chocolate, a handful of biscuits – but Alice's forgetting comes out of eating almost nothing at all.[16] Alice is a pecker, not a gorger. Perhaps that is why Carroll was so fond of picturing Alice Liddell and a host of other girl-child friends as little beggars. When we look at *Alice Liddell as 'The Beggar Maid'*, her cupped hand is a pocket not for change, or food, but for Carroll as a small White Rabbit to slip into – a hole in memory.

Although not named as such, nor even seen, Lethe, the meandering river of forgetfulness, is everywhere in the geography of *Wonderland* and *Through the Looking-Glass*. ('L, I *know* it begins with L' [177].) Alice drowns in Lethe, swallowing its waters as she does her very own tears. Forgetting is the only thing that Alice is unlikely to forget.[17] She is in her own way – via the waterways of her alter ego Lewis Carroll ('L, I *know* it begins with L') – consumed by the art of forgetting.

Memory is a storehouse, a cellar, a well, perhaps even a rabbit hole. Gaston Bachelard has argued that fears can be rationalized in the attic, even enlightened; but in the cellar, 'darkness prevails both day and night'.[18] 'The cellar dreamer knows that the walls of the cellar are buried walls,'[19] and the deeper Alice descends, the closer she comes to the dark place of forgetting. As Harald Weinrich writes in *Lethe: The Art and Critique of Forgetting*, 'Perhaps forgetting is also only, in trivial terms, *a hole in memory* into which something falls or *disappears*.'[20]

Death is the ultimate form of forgetting. On the most basic level, forgetting makes it possible to live without death, but forgetting is also death itself. In Milan Kundera's view, forgetting 'is the great private problem of man; death as the loss of self. But what of this self? It is the sum of

her cupped hand
is a pocket not for change, or food,
but for Carroll
as a small White Rabbit to slip into

everything we remember. Thus, what terrifies us about death is not the loss of future but the loss of past. Forgetting is a form of death ever present within life.'[21] In the great multiplication table of the ever-expanding worlds of the Dodo, Do-Do-Dodgson's writings and perhaps especially his photographs – themselves infinitely reproducible, never necessarily just one – are always already troubled by the mark of death.[22] When we look at Carroll's photograph of Alexandra (Xie) Kitchin underneath her umbrella, taken in 1875, we know today that she is dead. Nevertheless, she lounges before us as a child forever, protected against death by the wet collodion that holds her image. Yet Xie, like her parasol, is nothing more than paper. Photography operates as a trace of a moment gone forever. Photography is a hole that is made physical in the aperture of the camera itself, the iris of the eye. The hole, then, might signify death, but it is also a place into which death might disappear and be forgotten. Photography is a trace of a moment forever held, forever young, without death. The *mise en scène* of 'Alice' is a forgetting place, for-getting rid of death.

The hole and the possibilities of leaving it open are like an optimistic Once-upon-a-time O: a place not to fill, a stomach left hungry, a story promised but left untold. As Alice says to the Mouse at the Caucus-Race:

'You promised to tell me your history, you know,' said Alice, 'and why it is you hate – C and D,' she added in a whisper, half afraid that it would be offended again.
'Mine is a long and a sad tale!' said the Mouse, turning to Alice. and sighing.
'It *is* a long tail, certainly,' said Alice, looking down with wonder at the Mouse's tail; 'but why do you call it sad?' (33)

she lounges before us as a child forever

And much to our frustration and delight, the story is never told. C and D remain empty signifiers, for writerly readers to form (perform) their own 'long and sad tale' or even 'long tail' (33). Both *Alice* tales (whether you fall through her hole or go through her mirror) are more romp than story, not much of a narrative thread: there's no climax, no character development, no sentimentality, hardly a memory of what has

protected against death
by the wet collodion
that holds her image

happened just pages before. But that's just it: it's a staging of desire, a play left open – whether C and D are for Charles and Dodgson, Carroll and the Dodo or Cixous and Derrida. After all, Derrida, like Alice, loved cats and understood Dinah's purring as the ultimate deconstructionist utterance. To this effect, he cites the following passage from *Through the Looking-Glass*:

It is a very inconvenient habit of kittens (Alice had once made the remark) that whatever you say to them, they *always* purr. 'If they would only purr for "yes," and mew for "no," or any rule of that sort,' she had said, so that one could keep up a conversation! But how *can* you talk with a person if they *always* say the same thing?'
On this occasion the kitten only purred: and it was impossible to guess whether it meant 'yes' or 'no.' (377)

The kitten in question here is the offspring of Dinah, who starts both *Wonderland* and *Through the Looking-Glass*. Dinah is one of the very few things (whether they be people, places, pets, or objects) towards which Alice shows any conscious nostalgia. It is the cat – whether it takes the form of Dinah, or the metamorphosed form of the Cheshire Cat, or the form of a black kitten or a white kitten as birthed by Mother Dinah – that Alice misses. Alice tells us with atypical sentimentality that Dinah is 'a dear quiet thing [that] sits purring so nicely by the fire, licking her paws and washing her face – and she is such a nice soft thing to nurse' (26). In *Wonderland* and *Through the Looking-Glass*, cats can be understood as a metonymy for memory.

While Dinah is associated with saucers of milk and hunting mice, her displaced image as the Cheshire Cat is literally all mouth: '"Well! I've often seen a cat without a grin," thought Alice; "but a grin without a cat! It's the most curious thing I ever saw in my life!"' (67). Like the rabbit hole, this Cheshire Cat mouth is yet another spatiality of memory into which to fall. Anorectically metonymic, it feeds nothing. It stresses the void; rather than a recuperation of memory, it is its evacuation.

Second Empty Bite: Eating Words

Falling head-first right down that rabbit hole 'filled with cupboards', Alice initiates the eating down under by grabbing a jar labelled 'ORANGE MARMALADE', although 'to her great disappointment it was empty' (13). Likewise, she drinks language through a bottle (not empty) tagged 'DRINK ME' and chews language through a cake on which the words 'EAT ME' are spelled out in currants. In an echo of the Mad Hatter's paradox of whether the phrase 'I eat what I see' is the same as 'I see what I eat', Alice might say 'I read what I eat' is the same as 'I eat what I read'. Getting biblical with the Reverend Dodgson (yes, another hat worn by our Carroll/Dodgson mathematician, logician, writer, inventor, photographer, Oxford don), I cannot help but quote Jeremiah 15:16: 'Your words were found, and I ate them.' Carroll and his fictional Alice share the appetite of the withholding ascetic: their nutriment is textual; they eat words, not food.

When Alice eats the whole 'very small cake, on which the words "EAT ME" were beautifully marked in currants', she decides to 'set to *work*, and very soon finished off the cake' (18–19, emphasis mine). I have never found a small cake laborious to eat. Small words, on the other hand, can be a real bother, especially verbs – the category to which the word 'eat' belongs. As Humpty Dumpty claims, 'They've a temper, some of them – particularly verbs: they're the proudest – adjectives you can do anything with, but not verbs' (213). And let's not forget that Humpty Dumpty, who claims to be the Master of Language, is an egg, something to eat, and, like the Cheshire Cat, is all mouth – to the point that he verges on decapitation. '"If he smiled much more the ends of his mouth might meet behind," she thought: "and then I don't know *what* would happen to his head! I'm afraid it would come off!"' (210). It's all about displacement, about mouthing metonymy.

Eating as grammatical work is a form of anorexic labour (for the anorexic, eating is always work), in that it not only keeps desire in check (for one is never full/filled), but always embraces death. Death is the soulmate of the anorexic. Nevertheless, eating also keeps one close to death, in that a person must eat to grow older, grow towards death. The coupling of 'to eat is to die' with '*not* to eat is to die' is a double theme also found in J. M. Barrie's Neverland: a faraway island where Peter, a child who never grows up, hardly ever eats and is more fond of pretend food than he is of real food. As Wendy notices,

He could eat, really eat, if it was part of a game, but he could not stodge just to feel stodgy, *which is what most children like better than anything else*; the next best thing being to talk about it. Make-believe was so real to him that during a meal of it you could see him getting rounder.[23]

Likewise in Alice's tales, the excess of growing, of language itself, of babies turning into omnivorous pigs, is always matched by the impossibility of a full meal, a real meal.

Alice's orderly suppression of eating in *Wonderland* and *Through the Looking-Glass* is ultimately a purification of appetite. In the words of Adam Phillips, the world of the anorexic is one 'in which nothing can be eaten, nothing must be taken in.'[24] What might this suggest about narrative itself? Carroll claims a story gives us a framework, a menu to peruse, but then ultimately withholds the narrative, at least one that is conventionally told. Filled to the brim with rich words – which can never have only one meaning, but always already have layers of meaning – there is no food into which to sink our teeth. To go underground and through the mirror is to be at once anorectic and hedonistic. Carroll seemingly says, 'I would prefer not to tell a story,' just as the anorexic politely refuses to eat, claiming in a seemingly indifferent tone, with all the power of Herman Melville's Bartleby himself, 'I would prefer not to.'[25] Nevertheless, the anorexic knows how to present a meal and trim a table, just as Carroll gives us one of the most excessive, complex, often-quoted pieces of English fiction. A world is created in which *almost* nothing is eaten, and *almost* nothing can be taken in. This always-hungry world fills us with desire. We want to sit down and read/eat.

Even in his photographs, as in his *Alice* books, Carroll plays at eating without eating. (This eating without eating is not unlike every photograph being connected to the Real, without being the real thing.[26]) For example, in Carroll's 1857 photograph of Agnes Grace Weld as *Little*

Red Riding Hood, her unveiled basket exposes cakes that stage the act of eating, but do not look *really* delectable. We see in Agnes's menacing eyes the wolf's desire to eat Little Red, making us wonder whether Agnes is going to consume us as vampire viewers. Agnes, with her thick mane of hair, widow's peak and bat-wing cape, just might leap upon us, like Angela Carter's 'Wolf-Alice', 'to lick, without hesitation, without disgust with a tender gravity, the blood and dirt' from our cheeks and foreheads.[27] 'Wolf-Alice' is a surprising mix-of-a-story, suggestively borrowing from Jean-Marc-Gaspard Itard's *The Wild Boy of Aveyron*, 'Little Red Riding Hood', Bram Stoker's *Dracula* and *Alice's Adventures in Wonderland*. Lewis Carroll's 'Wolf-Agnes', like 'Wolf-Alice', appears to have also been 'suckled by wolves': both have been fed by related, if radically different, arterial-blood stories.[28]

In Carroll's 1864 photograph of Agnes Florence Price, the model holds a doll face-to-face, mocking the proper, nurturing mother; she is a duplication of Alice holding the Duchess's baby-turned-pig. As Nina Auerbach writes, 'the doll becomes less a thing to nourish than a thing to eat.'[29] But what kind of food is a toy doll?

Likewise, when in 1873 Carroll pictures Alexandra (Xie) Kitchin sitting on crates painted with Chinese floral patterns and bound tight with rope, with her cap on in *Tea Merchant (On Duty)* and again with it off in *Tea Merchant (Off Duty)*, there are no biscuit boxes among her crates of tea. How fitting that the focus is on tea, a drink free of calories but rich with energy-inducing caffeine. Tea, like coffee, is ascetic: it masks hunger; it feeds without food.

When Carroll endorsed the manufacturing of an Alice biscuit tin decorated with Tenniel's illustrations, he claimed unease with his story being used to sell a brand of biscuits. But perhaps his actual uneasiness was with the biscuits themselves. When Carroll gave many of the tins away to his little friends, he gave them without the biscuits.[30]

An eating disorder such as anorexia nervosa is the ultimate ordering of eating, a form of obsessiveness, which is often hailed in other aspects of daily life. Carroll himself was filled to the brim with his own obsessive orderliness. Each day, he lunched only on a glass of sherry and a biscuit.

Agnes Florence Price

what kind of
food is a toy doll?

Tea,
like
coffee,
is ascetic:

it masks
hunger;
it feeds
without
food.

In a more reflective but related way, his journals record dinner parties mapping where each guest sat and what each person ate. When packing for a trip, he wrapped each article of clothing in so much tissue paper that there was more paper than shirts, trousers, shoes or anything else. Carroll's pamphlet 'Eight or Nine Wise Words about Letter-writing', sold with the *Wonderland Postage-stamp Case*, included such precise directions (for example, for logging letters in and out) that one might never want to write one. Such order and etiquette, however, seemed only to fuel Carroll's own pen. It is estimated that he wrote over 100,000 letters in his last 37 years alone – and this is leaving off his first 29 years! What kind of eating is all of this licking of stamps and envelopes under the auspices of perfect order?

The *Wonderland Postage-stamp Case* envelope (which contains a simple fold-out cardboard wallet for stamps and the pamphlet on letter writing) features Alice nursing the Duchess's baby on the front, and the Cheshire Cat on the back. When one pulls out the interior stamp case, the Cheshire Cat becomes all mouth; the baby turns into an omnivorous pig. Of edible note, Carroll's rule for avoiding a letter that might 'irritate your friend' is all about taste and making it sweet. In his own words,

Another Rule is, when you have written a letter that you feel may possibly irritate your friend, however necessary you may have felt it to so express yourself, put it aside till the next day. Then read it over again, and fancy it addressed to yourself. This will often lead to your writing it all over again, taking out a lot of the vinegar and pepper, and putting in honey instead, and thus making a much more palatable dish of it![31]

To consume is to eat is to live – but to be consumed is to be eaten and to be eaten is to die. Consuming and being consumed is at the heart of many of Alice's strange conversations about who eats what; in other words, which animals and objects wear signs that say EAT ME and to whom such signs are directed. For example, Alice gets stuck on the question of whether cats eat bats and, sometimes, whether bats eat cats. She also toys with the Mouse, like a cat with a bird, by feeding him stories

The Wonderland

Postage-Stamp Case

PUBLISHED BY

EMBERLIN AND SON,

4, MAGDALEN STREET,

OXFORD.

(POST FREE, 13d.)

PRICE ONE SHILLING

Invented by

Lewis Carroll

MDCCCLXXXIX

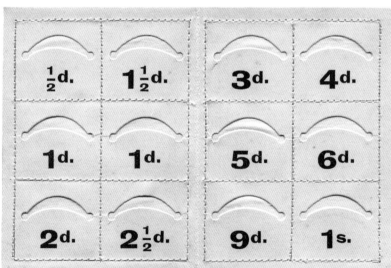

½d.	1½d.	3d.	4d.
1d.	1d.	5d.	6d.
2d.	2½d.	9d.	1s.

the Cheshire Cat becomes all mouth; the baby turns into an omnivorous pig

of Dinah. Likewise, Alice brags that Dinah is 'a capital one for catching mice' (26) and that she also knows 'a bright-eyed terrier' who 'kills all the rats' (27). When she is Tiny Alice, she fears that the 'enormous puppy' (44) might be hungry enough to eat her.[32] Most perplexing of all for Alice is when her neck grows so long that her head is high amongst the trees, causing the Pigeon to accuse her of being a cannibalistic serpent because she eats eggs:

'I've seen a good many little girls in my time, but never *one* with such a neck as that! No, no! You're a serpent . . . I suppose you'll be telling me next that you never tasted an egg!'

'I *have* tasted eggs, certainly,' said Alice, who was a very truthful child; 'but little girls eat eggs quite as much as serpents do, you know.' (55)

Emmet Gowin's photograph *Nancy, Danville, Virginia* (1969) looks like a 1960s Alice living in the American South. Her ripped and wrinkled full-of-memories slip feeds her 'sartorial ego' in an echo of Carroll's *Alice Liddell as 'The Beggar Maid'*. With her eyes closed and her long, gangly girl-arms twisted like Alice's serpent neck, Nancy holds out two eggs: like St Lucy's eyes, for the viewer to eat. Or, with further displacing violence, like Bataille's eggs, as the artist elin o'Hara slavick so provocatively suggests.[33] As one with her egg-eyes, Nancy sweetly, Aliciously, offers herself as something good enough to eat. We consume her cannibalistically. Gowin and Carroll nibble on what Maria Tatar has named 'folkloric cannibalism', as is found in the Grimms' 'Hansel and Gretel' and 'The Juniper Tree', or Perrault's 'Tom Thumb'.[34]

As the feminist literary theorist Nancy Armstrong has noted, 'all the problems with Alice's body begin and end with her mouth'[35] And yet, it hardly consumes anything at all. It is just there for getting, for forgetting.

Third Empty Bite: Kissing

Kissing, as first mentioned in regards to Antoni's *Tender Buttons*, 'involves some of the pleasures of eating in the absence of nourishment'.[36] Carroll enjoyed kissing his girl-child friends, as long as they were not so old as to wear their hair on top of their heads, or so far along into *grown-updom* that he would be required to tip his hat when greeting them (basically, they had to be under twelve years of age). He also liked to close his letters to his posse of girl-child friends by sending them ten million kisses, or 4¾ kisses, or a two-millionth of a kiss. In other words, he licked his letters closed with the same anorectic hedonism that fed his Alice stories. Carroll liked to call his beloved child-friend Alexandra Kitchin 'my dear Multiplication-Sign' – not just a diminutive 'Xie', but all the way down to 'X'.[37] Along with Alice and a whole chocolate box of other pretty young girls, Xie was one of Carroll's favourite subjects. And, of course, an X is a kiss.

Xs first became associated with kisses in the Middle Ages when, because most individuals were illiterate and could not write their names, documents would be scrawled with an X that would be followed by a kiss on an animal skin so thin that it served as paper. A little smack next to an X affirmed sincerity. X is also a kiss because it looks like two stylized people kissing. And most of all, X is a multiplier like Xie herself, like the infinitely reproducible photograph.[38] Both the X and the photograph are multipliers of delight and love, especially when developed on the body of Alexandra Kitchin.

However, calling Alexandra 'Xie' – and especially calling her 'X' – might have been less about kisses and more about Dodgson's debilitating stutter. Naming this beautiful girl X might have been a simple, if rather sexy, solution to pronouncing her difficult name.[39] If language is about eating words (reading words), then to eat/read Alexandra as X is not to eat/speak much at all. Likewise, when Alice as an alter ego of Carroll cannot remember her name and says 'L, I *know* it begins with L,' she is choosing anorectic speech as a solution to stammering speech. As Lindsay Smith makes clear, photography can also be read as avoidance of full speech, enabling Carroll to 'hold the child without the flaw of

Nancy sweetly, Aliciously, offers herself
as something good enough to eat.

language'.[40] If one cannot speak the name of the beloved, one can at least commemorate her with a photographic picture:

The connection of photography to stammering might be read as working in a way similar to that in which naming does . . . The photograph can't 'speak' the name of the absent loved one but it can otherwise commemorate that individual by triggering a temporal flight. By definition, the visual medium of photography can't figure forth a stammering subject but perhaps photography can come closer to so doing than any other visual medium.[41]

Carroll could imagine nothing lovelier than Xie before his lens. Amid such delicious anorectic Aliciousness is the story of a chocolate box, emptied of its chocolates but filled with delicious glass-plate negatives of Alice and her sisters.

In the late 1970s, the historian Colin Gordon found his way into the attic of Alice Liddell's granddaughter's home in Gloucestershire and there, within a chest of drawers, found an old wooden chocolate box, *Allen's Marvellous Chocolates*, whose confections had been eaten long ago. On the outside was the injunction 'Protect the contents from heat and damp.' On the inside, within a nest of synthetic straw, were glass-plate negatives of Alice and her sisters looking as delicious as ever, 'lolling on chairs' and 'masquerading' in costumes that Carroll kept for just such occasions.[42]

In the glass plate of Edith, Lorina and Alice Liddell for the photograph *Open Your Mouth and Shut Your Eyes*, their white cup-cake skirts are inversed as black, and their dark hair has turned preternaturally white.[43] With their mouths ready for kisses and cherries, we cannot help but read them as delicious confections more than good enough to eat. ('Eating and being eaten inspires one of the most common games adults play with babies' and children.[44]) Alice, the only one represented with an open mouth, is the subject of both a book and a photograph and serves as an evacuation of memory, a hole to fall into. Forever Liddell girls, Alice and her chocolate-box sisters are for forgetting; they are a kind of eating that makes forgetting possible.

'When we kiss,' writes Adam Phillips, 'we devour the object by caressing it; we eat it, in a sense, but sustain its presence.'[45] The kiss, then, is like a photograph. Capturing what is fleeting, the camera loves people and places not just as the conventional devouring eye, but also as a consuming mouth. Photographs as shutter kisses might be understood as an extension of kissing with the eye as if it were a mouth, like butterfly kisses. Both the kiss and the photograph are stories of taking and preserving an object, especially if the kiss is placed on the mouth, an action that 'blurs the distinctions between giving and taking'.[46] In other words, just as kissing can be described as 'aim-inhibited eating',[47] photographs can be described as aim-inhibited picture production: photography both takes and gives. In *Open Your Mouth and Shut Your Eyes*, Alice parts her lips for the two cherries in her sister's hand. She is caught/consumed by the camera, closing her eyes and opening her mouth as if ready to kiss. The 1850s have been appropriately labelled 'the culinary period of photography' because, during this period, photographers held their stolen images, not with traditional photographic chemicals, but in sugar, caramel, treacle, malt, raspberry syrup, ginger wine, sherry, beer and skimmed milk.[48]

Fourth Empty Bite: Romancement

Leaving the Alice stories aside, I want to close with a lesser-known story by Carroll, 'Novelty and Romancement', a tale that is far too dark and strange to ever be of interest to most children today (but one Lacan would have loved: a sort of witty version of Edgar Allan Poe's 'The Purloined Letter'). This sad tale involves one Leopold Edgar Stubbs, who quite by chance happens upon Simon Lubkin's shop and its signboard SIMON LUBKIN, DEALER IN ROMANCEMENT. Stubbs concludes from the sign that he can buy and readily consume something that will 'connect the threads of human destiny'.[49] Sadly, however, as if lacking the most elementary introduction to the field of semiotics, he has misread the advertisement:

Standing before that base mechanic's door, with a throbbing and expectant heart, my eye chanced to fall once more upon that signboard, once more I perused its strange inscription. Oh! fatal change! Oh! horror! What do I see? Have I been deluded by a heated imagination?

A hideous gap yawns between the N and the C, making it not one word but two![50]

Romancement has turned into Roman cement. Force-feeding every space with yet another twist of the letter (whether in a book, a poem, a pun or the post), Carroll plays at forgetting the 'hideous gap' between the words 'Roman' and 'cement' while hailing it at every turn. We dream of romance; we are constricted and weighted down by cement.

In 'Eight or Nine Wise Words about Letter-writing', Carroll insists on logging every letter received and every letter sent, carving out a space for every letter with which a person comes in contact. Despite such vigilant record-keeping, letters come and go, even after death. Letters are lost. Some sit forever undelivered at the Dead Letter Office (where Melville's anorectic Bartleby is an employee). Many are sent to the wrong address. Some are just meant for forgetting. Nevertheless, there are plenty of envelopes to lick closed without fear of absorbing the nourishment (the meaning) that each letter holds. The envelope is a spatiality, a rabbit hole, a cat hole, a mouth. The stamp is for dessert.

———

an

evacuation of

memory, a hole

to fall into

3 A Raindrop Unfallen:
Innocence and Jacques-Henri Bernardin de Saint-Pierre's *Paul and Virginia*

What is innocence? 'A Raindrop Unfallen' looks at Jacques-Henri Bernardin de Saint-Pierre's tragic fairy-tale romance, Paul and Virginia *(1788), alongside Julia Margaret Cameron's 1865 photograph of the same title. Bernardin's* Paul and Virginia *is the tale of two children on the idyllic Île de France (now Mauritius), whose love encodes an eroticized innocence, which is made photographically explicit in Cameron's re-imagining of the fairy tale with two local children from the Isle of Wight. Other artworks play into Bernardin's story, including a twenty-first-century science experiment that allows a single raindrop to float mid-air without ever falling and a pair of nineteenth-century 'freed slave' dolls that dramatize the colonialism and racism of Bernardin's not-so-innocent parts. At the heart of 'A Raindrop Unfallen' is a fresh look at innocence, redefining it as an inability to remember.*

I reach

into the air

and uncatch

innocence

(ungraspable

as a raindrop

unfallen)

Innocence Cannot be Caught

Innocence is derived from the Latin *nocēre* (meaning to hurt, injure) and the negative *in*. Innocence quivers on an impossible, or nearly impossible, state of being: to be unharmed or uninjured. It is easy to believe in innocence, but it is hard to get a hold of it. As James Kincaid has astutely, and very unromantically, remarked: 'Innocence is a lot like the air in your tires: there's not a lot you can do with it but lose it.'[1] Strange innocence is fleeting (if it exists at all).

The photograph by the American pictorialist George Seeley, entitled *The Firefly* (1907), makes me *think innocently*. (A copy of Seeley's photograph has been taped to my wall for over a decade. I am drawn to it. I cherish it. I look at it often. 'This photograph has *worked* within me.'[2]) In it, I think I see innocence. But where? At first I think it is simply in the beautiful face of the androgynous child-adolescent. Then, I think I see innocence in the little explosion clutched by the youth. But no. Like Barthes after *punctum,* my 'thinking eye' (*oeil qui pense*) wanders and tries to hold, but must not snatch.[3] I reach into the air and uncatch innocence (ungraspable as a raindrop unfallen) and find it traced by the falling-star light of the firefly, like the trail of a child's 'sparkler' on the Fourth of July. Innocence is strange and otherworldly.

A Raindrop Unfallen

Once upon a time, there was a real glistening raindrop, a beautiful miniature world, which could be held, impossibly, in the air, never dropping to the ground. It all began with a magical machine made in England in the early 1970s by the Physics Department at the University of Manchester Institute of Science and Technology. (Manchester, of course, also happens to be a particularly rainy part of the rainy United Kingdom: a very fitting place to make raindrops that never fall.) Decades later, the British artist Alistair McClymont came across the experiment and was beguiled. With a self-proclaimed childish glee for science, McClymont set about building an artist's reconstruction of the physicists' apparatus. By 2012, after two years of experimentation, McClymont was able to make a raindrop that did not fall, apprehending it above a specially designed wind tunnel. Like a stuttering word, the lone raindrop shudders in its suspension. McClymont's dreamlike raindrop whispers micro-worlds detained: a little crystal biosphere; a very small snow globe; a tiny glass jellyfish; a frozen Tom Thumb soap bubble. Of interest are its camera-lens properties: looking through it reveals a contained world that is upside down and back to front.

A raindrop is ordinary, but you never see just one, which makes McClymont's singular raindrop extraordinary. As if it were the last dodo on Mauritius (formerly called Île de France), the raindrop quivers with extinction. It shakes with the wind, like the solitary surviving *Hyophorbe amaricaulis* (also known as the 'Loneliest Palm'),[4] which grows in the botanical gardens of Curepipe (an inland town in Mauritius) and is the only known example in the world. The 'Loneliest Palm' stands thirty

*the lone
raindrop
shudders in
its suspension*

feet high and is surrounded by scaffolding; it 'is as close to extinction as a non-extinct species can be'.[5]

McClymont's raindrop may quiver in fear, but it also suspends time, by not falling. A drop of pure rain that never hits the ground is innocence uninjured, escaping the ravaging hands of tick-tock time. As if . . . in a fairy tale. As if . . . in Jacques-Henri Bernardin de Saint-Pierre's 1788 book, *Paul and Virginia*: the once famous, now rarely read, tragic fairy-tale romance of two children, innocent as birds, havened on the Île de France.

Living on an Edenic island, Paul and Virginia (born in the same year, twins of a sort, who are compared to 'the children of Leda'[6]) are raised by their two respective single mothers: Madame de la Tour and Marguerite. Each woman *mothers* both children and all four live idyllically. The children are described as passing their early days in 'innocence', with conversation 'as mild and innocent as their excellent meals'.[7]

The beginning of the story is a lactating, redoubling *mise en scène* of two mother-lover-friends and their children-brother-sister-lovers:

Their mutual affection redoubled at the sight of their children, each of whom was the fruit of an unfortunate love. They delighted to bathe them together and to put them to sleep in the same cradle; often one would give her milk to the other's child.[8]

Paul and Virginia

The children will grow up to call each other brother and sister. 'When they were able to speak, the first words they learned to exchange were "brother" and "sister".[9] Each child will refer to both mothers as 'mother'. The brother and sister raised by two mothers will fall in love. Incest, homoeroticism and innocence are the faces in the clouds that blush sanguine coral amid the fluff of grey clouds, which threaten to cry stormy tears over the island of Paul and Virginia.

In 1864, the Victorian photographer Julia Margaret Cameron used her pencil of light, her camera, to photo-graph (light-write) the lightly incestual (brotherly-sisterly) *Paul and Virginia*. Cameron's Orientalist reading of two deliciously seductive children who lived near her on the Isle of Wight, her own Île de France, features Freddy Gould (the son of a fisherman) and Elizabeth Keown (the daughter of a military officer stationed on the island). Elizabeth gives us the unfaltering stare of the child. Freddie's bedroom eyes are arresting. The two children are androgynous, are lookalikes, are twinning sameness. The poses and expressions of the children, along with their bare skin, tangled and tousled hair, coupled with the treatment of the photograph, with its soft in-and-out-of-focus focus, touched-all-over smudges on the plate, even feet that have been drawn over (see Freddie's scritch-scratched toes), are typically Cameronesque.[10] The photograph speaks erotically. Cameron's is a sloppy, seductive handling of the child and sexuality at once.

By fixing Bernardin's utopian fairy tale as a photograph, Cameron's *touch* effectively troubles the waters of the sanctuary of a presumed innocent Edenic pre-adolescent life. Nevertheless, I seek to find a raindrop unfallen, as innocence differently maintained. Not as something with which to *unjustly* clothe the child's body, in order to make them paradoxically that much more desirable, more taboo, as has been so justly argued by James Kincaid. Rather, as a way of thinking freely, laterally, horizontally, sibling-wise, without the fall of Freud's Father-Mother-Child Oedipal troubles. I grab at the air for an innocence worthy of detention.

Infant Bridal

Paul and Virginia are raised with tropical wedding bells in the air:

Already, over their cradles, their mothers were talking of the day
when they would marry . . .

. . . nothing could compare to the attachment already displayed . . .
I never came here without finding them both naked, as is the custom
in this country, scarcely able to walk and supporting each other by
the hands and under the arms, like a picture of the twins in the constellation of Gemini. Even the night could not part them; they would
be found lying in the same cradle, cheeks and breasts pressed together, their hands round each other's neck, embracing as they slept.[11]

This pressed embrace of Paul and Virginia is echoed again and again
by Cameron. See for example her *The Double Star*, *The Infant Bridal* and
The Turtle Doves (all from 1864). The latter (modelled by Elizabeth
Keown and her sister Alice) has been haphazardly cut into the shape of
an oval raindrop. The photograph's title has been written on the back of
the photograph and has seeped through in reverse, like 'Looking-Glass'
letters in silver milk. Alice Keown's open mouth draws me in like a breath
taken. The openness speaks, I think, innocently.

In *Goodnight Kiss* (1988), the American photographer Sally Mann has
redoubled this open mouth of *The Turtle Doves*. With even more water-baby
focus,[12] the turning of one child's head turns all eyes to the soft mouth of
Mann's *Goodnight Kiss*. Mann, unlike Cameron, does not feature neighbour
children, but rather her own two daughters: Jessie and Virginia. Open-
mouthed three-year-old Virginia resuscitates her illustrious name into the
mouth of her older sister. Virginia Mann is a twentieth-century guiltless
girl, whose name is rooted in 'virgin'. 'Virginia' echoes the Virgin Mary
and Queen Elizabeth I of England. It hums the state of Virginia (Mann and
her children both grew up in Virginia). It sings Virginia Carter, the name
of the woman who was a second mother to Sally Mann. (Virginia Mann
is named after Virginia Carter.) It resonates the author of *The Waves* and
To the Lighthouse and *A Room of One's Own*. Virginia Woolf just happened

to be the great-niece of Cameron.[13] It warbles countless other Virginias, including the one who was loved by Bernardin's Paul.

But Paul and Virginia are not only about their pre-Oedipal Double-Star-Infant-Bridal-Turtle-Doves-Goodnight-Kiss years. Their island is ripe with erotic metaphors, suggestive of the intensity of the changing adolescent bodies of Paul and Virginia. When the children enter their twelfth year, the two coconut trees tha were planted at the time of their births cry out with sexualized teenage lankiness and loneliness. Together, they are under threat, like the island itself, which was invaded by the Dutch in 1598, only to be colonized by France and then captured by Britain in 1810. (Though still infused with beauty, 'today, Mauritius is a "trashed island".'[14]) In the words of Bernardin, the two coconut trees

grew in the same proportion as the children, being somewhat unequal in height, and at the end of twelve years reached above the roofs of … [their respective mothers'] cabins, intertwining their palms and letting their clusters of young coconuts hang above the surface of the pool. These two trees excepted, they had left the hollow below the rock with no ornaments but those of nature. On its damp brown slopes great tufts of maidenhair beamed like green and black stars, and bunches of hart's tongue, hanging down like long ribbons of purplish green, waved at the wind's pleasure. Nearby were borders of periwinkles, whose blossoms are so much like those of the red gilly-flower, and pimentos, their blood-red pods more brilliant than coral. Round about, the balsam-plant with its heart shaped leaves, and basil with the odour of cloves, gave out the sweetest perfumes.[15]

With an eye on these two adolescent, brotherly-sisterly, self-same coconut trees, one might imagine Virginia proclaiming to Paul, as Catherine does to Heathcliff, in Emily Brontë's *Wuthering Heights* (1847): 'He's more myself than I am. Whatever our souls are made of, his and mine are the same.'[16] This untroubled utopia is short-lived, like childhood, like a moment captured by the camera. Life soon moved beyond the frame of childhood (of the photograph). Before long, Paul and Virginia are threatened by a stormy adolescence and, with it, erotic desire. Sexual relations between Paul and Virginia, who are not brother and sister, yet are not *not* brother and sister, would not be incest, yet would not *not* be incestuous. Each as an umbrella to the other, Paul and Virginia seek shelter from the falling rain. In the words of the narrator:

Whenever one of them was to be found, the other was to be close by. One day, as I was coming down from the top of this mountain, I noticed Virginia running from the end of the garden towards the house, the back of her petticoat thrown up over her head as protection against a sudden shower. From a distance I thought she was alone, but as I came forward to give her my arm I saw that she was holding Paul's – he was entirely covered by the same canopy – and they were laughing, both of them, to be sheltering together under an umbrella of their own invention. The sight of these two pretty heads encircled by the billowing petticoat brought to my mind the children of Leda, enclosed in the same shell.[17]

a twentieth-century guiltless girl, whose name is rooted in 'virgin'

Innocence re(a)d

As the children find themselves deeper and deeper in the (rain)forest of adolescence, the novel blushes more red. Hormone-fed Virginia finds herself 'troubled by a strange ailment'[18] – teenage love:

Her skin took on a yellow tint; her fine blue eyes became shot with black; all her body felt languid and oppressed . . . She would suddenly assume a joyless gaiety or appear dejected without cause . . . Sometimes at the site of Paul, she would run playfully towards him; then, having nearly reached her goal, she would stop, seized with a sudden embarrassment; her pale cheeks would flush deeply and her eyes no longer dare to rest on his.[19]

'Possessed with a consuming fire',[20] Virginia hungers for her 'brother'. The mothers understand this appetite. It is time for the 'infant bridal' to become real, more than a Tom Thumb wedding. Yet the sweet betrothal is sure to lead to an impoverished future for their children and themselves. The mothers are growing old. Everyone is ageing, despite the utopian no-time, u-chronia that their island life tries to maintain.[21]

Paul and Virginia had no clocks or almanacks, no books of chronology, history of philosophy. They regulated their lives according to the cycles of Nature. They knew the hours of the day by the shadows of the trees, the seasons by the times when they flower or fruit, and the years by the number of their crops. As a result, the most delightful images were scattered through their conversations. 'It is dinner-time,' Virginia would say to the family, 'the shadows of the banana-trees are at their feet;' or, 'Night will fall soon, the tamarinds are closing their leaves.'

'When will you come and see us?' some girls who lived nearby would ask. 'At sugar-cane time.'[22]

Then suddenly, fairy-tale hope arrives and the action of the story moves forward with great force, like a tempest. With the promise of riches, Virginia's ailing and moneyed aunt in France persuades her niece to set sail for the continent. Paul and Virginia will be wealthy and live happily ever after. But at a cost: Virginia will have to be educated and turned into a European lady and must leave Paul behind, until the end of her aunt's life, when she will inherit the wealth. Nevertheless, Virginia embraces the sacrifice and sets sail. Paul, of course, is left devastated and empty. A year and a half later, Virginia, the girl-turned-woman, comes home to the Île de France, only to be greeted by a great hurricane. Her ship becomes stuck offshore, near the north of the island, close to the district called La Proudre d'Or (Gold Dust). Paul hears of Virginia's near-arrival and of her ship in distress. He rushes to meet Virginia. This is the end of everything. Standing in the stern-gallery, a bit like Kate Winslet in James Cameron's film *Titanic* (1997), Virginia stretches her arms towards Paul, whom she sees on shore. She waves her hand, as if to bid . . . an eternal farewell. Only one of the sailors had remained on deck, all the others having cast themselves into the sea. He was completely naked and muscular as Hercules. We saw him approach Virginia with respect, throw himself down before her and even do what he could to remove her clothes; but she, turning away her eyes, rejected with dignity his attempts to help her . . .

But at that very moment a mountain of water of terrifying size swept in . . . At this dreadful sight the sailor sprang alone into the sea; while Virginia, seeing that death was inevitable, kept one hand on her billowing clothes, placed the other on her heart, and raising upwards eyes shining with serenity, seemed an angel taking flight for heaven.

Alas! O dreadful day! All was swallowed up.[23]

Virginia's death is sexually clothed in determined chasteness. She will not undress.

Virginia is swallowed up by the sea, as if she were the Little Mermaid: there is nowhere else to go. Both Bernardin and Hans Christian Andersen tell tales of aroused feminine desires absorbed by a Christianized *mise en scène*. By necessity, both *Paul and Virginia* and 'The Little Mermaid' have unhappy, sacrificial fairy-tale endings. Andersen's heroes and heroines, unlike the central characters of the Brothers Grimm and Charles Perrault, do not find an earthly happily ever after. 'The Little Mermaid' is no exception: 'One more time, with her eyes half glazed, she looked at the prince. Then she threw herself from the ship into the sea, and she felt her body dissolve into the foam.'[24]

Jean-Baptiste Huet, the painter and textile designer, produced a beautiful red and white *toile de Jouy* of *Paul and Virginia* as an archipelago of the doomed romance (1802). Although the fabric is now faded and worn, the little islands stage scenes from the story: the two mothers caring for their children (looking like Mary and Elizabeth, with John the Baptist and Jesus), their housedog Fidele looking on; Paul pleading to Virginia to stay and not leave on the ship; the discovery of Virginia's body after the shipwreck; Virginia's pair of goats. Huet's design for Paul and Virginia 'encircled by the billowing petticoat', as if they had borrowed

the cloak of Little Red Riding Hood is a nod to *Le Petit Chaperon rouge*.[25] Already a part of the oral tradition of France, the first published version of *Le Petit Chaperon rouge* was in 1697 in *Histoires ou Contes du temps passé, avec des moralités*.

The film-maker, artist and writer Derek Jarman gets at the red heart of it: 'I blink there's Red Riding Hood in the dark forest. A bright red cloak in the gathering gloom. The red-eyed wolf licks his scarlet chops.'[26]

Virginia blushes, blooms, bleeds and cloaks fairy-tale red. 'Paul . . . would crown her with a garland of red periwinkle blossoms which set off her fair complexion.'[27] Virginia looks lovely in the simple red hand-kerchief, her own *chaperon rouge*, which she ties around her head. Recall how the periwinkle flowers that flourish near the two coconut trees are like the blossoms of 'the red gillyflower, and pimentos, their blood-red pods more brilliant than coral'.[28]

Forgoing Huet's once vibrant red, the French painter Pierre-Auguste Cot spins Paul and Virginia's 'billowing petticoat' out of gold and names

it *The Storm*.[29] Compared to Huet's modest little print, Cot's golden rain romp is Bouguereau saccharine-sweet. In Cot's fantasy, a golden silk tent billows over the blossoming-into-adolescence-children: Virginia in transparent tulle, like Easter confectionery, and Paul sporting Dionysus skins with a blue sash to hold his drinking horn. They are dusted in La Proudre d'Or excess and served up in an elaborate gold g(u)ilt frame. More in keeping with Bernardin is Huet's tent of Little Red Riding Hood red, not Cot's Rumpelstiltskin greedy gold.

Innocence Does Not Eat Time

Paul and Virginia are in a race against time: against *falling* into their impending sexuality; against taking a bite from the apple; against the Fall of Man spelled out in Genesis. As if trying to eat in an Eden before the Fall, Paul and Virginia spend their days in a world of *natural* eating, imagined as preternaturally pure, as almost without desire.

While Paul and Virginia may indulge in the almost decadent consumption of 'sherbets and cordials from the juice of sugar-cane-lemons and citrons',[30] they nevertheless imagine themselves as birds, understanding their hunger as always satisfied, as free of starving desire. In the words of Virginia: 'God . . . answers the cries of the little birds when they ask Him for food.'[31] Their eating is innocent: 'for which no animal had paid with its life . . . Gourds brimming with milk, fresh eggs, rice-cakes served on banana leaves, baskets of sweet-potatoes, custard-apples, mangoes, oranges, pomegranates, bananas and pineapple provided at once the most nourishing dishes, the gayest colours and the sweetest juices.'[32] Their eating is at its best when unsullied by labour, as when Paul and Virginia eat from 'banana-trees whose substantial fruit furnished them with a dish ready-prepared and whose long, broad and glossy leaves served as linen for their table.'[33]

St Paul the Hermit, the first Christian hermit, for whom Marguerite named her son, also ate innocently, even clothed himself innocently. He lived in a cave for almost a hundred years; a nearby palm tree furnished him with fruit for food and leaves that he wove into clothing. Along with water from a stream, the palm tree was all that he needed, was in a sense his self-same Virginia (his coconut tree, his 'Loneliest Palm'). Around his neck, Bernardin's Paul wore a tiny miniature of St Paul the Hermit: it had once belonged to his mother. When Virginia set sail for France, Paul gave the miniature portrait to his sweetheart-sister: she never took it off and died with its 'innocence' clenched in her hands.

'The Magic Negro'

Like Thomas More's *Utopia* (1516), further dystopia nestles inside the paradise of *Paul and Virginia*, through the body of the slave. In the case of More, slavery is justified as a good solution for problem people: like those 'enslaved for some heinous offence' or others who are 'hard-working penniless drudges from other nations who voluntarily choose slavery in Utopia'.[34] Bernardin's utopia is marred with the problem that the novel justifies slavery by making the survival of Paul and Virginia and their two mothers dependent upon it. Bernardin, as if making a Hollywood film, makes use of what the *New York Times* writer Nelson George refers to (in his review of Tate Taylor's 2011 blockbuster *The Help*) as '"the Magic Negro," a character whose function is to serve as a mirror so that the white lead can see himself more clearly, sometimes at the expense of the black character's life'.[35]

The two slave characters in Bernardin's novel, Marie and Domingue, nourish the 'happy lives' of Madame de la Tour, Marguerite, Paul and Virginia. Domingue was a 'Yolof Negro' (from Gambia); Marie 'had been born in Madagascar'.[36] Madame de la Tour owned Marie from the time of her marriage and Marguerite had borrowed 'a small sum, enough to acquire an old Negro'.[37] Fortuitously, Marie and Domingue meet. The man slave and the woman slave marry and are scripted as being 'happy' to make those who enslave them 'happy' through their 'unremitting labour'.[38]

Domingue, Marguerite's Yolof Negro, although no longer young, was still strong and active and joined experience to his native good sense.

He cultivated the ground that seemed to him most fertile, whether on Marguerite's property or Madame de la Tour's choosing for each the most suitable kind of seed . . . Along the river and around the cabins he set banana-trees, which give long clusters of fruit and cooling shade all the year round, and a few tobacco plants to lighten his hours of care and those of his good mistress . . . He was strongly attached to Marguerite and hardly less so to Madame de la Tour, whose Negress he had married when Virginia was born. She was called Marie and he loved her passionately. She had been born in Madagascar and had brought with her some of the crafts of her birthplace, especially the weaving of baskets . . . Skilful, neat and faithful, she saw to the preparation of meals, raised a few chickens and from time to time went to Port Louis to sell what the two families produced in excess of their needs, which was indeed very little.[39]

her
black
skin has
torn to
reveal a
hole of
white
cotton

Marie and Domingue are lovable passive 'Magical Negroes', shadowed by the *Uncle Tom's Cabin* yet to be written: Domingue as an 'Uncle Tom' for bringing food to the two mothers and their children; Marie as a 'Mammy' for more maternal care in this isolated matriarchal family.

Marie and Domingue are rendered like the homespun, elegant black dolls (1834–6), pupas, housed in Manchester's Whitworth Art Gallery. It is believed that the dolls may have been made to mark the freeing of slaves belonging to Ralph Henry Samuel, a textile merchant from Liverpool who also ran a successful cotton plantation in Rio de Janeiro.[40] The 'Marie' doll holds a white baby like so many Mammies before her and after her, all the way up to *The Help*. The 'Mammy' is worn: her black skin has torn to reveal a hole of white cotton. The 'Domingue' doll is very fashionably dressed in a fancy-print short coat. On his head he balances a large box covered in indigo-blue-coffee-brown-vanilla-ivory-cinnamon-patterned fabrics (perhaps like those sold by the textile merchant who once owned him). A smaller, closed silver box, without a golden key, is belted on top. While Paul and Virginia and their two mothers are free of possessions not made by their own hands ('halved gourds were all they had for dishes and banana-leaves for table-linen'[41]), they own

their beloved doll-like Marie and Domingue, as they do their dog Fidele. The carefully calculated 'stitch in time saves nine' words of Bernardin (stylistically a reduplication of the supposedly simple, utopian living of *Paul and Virginia*) cannot stitch fast enough to secure this hole in the text. Nature is always historical (damaged, bigoted, violent, troubling); there is no way around it.[42]

Given that the word 'doll' comes from the Latin *pupa*, hence the French *poupée*; given that play and imagination magically animate the doll; given that the pupa is the chrysalis before it becomes a butterfly and flies away 'free' – these Liverpool dolls, along with Domingue and Marie, are inert pupae in a troubling 'utopia' that cannot break free from the constraints of the magical happiness that they are indentured to provide, even when set free.

The bigotry of the novel plays through Bernardin's text, like the outdoor plays in the forest staged by Paul and Virginia. Sometimes, Virginia 'would perform a mime with Paul in the *native* fashion. Mime is the first language of man . . . so natural and expressive that the children of white settlers lose no time in learning it themselves once they have seen it practised by the black children of the island.'[43]

———

I stop and wonder with the too-easily compartmentalized 'white guilt' of my American homeland. My elderly mother's life was lovingly sustained by the help of Gloria: an African American woman who breathed new life into my mother, who had Alzheimer's. I am not beyond (The) Help. For a brief time, Gloria was a kind of mother to me, although she was the same age as I was; for she taught me how to mother my mother, who had become my father's other little girl.

Innocence is Not Guilty

One thing is for sure: innocence zigzags with guilt, is in touch with it. As an adult, I know fully well how it feels to feel guilty. Innocence, however, like a raindrop *unfallen*, cannot be felt. It just is. I can claim innocence, but I cannot feel it.

Innocence is impossible to hold. Nevertheless, I believe that innocence, dare I say it, is real. Innocence is 'a tiny bead of pure life'. But how to get a hold of it, without harming it?

Innocence Cannot Remember

'Where we goin' George?'

The little man jerked down the brim of his hat and scowled over at Lennie. 'So you forgot that awready, did you? I gotta tell you again, do I? Jesus Christ, you're a crazy bastard!'

'I forgot,' Lennie said softly. 'I tried not to forget. Honest to God I did, George.'

John Steinbeck, *Of Mice and Men*

Although centuries and cultures away from *Paul and Virginia*, the American novella *Of Mice and Men*, written by John Steinbeck in 1937, gives the most moving account of (strange) innocence I know. In *Of Mice and Men*, innocence is the inability to remember.

In the story, two drifters, George Milton and his 'simple' friend Lennie Small, come to work on a ranch in the fertile Salinas Valley. Lennie is big, is grown-up (overgrown), but struggles with his small intelligence and his inability to remember. George scoffs at Lennie for constantly not remembering: Lennie cannot remember to stroke soft things gently.

Lennie is described as 'a kinda nice fella. Jus' like a big baby.'[44] When George takes a petted-dead, pilfered mouse away from his companion, 'he heard Lennie's whimpering cry' and says to him: 'Blubberin' like a baby! Jesus Christ! A big guy like you!'[45]

Lennie is likened to animals and often speaks of them. When George demands Lennie to give up the dead mouse in his pocket, the two become a master and his dog:

George's hand remained outstretched imperiously. Slowly, like a terrier who doesn't want to bring a ball to its master, Lennie approached, drew back, approached again. George snapped his fingers sharply, and at the sound Lennie had the mouse in his hand.[46]

Lennie's love of softness, the texture of innocence, is just about all that his small mind has room for. Only softness occupies this *bête*. As a noun, *bête* means beast or animal. As an adjective, *bête* means not very bright and lacking in judgement; stupid; inept.

Lennie, *la bête*, catches mice like a terrier and squirrels them away in his pockets like stolen goods. Lennie strokes and strokes innocent mice too much with his too-big fingers. Lennie's great hope is to own pet rabbits, 'Furry ones, George, like I seen in the fair in Sacramento'.[47] In 1966, the Sacramento painter Wayne Thiebaud created a white rabbit, drawn out of Lennie's dreams, with lipstick-like oil pastel, thick as cake icing. Like cotton candy at the Sacramento State Fair. Thiebaud's *Rabbit* is sweet, makes your teeth ache. But dreams cannot be touched.

Lennie's love for softness is without intelligence: he does not separate the softness of animals from the softness of women. Lennie gets caught not only for over-petting mice, but for stroking a woman's soft skirt. Finally, to his tragic end, Lennie is drawn to the soft hair of Curley's wife. (Curley, the son of the superintendent of the ranch, is a small man with 'coarse hair' and a Napoleon complex.[48]) Curley's wife invites Lennie Small to feel her hair: 'Feel right aroun' there an' see how soft it is.'[49]

Lennie's innocence is his inability to remember. If you cannot remember, you cannot have knowingess. You cannot be held responsible. You cannot be guilty. But to be innocent is always already to be 'not guilty'. The two are inseparable, like Paul carrying Virginia on his back. ('The noise of the water so frightened Virginia that she was afraid to wade across. So Paul took her on his back. Stepping from one slippery stone to another, he carried her over the turbulent water to the other side, telling her as he went: "Don't be afraid; with you I feel very strong."'[50])

When heartbreaking Lennie tries to get a hold of innocence, he kills it. George to Lennie: 'you've broke it pettin' it.'[51]

Raindrops fall. 'Grief is a Mouse – '[52]

4 Poto and Cabengo

'Dugon, haus you dinikin, du-ah,' says Poto.
'Snup-aduh ah-wee diedipana, dihabana,' replies Cabengo.

Poto and Cabengo were twin girls who came to fame on the 1970s for their captivating use of a private, invented language. These little dark-haired princesses of words were chirpy and sweet and seemingly oblivious to the world outside of their bubble. Moving about and sounding like humming-birds, the girls were unreal, like something from a fairy tale. They became a media sensation. The whole world (parents, educators, therapists, the newspaper-reading public, television-watchers, even a Hollywood movie producer) wanted to believe that these beautiful girls, made of staccato rhythm, were magical. But, with further examination by the experts, it turned out that they did not practice Alicious 'Jabberwocky'. Nor did they have the good luck of Snow White. (They were not able to cough up the poisoned apple that an all-consuming commodity culture had fed them.) They lost their special voices.

In real life fairy tales do not come true.

Once upon a time there were two little twin German-American girls named 'Poto' and 'Cabengo'. They were remarkable and captivating for their fast-speaking cryptophasia or 'twin language'. Poto's *real* name was Grace. Cabengo's *real* name was Virginia. 'Poto' and 'Cabengo' were their concocted names for each other. Their parents called them Gracie and Ginny. These twin 'princesses of words' were chirpy and sweet.[1]

In the 1970s, at the tender age of six, Poto and Cabengo became a media sensation. Newspapers from San Diego to New York pondered and questioned: had the twins invented their own secret language? Were the gibberish-talking twins possessed? Did their high-pitched rapid-fire

Martian-speak offer a key to the origins of the development of speech? Even the BBC made a visit to their cramped apartment in Linda Vista, a suburb of San Diego, California – 25 miles from the Mexican border.

Their mother, Christine, was born on a farm outside Berlin. Their father, Tom, was born in the American South (Atlanta, Georgia); he was a one-time Air Force man. He met Christine in Munich at an Oktoberfest party.

When they were born, little Gracie and Ginny suffered from convulsions. The parents were told that the girls were cognitively disabled. Tom came home and punched a hole in the wall. Christine's nerves became so bad that she could no longer hold down a job. Out of fear for their girls, Christine and Tom isolated their fluttering twins from the *real* world, that *real* world in which the parents were enduring lives of blasted hope: both economic and familial. (Yet years later, when the girls were tested by therapists, they were found to have relatively normal IQs.)

Poto and Cabengo lived not only with their parents, but also with their maternal grandmother, who knew only five English words, more or less. The family was poor. They lived on food stamps, welfare and the occasional house sale by their tragically financially unsuccessful realtor father. Living space was cramped. The 'compound in which they lived had been built after WWII for returning Navy personnel'.[2] The twins shared one of the rented apartment's two bedrooms with their grandmother. The 'taciturn grandmother' spoke to them in German, dressed them, cared for them, kept them immaculately clean, and loved them with a sternness straight out of an August Sanders portrait.[3]

Poto and Cabengo lived in a secluded post-war cement garden. With gasps of green grass and a bit of moist earth, their voices were strong, bright yellow dandelion flowers that burst out of the cracks, somehow overcoming the tyranny of the cement that imprisoned them and the harshness of the too-sunny weather.

Seemingly oblivious to the world outside of their bubble, Poto and Cabengo played with language and themselves. With their dark feline-shaped eyes and dark blue-otter-coloured irises – and their long thin arms like the new wings of young swallows – and their smooth, pixie-cut hair and their long, sun-tanned, clean legs hoofed with white sandals, always paired with tidy white bobby-socks – they galloped, trotted, flapped, soared, chattered, squeaked, tweeted, sang and chirped a poetry of unknown semantics (an unwritten concrete poetry) through the perennial fair-weather air of San Diego. Imagined and imagining creatures, they moved about and stared like little animals and over-wound wind-up toys. (Was there a wind-up key between their wing-like scapulae?) All the while Poto and Cabengo appeared wise and knowing, with a bit of malice – a bit of Alice. They were Alice-Malices.

Poto and Cabengo were unreal, like something from a fairy tale.

The Magic of Film

In 1980, the Sorbonne-educated film-maker Jean-Pierre Gorin (known for working with Jean-Luc Godard on several films, most famously *Tout va bien* and *Letter to Jane*, both from 1972) made a film about the twins entitled *Poto and Cabengo*: a documentary, purposely unhinged, spoken like a pondering essay, taking on the strategies and sensibilities of the 'film essay' or the 'cine-essay', hearkening other French film-makers, such as Chris Marker and Godard himself.[4]

For *Poto and Cabengo*, Gorin uses his own voice for the voiceover: charming up his French accent, whimsically using his 'outsider English' to make a point. He too is a foreigner to English, like the girls themselves. Flirting with his listening audience, his accented voice playfully withholds, not unlike the chatter of the twins, which also keeps meaning at bay. We are not sure what to think. Where is he taking us?

Gorin's voiceover notes that the story of Poto and Cabengo is a 'fairy tale' that everyone wanted to believe.[5] But the yellow-brick road stops short of the kingdom of the fairy tales.

The story of Poto and Cabengo echoes Jean-Marc-Gaspard Itard's 'fairy tale' of a foundling, who was found, or more precisely caught, in a French forest in 1797. The story became the subject of his study: *The Wild Boy of Aveyron*.[6] François Truffaut's 1970 film *Wild Child* (*L'Enfant sauvage*) is based on Itard's story. 'On 6 June 1969, Truffaut declared that he had found [his wild child] "his little boy": "He's a very handsome child, but I think he really looks like he came out of the woods.'"[7] And like Itard's 'Wild Boy', things do not turn out so well for the girls.

The whole world (parents, educators, therapists, newspaper-reading public, television watchers, even a Hollywood movie producer) wanted to believe that these beautiful girls, made of staccato rhythm, were magical.[8] Poto and Cabengo embodied innocence, invention, utopia. They echoed (echoed) each other in hopeful song, as if in a wishing (wishing) well like Disney's Snow White. And they Tweedledee-dummed each other in *Looking-Glass* chatter.

Two Alices in Reverse

'Twas brillig, and the slithy toves
    Did gyre and gimble in the wabe:
All mimsy were the borogoves
    And the mome raths outgrabe.

Lewis Carroll, 'Jabberwocky', *Through the Looking-Glass*

Gorin refers to Poto and Cabengo as 'two Alices in reverse', alluding to *Through the Looking-Glass*, the second of the Alice stories, which emphasizes not her growing and shrinking, but rather the inadequacies of language. On 'the other side' of the looking-glass, Alice cannot read the Jabberwocky poem because it is in a language that she does not know *and* it is in a 'Looking-Glass book'. She soon discovers that it must be held up to a mirror to make the words 'go the right way again'.[9] Nevertheless the words remain impenetrable: *brillig*, *slithy*, *gyre*, *wabe*, to name but a few of the strange portmanteau words that make up the Jabberwocky poem,[10] which could have come out of the mouths of Poto and Cabengo. In *Through the Looking-Glass,* Alice experiences words as empty things (like mirrors), whose meaning is determined (or reflected) solely by the speaker (or user), a point made *clear* by Humpty Dumpty.[11] The foolish egg, full of himself, foolishly suggests that he is the master of language, before 'a heavy crash shook the forest from end to end',[12] and he falls to his shattered end:

LIFE

ALICE IN WONDERLAND

APRIL 28, 1947 **15** CENTS
YEARLY SUBSCRIPTION $5.50

REG. U. S. PAT. OFF.

'When *I* use a word,' Humpty Dumpty said, in rather a scornful tone, 'it means just what I choose it to mean – neither more nor less.'

'The question is,' said Alice, 'whether you *can* make words mean so many different things.'

'The question is,' said Humpty Dumpty, 'which is to be master – that's all.'[13]

Poto and Cabengo's speech therapist at San Diego's Children's Hospital, Alexa Romain, seemed to miss the point (that *all* language is nonsense, more or less), when she claimed that the twins' 'Jabberwocky may really be a comprehensive language within a structured syntax'.[14] The *New York Times* jumped on this line, which Gorin highlights in his film. Through the mouth of the 'master' Humpty-Dumpty speech pathologist (Romain) all pleasure and play is usurped form Carroll's 'Jabberwocky' (a word of his invention from 1871). In turn, all pleasure and play is also usurped from Poto and Cabengo's Jabberwocky.

(Note: Today, I am charmed by *Poto and Cabengo*'s references to *Alice*. Long ago, when I was a postgraduate student at the University of California, San Diego, where Jean-Pierre is now Professor Emeritus, he

suggested to me that I work on *Alice*. I jumped on the idea with *Alice Malice:* a performance that I staged with another pair of *real* little girls living in San Diego, a live white rabbit and a live piglet. In *Alice*, I found my voice.)

Dressing Up their Speech Aliciously

Two 6-year old girls, faces slight, are rearranging furniture in a large dollhouse. They have short brown hair, little print dresses and eyes that scrunch with concentration as they examine each new piece of furniture. Their conversation, to the untrained ear sounds like this:

'Genebene manita,'

'Nomemee.'

'Eebedeebeda. Dis din qui naba.'

'Neveda. Ca Baedabada.

'Ga.'

Cynthia Gorney, 'My Sister, My Self', *Washington Post*, 17 July 1979

Poto and Cabengo's grandmother took particular care in designing and sewing 'little print dresses' for Poto and Cabengo. Like well-turned-out paper dolls, the twins wore a host of frocks, not unlike Alice's various fashions over the decades, designed first by John Tenniel and then by the many illustrators who followed him. Distinct, however, was the touch of Germanicity (seemingly from another time) in the grandmother's choice of details, fabric colours and patterns, often using pattern with pattern: one pair of dresses features panels of large red roses sewn with panels of checked purple and white gingham. Plus: smocking; mushroom and little-blonde-girl appliqués; short puff sleeves; lace trim; large round red buttons; red plaid.

The dresses were always short-sleeved or sleeveless, with short skirts, exposing the long coltish brown legs and arms of Poto and Cabengo. Their dresses gave a childish taste to pre-adolescence, yet to come. As Humbert Humbert exclaims of his 'Lottelita, Lolitchen': 'Lolita! . . . The

ng voice.

like well-turned-out paper dolls

the touch of Germanity (seemingly from another time)

fragility of those bare arms of yours – how I longed to enfold them, all your four limpid lovely limbs, a folded colt.'[15]

Like their linguistic life, Poto and Cabengo's sartorial life was rich. The dresses were another way to isolate them. It kept them enclosed in a magical bubble of a world: their room of their own.

In a gather of light cotton pleats, puckers and ironed smoothness, the girls moved like 'hummingbirds',[16] and sounded like a vinyl LP of Disney's Snow White singing 'I'm Wishing' played at 45 rpm. Delicious-looking and delightful, you felt an urge to eat Poto and Cabengo. Their dresses, ever so slightly, catching the sound of their chattering – the taste of their favourite food (potato salad) – the scent of Niagara Falls Spray Starch – the smell of the grass outside of their apartment, soured with Southern California sun and Pacific Ocean humidity – the dry alkaline smell of cement that they swept up with their twin brooms, along with bits of grass, dirt, pebbles, little dead bugs, and other such debris from the clean sidewalk that led up to their unremarkable front door.

Poto and Cabengo were difficult to catch, not only physically, but especially aurally.

1. poo day dooz

po day tas ta led

Poto and Cabengo had sixteen ways to pronounce a beloved food: potato and its supreme German gourmandet form of potato salad:

2. pu da tut

3. bus da dus

1. *poo day dooz*
2. *pu da tut*
3. *buh da duh*
4. *puh tay toe sa led*
5. *po ta too*
6. *puh day too tah*
7. *po da tuht*
8. *po da too*
9. *po day tah ta led*
10. *put ah ta let*

4. pus tay toe sa led

5. po ta too

6. pus day too tas

7. po da tust

8. po da too

9. po day tas ta led

10. put as ta let

117

However, despite the richness of their language play, the results were disappointing for scientists. As writer Jon Lackman points out:

Scientists eventually discovered that like most cryptophasics the girls had invented very little truly new vocabulary. They were just very badly pronouncing English and German, the two languages spoken at home. For example, instead of 'Dear Cabengo, eat,' Grace once said, 'Liba Cabingoat, it.' They were particularly hard to understand because they spoke rapidly and their pronunciations changed constantly. Adding to their disappointment, the scientists couldn't even use their hard-won knowledge of the girls' babble to converse with them. When the girls heard it out of adults' mouths, they couldn't stop laughing.[17]

Gold in the Cement

Jean-Pierre once told me that all he could offer to Poto and Cabengo was food. He used to cook for the girls at his apartment. ('Dear Cabengo, eat' – 'Liba Cabingoat, it.') Jean-Pierre has been described as a Marxist who can cook. (He was once married to the famed chef, cookbook author and Berkeley restaurateur Alice Waters.)

In his film, Jean-Pierre takes Poto and Cobengo to his place to prepare a picnic. The twins help out with boiling eggs and slicing cucumbers. Jean-Pierre holds up a thin cucumber slice up to the eyes of one girl and shows her the light shining through the seeds. For Jean-Pierre and Poto and Cabengo (with their sixteen names for potatoes/potato salad), language is their food, their cuisine, their particular way to philosophize.

Jean-Pierre once made me and a group of students fresh-cooked golden corn from Chino's Farm, in nearby Rancho Santa Fe, not far from UC San Diego. We boiled it on a camping stove, right outside the Art Department office, which is housed in a Brutalist-style poured concrete building. I had never had and will never again taste corn so fresh and sweet. Spontaneous, raw and free like Jean-Pierre's film-making. Like

enclosed in a magical bubble

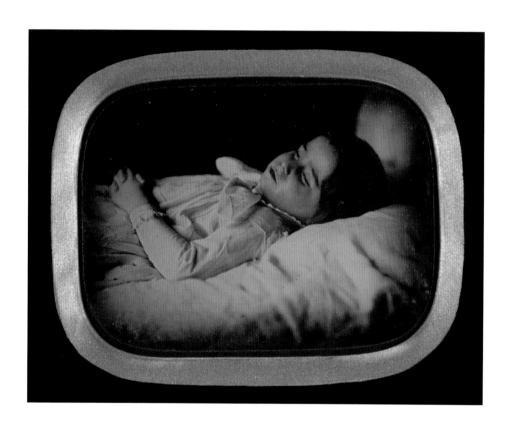

'Then they wrote
her name on the coffin
in gold letters.'

the speech of Poto and Cabengo. Like a bright yellow dandelion flower bursting out of a crack in the cement.

Gold in the Forest

The treatment of the child in the fairy tale is often viewed as particularly unfeeling with its focus on abandonment, written in a matter-of-fact style. Stories like 'Hansel and Gretel', with their 'tone licked clean', send children out to 'the middle of the forest where it's most dense' among the 'wild beasts'.[18] Such is the case of Little Snow White and Hansel and Gretel, where children are threatened to be eaten by wild animals and terrifying women. As the witch says to Gretel: 'I don't care whether your brother's fat enough or not. He's going to be slaughtered and boiled tomorrow.'[19]

Yet, in the Grimms' stories, mistreated little guys and gals work to overcome their situation and achieve riches. As Ernst Bloch writes: 'Fairy tales always end in gold. There is enough happiness there.'[20] Hansel and Gretel outsmart the witch and fill their pockets with jewels and pearls. And Little Snow White escapes the abuse of the queen by becoming a pupa and falling into a long sleep, as she awaits her final becoming as a butterfly-princess. The dwarfs 'intended to bury her, but she looked more alive than dead and she still had such pretty cheeks. So instead they made a glass coffin and placed her inside so that she could easily be seen. Then they wrote her name on the coffin in gold letters.'[21]

Of aurelian interest is the fact that Little Snow White was placed in a glass coffin, trimmed in gold, as if she were trapped in a daguerreotype. (The daguerreotype, which was invented in 1839, produces its images in 'finely divided grains of mercury-silver amalgam on the surface of a polished, silver-plated copper sheet'[22] – making images appear as if they were floating on small mirrors. Precious and unique objects, they were often placed in ornate settings, including gold boxes and frames, and kept under glass. Cheeks and lips were sometimes hand-coloured with red.) The story of 'Little Snow White' encases all of the material trappings of the daguerreotype yet to be invented: gold, glass, the mirror, a spot of red. And like all photographs, the daguerreotype freezes the moment (including of course, childhood and youth) forever.

When the prince happens upon Little Snow White in her glass coffin, he cannot get enough of her beauty. He tries to get the dwarfs to 'sell him the coffin with the dead Little Snow White inside. But they wouldn't accept all the gold in the world for it.'[23] Nevertheless, they agree to give her to the prince as a 'gift'.[24] At home in his castle, the prince orders his servants to carry Little Snow White everywhere so that he can be with her as much as possible, hardly ever taking his eyes off her. Her image feeds him with longing desire, so much so that 'he couldn't eat a thing unless he was standing near the coffin'.[25] Finally (when the prince has to leave the room), a servant becomes fed up with carrying Little Snow White all about and opens the coffin, lifts her into the air, and says: '"Why must we be plagued with so much work all because of a dead maiden?" On saying this he shoved Little Snow White's back with his hand, and out popped the nasty apple that had been stuck in Little Snow White's throat and she was again alive.'[26]

Of oralian interest, she got her voice back.

The Last Birthday Party

The Cement Garden (1978) is Ian McEwan's shocking story of four children, who first lose their father, then their mother and then go on to create a new family order without adults. They manage on their own, without parents, in a post-war home of cement and very few trees – along with a sense of adventure, a little incest and plenty of teen angst. At the start of the book, Jack, the narrator, is fourteen. His siblings are Julie (seventeen), Sue (thirteen) and Tom (six). (The book was made by Andrew Birkin into a film in 1993, under the same title, with Charlotte Gainsbourg triumphing as adolescently alluring Julie.) The children keep the death of their mother a secret, so as to avoid foster care, by burying her in cement in the cellar of their bleak home. The result is a perverse *Lustgarten*, which is no garden for tending, but a tomb in which the mother is preserved like a photograph, like a fly in amber, only the golden resin is cement. Among the many hopeless moments of the story, Jack recalls Julie's tenth birthday and the sense of doom she felt. As Jack tells us:

My mother remembered a party we had on Julie's tenth birthday.
I remembered it too. I was eight. Julie had wept because someone
told her that there were no more birthdays after you were ten.[27]

At around the age of ten, Poto and Cabengo are sent to school and are separated from each other, thereby losing their rapidly beaten fairy-tale voices and their childish innocence. *It was their last birthday party*. Unlike Little Snow White, they were unable to cough up the poison apple in order to get their voices back. Removed from their cement garden, a drab, depressing apartment complex which was their fairy-tale forest, the little girl-bird twins were not so much released into the outside world as they were kidnapped by it. A 2002 American television show on twins reported:

Though therapy eventually cured Virginia and Grace of their secret
language, they are still developmentally disabled. Now approaching
30, the twins continue to experience speech problems and mental
delays. Grace, who has achieved a higher level of functioning than her
sister, works at a McDonald's cleaning tables and mopping. Virginia
works at a job-training center and performs assembly-line work.[28]

Pierre Huyghe's 1997 four-minute film *Blanche-Neige Lucie* is a tiny documentary about the French singer Lucie Dolène, who dubbed Walt Disney's 1962 French version of *Snow White*. When the Disney film first came out in 1938, Dolène, as a child, sang for her school party: 'Someday my Prince Will Come'. It was a sign of things to come. Later, as a professional singer, Dolène was chosen to be the voice of Snow White: a 'light soprano, but not too lyrical, a small resonant voice, childlike'.[29] (Indeed it had a Poto and Cabengo touch.) As she says: 'When I gave my voice to that character, that beautiful little princess, graceful and innocent, I was Snow White.'[30] But when the Disney film was rereleased, with Dolène's

they are

eaten by

the real

world and

that's it

voice retained, she was not contacted or compensated. In November 1996, Dolène, as the interpreter of French Snow White, won her case in court. Dolène got her voice back.

This was not the case with *Poto and Cabengo*, the latter a story of loss: the last birthday party.

There is no golden-Grimm ending to the dystopian fairy tale of *Poto and Cabengo*. When the girls leave their cement garden, they are eaten by the real world and that's it.

———

5 Speaking in Glass

'Glass is dead matter transformed by human labor and by breath,' writes Isobel Armstrong. Turning sand into glass has a fairy-tale quality, which we readily equate with the enchantment of Cinderella. We associate glass not only with magical transformation, but with epiphanies. Etymologically, 'epiphany' comes from the Greek 'to show'. Glass shows in eyeglasses, microscopes, telescopes, magic lanterns, shop windows, curiosity, crystal balls, display cases, even the barometer, which shows us the weather. Epiphanies manifest when an individual 'has a vision'. Glass crosses boundaries, it steps over: it breathes in life of a different order, like the fairy tale itself.

First Shoe Made of Glass

Once upon a time, when I was a child, bronzed baby shoes were all the rage and were common as weighty souvenirs of the babies that once pattered around the household. The little cast-bronze boots were made for walking backwards and holding time still. These ornaments – under a lamp, on a side-table, or over the mantel of the fireplace – are found in those houses that gave birth to children in the 1950s. Pick one up – kitschy and epitaphic – feel the worrying, even sickening heft of nostalgia.

Dust gets in the air. Yet dust is not only 'mundane': it is 'magical'.[1] Walter Benjamin reminds us of this fact in his enchanting, fragmented collectomania entitled *The Arcades Project* (first imagined with the more magical title of 'Paris Arcades: A Dialectical Fairyland'). There, Benjamin drifts: 'Mystery of dustmotes playing in the sunlight. Dust and the "best room".'[2]

In J. M. Barrie's *Peter Pan*, fairy dust enables flights to Neverland:

No one can fly unless the fairy dust has been blown on him. Fortunately . . . one of . . . [Peter's] hands was messy with it, and he blew some on each of them, with the most superb results . . . Up and down they went, and round and round. Heavenly was Wendy's word.[3]

As the Surrealist Georges Bataille wrote in his journal: 'The storytellers have not realised that the Sleeping Beauty would have awoken covered in a thick layer of dust.'[4]

Jonny Briggs's glass *Shoe* (2011) is a cast of his first toddler shoe, made in glass, rather than the traditional, heavy, opaque, coppery bronze. Unlike the leather of the original shoe, glass does not smell or expand. As a material, glass does not lend itself to nostalgia. Briggs's glass shoe slips and slides on metonymy. Like Alice after the White Rabbit, Briggs's glass shoe is a carrot on a string (more accurately a *glass* carrot), always before us – 'eternally stretching forth towards the *desire for something else*'.[5] Like Carroll's Alice stories, it is a 'weapon against nostalgia'.[6] I want to throw this glass shoe. It makes me into a *nostalgia-clast*.

Marcel Proust's famous nostalgic, involuntary memories provoked by the taste and smell of a crumb of madeleine dipped in tea, or the feel of a starched napkin on one's face, or the sound of a chance knock of a spoon hitting a china plate, or a trip on an uneven paving stone in front of St Mark's in Venice, sent the author flying utopically to the past in the present. Briggs's shoe is *not* for nostalgically tripping on uneven paving stones in Venice, which just happens to be the home of some of the greatest glassmakers in history. We cannot taste the past in Briggs's shoe with its tongue made of glass.

In 1997, the German artist Asta Gröting made models of intestines out of clear glass, leaving the viewer in a state of wonder: the inside became outside; the abject became clean. Likewise, the American artist Kiki Smith has made a glass stomach: impossibly empty and anorectic. With glassy charm, Smith's sperm made of glass are Surrealist tadpoles rushing to Cinderella's ball.

Glass is difficult to see and smell. Glass is seemingly odourless. Glass smells Petri-dish clean, green (but not in a plant sort of way), manufactured and smooth. Glass smells of nothing, which is a smell, just as silence is a sound and blankness is a picture.

a glass stomach: impossibly empty and anorectic

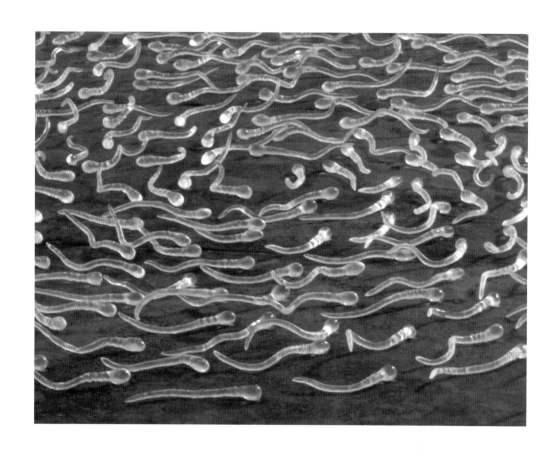

sperm made
of glass are
Surrealist tadpoles

Ontologically, the glass shoe is a missing story. For not only is Briggs's foot missing from the shoe, but the material of the shoe itself appears to be missing. Taking the Freudian path, there is nothing sexual or fetid in Briggs's glass shoe, as there is in Robert Gober's child's wax brogue, which has sprouted human hair (*Untitled*, 1992). Wax, like leather, shows wear, holds a scent, softens to the touch. The hairs are suggestive of the new growth of pubic hair. Scale-wise, Gober's T-strap, measuring in at 9 × 18 × 7.5 cm, is too large for a baby's first steps; it is toddler size. I measure my son's nostalgically saved leather shoes from when he was aged three and discover that they are exactly Gober-size. Gober's shoe is impressed with Barthes' aforementioned observation that it is around the age of three when the little human 'invents' at once sentence, narrative and Oedipus narrative.[7]

To never grow up is a weapon against nostalgia, perfected by Oskar in Günter Grass's *The Tin Drum*. 'On his third birthday our little Oskar fell down the cellar stairs, no bones were broken, but he just wouldn't grow any more.'[8] Oskar's fall was self-induced.

Briggs blew the dust off his old, modest, Clark's childhood shoe, transforming it into magical Cinderella glass. In the words of the artist:

I filled the shoe with clay; then I made a three-part plaster mould around it that I could easily pull apart and put back together again, with a funnel running through the top. The glass was then *blown* into the shoe – it was so hot in there! It took four tries, and then the plaster mould exploded in the heat. This happens to all moulds. The glass took a day to cool, and then I worked on it, cutting away the glass funnel that surrounded the ankle of the shoe, sanding the holes with a file, and finally polishing it.[9]

Briggs's boyish, fairy-tale glass slipper is a longing for childhood: but this shoe can no longer fit. To wear it would shatter the glass. Perhaps it is not surprising that Grass's Oskar could break glass with his voice. As Oskar notes:

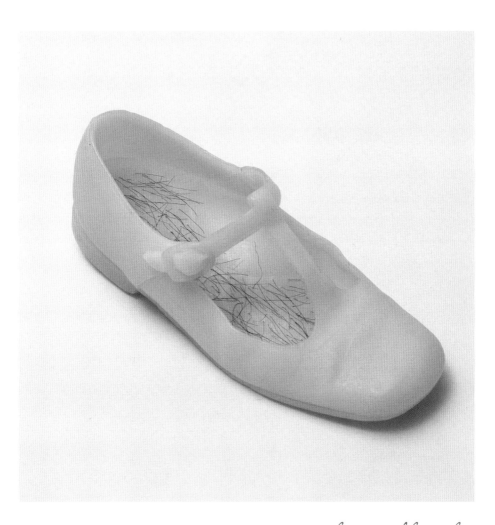

has sprouted human hair

I had the gift of shattering glass with my singing: my screams demolished vases, my singing made windowpanes crumble and drafts prevail; like a chaste and therefore merciless diamond, my voice cut through the doors of glass cabinets, and without losing its innocence, proceeded to wreak havoc on harmonious graceful liqueur glasses, bestowed by loving hands and covered with a light film of dust.[10]

An elfin boy photographed by Sean Graff holds up a circle of glass close to his face: he looks as if he is in a bubble. It is as if he has been grown in a glass Petri dish. The glass magnifies and expands the boy's head; he becomes once again his foetal self. His ear, under glass, is now not yet developed. A flipper, not an ear. His tadpole body, in contrast to the expanded head, appears small and slender. His hair seems to look thinner, like lanugo, the very fine hair that covers the bodies of many newborn babies at birth, before falling out. The skin whiter, like an albino seal, and more delicate: foetal skin. His double-jointed fingers even stranger, amphibian. He is a not-yet-boy under glass. To grow will break the glass.

Briggs's glass shoe beguiles, not unlike those famous scentless glass flowers of Harvard's Botanical Museum made by father and son Leopold and Rudolf Blaschka (who lived and work in Hosterwitz, near Dresden, Germany). Leopold had enjoyed success with the production of jewellery – embellished with glass forget-me-nots, violets, roses – as well as glass eyes (for ocular prostheses and taxidermy). In 1863, coinciding with the aquarium craze that had begun in England in the mid-nineteenth century,[11] Leopold began to make lovely glass models of invertebrates, with Rudolf assisting him from 1876. They were made and sold as models for teaching, but their beauty far exceeds the edifying intention. The *real* glasslike transparencies of sea creatures, such as jellyfish, sea slugs and anemones, undoubtedly were an endless sense of wonder for the Blaschkas. Their very small *Athecate Hydroid* (a kind of jellyfish) is a case in point. Behind its glass display case, this jellyfish appears as a magical wand of glass. (With a touch of her wand, Cinderella's fairy godmother

133

To grow will break the glass.

made all of the transformations possible, including 'the slippers made of glass, as pretty as could be'.[12])

Later, working from 1886 until 1936, father and son began to make glass flowers, again for the purpose of teaching botany, and again their beauty exceeds their edifying intention. They were first commissioned by Professor George Lincoln Goodale, founder of Harvard's Botanical Museum, where today there are now over four thousand models, representing more than 830 plant species. 'The Blaschkas fashioned their glass models by flame-working. They heated glass tubes and rods in a flame until they became soft and could be pulled into different shapes with tweezers, cut unto the required sizes with scissors, and attached to one another by fusion.'[13] To transport these exceedingly delicate princess-and-the-pea flowers (from Germany to Boston and for touring exhibits) required endless wrapping. Just one fragile model resulted in an enormous package, which looked as if it could have been made by the conceptual artists Christo and Jeanne-Claude.

In 1976, the Steuben Glass Company arranged for a special month-long exhibition of the glass flowers for their showroom on Fifth Avenue, New York. 'The models . . . were to be flown from Boston to New York in a small plane. But the question of how they could be safely transported over the icy, potholed streets to Logan Airport in Boston and from La Guardia to Manhattan remained.'[14] To ensure a smooth ride, these flowers, which are forever in bloom and never die, were (ironically) driven in two black hearses by drivers in funerary dress. Fittingly, the weather was snowy. For glass, like frozen ice, is associated with winter, death and photography.

The glass of early glass-plate negatives (as we saw with *Open Your Mouth and Shut Your Eyes*) doubles up the photograph's inherent immobilization. The subject is frozen in Snow-Queen-ice-like glass, just as she was at the time of life *taken* by the camera, the body forever iced in the dress of 'that day and age'.[15] As Andersen writes of his frozen, yet alive, Snow Queen: 'she . . . was made of ice, dazzling, glittering ice, and yet she was alive'.[16] Like a camera, the Snow Queen kisses her subjects, with cold death:

glass, like frozen ice, is associated with winter,
death and photography

She kissed him on the forehead. Ooh! It was colder than ice; it went right to his heart, which was already half ice. He felt as if he would die . . . 'No more kisses for you,' she said. 'Or I might kiss you to death!'[17]

In the glass plate for the picture of the open-mouthed child taken by an unknown photographer in northern England in about 1900 (the photographic print developed from this negative first appeared in the Preface of this book), we witness the icy kiss of photography. The toddler sits on a blanket of snow. The mouth opens to a snowball. The child's heart is half-frozen.

Under the spell of the Blaschka flowers, I am charmed to learn that at one time old photographic plates were reused to build greenhouses. The images on the glass plates would still be faintly visible.[18] The magic and 'value' of glass 'exceeded that of the image'.[19]

Like a photograph, the perfection of the glass flowers is that they never fade. In *Through the Looking-Glass*, Alice leans over the side of her river rowing boat, in order to pick bunches of darling scented 'dream-rushes',[20] which beckon her, like little girls summoning Carroll's camera. 'There's was always a more lovely one that she couldn't reach.'[21] When she began to arrange her 'new-found treasures',[22] she was very disappointed to realize that the flowers faded (just as Carroll's girl-child models would always grow up):

The rushes had begun to fade, and to lose all of their scent and beauty from the moment that she picked them. Even real scented rushes, you know, last only a very little while – and these, being dream-rushes, melted away almost like snow, as they lay in heaps at her feet.[23]

Polar opposite to Alice's dream-rushes that melt like snow and lose their scent (even faster than 'real' flowers) and the Blaschkas' icy-glass posies, which are always already fragrance-free, is the stinky Gulliveresque *Amorphophallus titanum*, which can reach over six feet in

The mouth opens to a snowball.

height. Its grotesque but beautiful bloom (reaching four feet in diameter) smells of rotting meat, hence its nickname, 'Corpse Flower'.

The Blaschkas' foot-long glass pitcher plants (*Nepenthes sanguinea*) are among the largest flowers displayed at Harvard. Pitcher plants grow large with Jack-and-the-beanstalk fervour. One species develops 'pitchers as long as thirty-six inches'.[24] Their fairy-tale size sustains their curiously carnivorous oralia. 'The edge of the pitcher is curved inwards and has honey glands that attract insects, which are then drowned in the water collected in the pitcher and are eventually digested.'[25] They are also charmingly sartorial. The Blaschka pitcher-plant slippers made of ballet-shoe-pink glass have the curled toes of Mojari slippers. Although not as elegant as the famous real slippers, possibly worn by Nizam Sikander Jah of Hyderabad, made with real gold thread and encrusted with emeralds, rubies, sapphires and diamonds, the Blaschka slippers have a magic of their own. They are Cinderella and the *Arabian Nights* at once.

real gold thread and encrusted with emeralds,
rubies, sapphires and diamonds

In the German fairy tale entitled 'The Tale of Little Mook', written by Wilhelm Hauff (1802–1827),[26] the author lifts characters from bazaars and mosques, adopting 'the latest oriental trappings with enthusiasm'.[27] Written under the sparkle of a recent translation of the *Arabian Nights* into German,[28] Hauff's sixteen-year-old Little Mook becomes a servant to the unsympathetic Madame Ahavzi's cunning cats, wicked little felines who are waited upon like royalty. Little Mook escapes his terrible plight when he discovers in a locked room a pair of gigantic magical slippers. The slippers enable magic-carpet flight. I smile at the 'little fringed hairy wings' clearly visible on the open heels of the Blaschka Mojaris made of glass.[29]

First Slippers Made of Glass

'Animals', suggests John Berger, are 'our first metaphor'.[30] Glass is, perhaps, our first epiphany.

Pliny the Elder's encyclopaedic *Natural History* narrates the epiphanic discovery of sand turning into glass. Magical and scientific, like all impressive cuisine, it is a story of cooking:

A ship belonging to traders in soda [nitrum] once called here, so the story goes, and they spread out along the shore to make a meal. There were no stones to support their cooking-pots, so they placed lumps of soda from their ship under them. When these became hot and fused with the sand on the beach, streams of unknown translucent liquid flowed, and this was the origin of glass.[31]

Glass is the magical transformation of sand into glass: the ice, diamonds and spun sugar of the fairy tale. The dreams of the Sandman. Benjamin writes poetically of the glass worlds of the fairy tale and toy, including glass globes of snowy landscapes that could be brought back to life (unfrozen) with a shake. In his *Berlin Childhood around 1900*, Benjamin recalls the voice of his aunt, 'fragile and brittle as glass',[32] who always saw to it that someone immediately set before him a very special toy: a 'large glass cube, containing a complete working mine, in which miniature miners, stonecutters, and mine inspectors, with tiny wheelbarrows, hammers, and lanterns, performed their movements precisely in time to a clockwork'.[33] Likewise, as a child, the news of the Crystal Palace reached Julius Lessing like fairy tales of old, as quoted here by Benjamin in his 'dialectical fairyland':

I myself recall, from childhood, how the news of the Crystal Palace reached us in Germany, and how pictures of it were hung in the middle-class parlors of provincial towns. It seemed then that the world we knew for old fairy tales – of the princess in the glass coffin, of queens and elves dwelling in crystal houses – had come to life.[34]

Glass 'is dead matter transformed by human labour and by breath'.[35] Turning sand into epiphanous glass has a fairy-tale quality which we readily equate with the enchantment of Cinderella. Beyond the story's use of the resplendent glass slipper, there are further magical transformations: a pumpkin turns into a 'beautiful golden coach'; six live mice become 'a team of six horses, with prettily dappled mouse-grey coats'; a rat transforms into 'a great fat coachman, with one of the finest moustaches that had ever been seen'; six lizards metamorphose into 'six footmen, their uniforms in gold braid'.[36] Glass crosses boundaries, it steps over; it breathes in life of a different order.

It was Charles Perrault who in 1697 cast Cinderella's slipper in glass, calling his story *Cendrillon ou La Petite Pantoufle de Verre*. It was popularly suggested by Balzac (without any evidence) that the glass shoe was a misstep, a mistaken substitution of the French word *verre* (glass) for *vair* (the old word for squirrel fur). Today, folklorists embrace Perrault's intention, the glass slipper clearly signalling an intentional, studied emphasis on the magical. (In the Grimms' version, the slippers, as well as the stockings and dress, are gold: 'Then a dress fell down, and it was even more glorious and splendid than the previous one. It was made out of gold and precious gems. In addition there were golden gusseted stockings and gold slippers.

And after Cinderella was completely dressed, she glistened really like the sun at midday.'[37] But for most of us, Cinderella's slippers have to be glass. Glass is more magical, more transformative, more otherworldly than precious gold.)

A real pair of moles (slaughtered in the hundreds to clear golf courses) is translated by Studio Van Eijk & Van der Lubbe into curious readymade slippers from nature. Materially, the *Moulded Moles* play out the bodily outcries of real fur that magical glass outvies. The nose of a mole makes a perfect fashionably pointed toe, while also pointing to the shoe as ripe with smell metaphors. The artists' refusal to remove the nose, feet, eyes and mouth is a statement about cruelty to animals in the service of fashion. *Moulded Moles* are made under the dark shadow of the nineteenth-century craze (which lasted well into the twentieth century) for fox heads, tails and feet as ornamental to the fur stoles that women swathed across bare arms and shoulders. With surreal drama, Van Eijk & Van der Lubbe emphasize where fur, and by extension other animal products, come from, lest we forget.

Francesca Woodman suspends her vintage fur stoles, with intact head, tails and feet, on a clothesline stretched across her studio. Behind her hanging beasts, she stands naked on her toes, arms stretched upward and off the frame. One boneless, muscleless furry being blocks out the pudenda of this self-induced performance of 'Venus in Furs'.

Delightful by way of revulsion, the eight little feet of the poor *Moulded Moles* would drag and scrape their tiny toenails with every shuffling step of its wearer. The slippers are a European size 32, just the right size and shape for the daughter of the incestuous king in the Grimms' 'All Fur'. In the Grimms' story, the beautiful daughter with the same golden hair as her dead mother hides from her incestuous Humbert Humbert father, disguised wearing 'a cloak of a thousand kinds of pelts and furs'.[38] In the context of the fairy tale, the moles add a sexualized beastly turn. No wonder Cinderella's glass shoes have become so enduring.

See-through glass and the story of Cinderella are mutually reinforcing grammars of epiphany. Etymologically, *epiphany* comes from the Greek for 'to show'. We associate glass with showing, including

The nose
of a mole
makes a perfect
fashionably
pointed toe

Venus in Furs

eyeglasses, microscopes, telescopes, magic lanterns, shop windows, curiosity, crystal balls, display cases, even the barometer, which shows us the weather. Epiphanies manifest when an individual 'has *a vision*'.

By the end of *In Search of Lost Time*, Marcel Proust writes that his long novel should be understood not as words on paper, but as a magnifying glass (*verre grossissant*) for finding our own epiphanies: 'My readers' are 'readers of their own selves, my book being merely a sort of magnifying glass like those which the optician at Combray used to offer his customers – it would be my book, but with its help I would furnish them with the means of reading what lay inside themselves'.[39]

In Megan Powell's *Portal* (2014), a young woman floats in a circle of domestic wallpaper flowers, a spring moon with the blue of the sky, a circular lily pad on an azure lake. She's the princess without the *'plip, plop, plip, plop'* frog eating off her plate.[40] The sleeves of her creamy blouse are punctuated with tiny black full-stop buttons. A portal, like the O that began this book, is also an entry, like an eye, like a mouth. The delicate young Mia Farrow-esque woman (both the actress and the model have perfect round faces, large round eyes) holds a magnifying glass over her closed eye, as if it were a monocle worn by Proust's character Swann, who happens to be an art connoisseur writing on Vermeer. (The monocle is Swann's metonymic sign.) But *Portal*'s magnifying glass has a very curious effect: it *inverts*, even displaces the eye, as a way to see *inwards*. Her monocled eye takes her down, down, down the rabbit hole. This woman, so still, not even a twitch of the nose, appears frozen. The magnifying glass is an epiphanic portal to see what lies within herself.

A mirror is made of glass. In France, people once said *glace* for mirror. Cinderella's wicked stepsisters had 'looking-glasses in which they could see themselves from head to foot'.[41] Likewise, Alice is to the 'looking-glass' what Cinderella is to the glass slipper. In the Grimms' 'Little Snow White', the wicked Queen asks of the mirror: 'Mirror, mirror, on the wall, who in this land is fairest of all?'[42] Recall from the last chapter how the dwarfs, horrified by the thought of burying the seemingly dead Snow White in the ground, place her in glass. A later version of the Grimms' 'Snow White' notes how the transparent glass

Her
monocled
eye
takes
her
down,
down,
down
the
rabbit
hole.

coffin 'allowed Snow White to be seen *from all sides*',[43] emphasizing the metaphors of the multiple images (real and psychological) induced by the mirror.

According to Jacques Lacan ('The Mirror Stage as Formative of the Function of the I as Revealed in Psychoanalytic Experience', 1949), when the child first sees himself or herself in the mirror, it is a moment of mis-recognition. For a mirror is an empty glass, *showing* whoever happens to be standing in front of it. (Glass is an empty word without a good etymology.) Like the pronoun I, the mirror is a vacant receptacle, pro-miscuously representing any person that arises to use it.

The child experiences his or her Lacanian mirror moment between the ages of six and eighteen months – roughly when a child is taking his or her first steps. As a small child, the mirror seems a perfect *fit* – 'that's me!' – not unlike Cinderella's glass slipper, which slips on so easily. Believing in the fairy-tale vision of a whole, perfected, unfragmented, unshattered Self, the child enters a state of 'jubilant assumption'.[44] 'Jubilant assump-tion' is an ecclesiastical vision, summoning the Assumption of the Virgin. The epiphany for the child's sense of self and for Cinderella's transforma-tion into the princess turns on glass.

Glass Voice

When I say the Sandman's coming, I only mean that you're sleepy and can't keep your eyes open – just as if sand had been sprinkled into them.
E.T.A. Hoffmann, 'The Sandman'

'Nathanael' (in E.T.A. Hoffmann's famed dark tale) tells the reader that as a child he was 'filled with curiosity about this Sandman and his relation to . . . children'.[45] When Nathanael finally takes the initiative to ask the old woman who looks after his little sister what kind of man the Sandman is, she replies:

'Why, Natty' . . . 'don't you know that yet? He is a wicked man, who comes to children when they don't want to go to bed, and throws handfuls of sand into their eyes; that they makes their eyes fill with blood and jump out of their heads, and he throws the eyes into his bag and takes them into the crescent moon to feed his own children, who are sitting in the nest there; the Sandman's children have crooked beaks, like owls, with which to peck the eyes of naughty human children.[46]

A butterfly tongue. A proboscis.

As an adult, Nathanael will displace the fantastical tale of the Sandman onto a menacing glassmaker by the name of Coppolla, the double little os of his name like piercing eyes. Coppolla sells and makes all kinds of things made of glass, including barometers, lorgnettes, spectacles and telescopes, large and small. Coppolla (with the assistance of the physicist named Spallanzani) will create the perfect female automaton: perfect clockwork, perfect glass eyes, and the ability to perform 'a bravura aria in a clear, almost shrill voice, like a glass bell'.[47] Nathanael cannot but help fall in love with this girl-doll, whose O-name is Olympia.

In Francesca Woodman's photograph entitled *Talking to Vince* (1975–8), she gives herself a glassy voice in the form of a see-through banderole that unrolls from her mouth like religious liturgy in an illuminated medieval manuscript. (Vince was a glass blower.) Cursive glass Os spew out, one after another. A butterfly tongue. A proboscis.

In 'Butterfly's Tongue' (1996) by Manuel Rivas, a schoolteacher has finally acquired a microscope for his young students. At the start of the story, the teacher poetically describes to his students how a butterfly uses its proboscis:

The butterfly's tongue is a coiled tube like the spring of a clock. If a flower attracts the butterfly, it unrolls its tongue and begins to suck from the calyx. When you place a moist finger in a jar of sugar, can you not already feel the sweetness in your mouth, as if the tip of your finger belonged to your tongue? Well the butterfly's tongue is no different.[48]

The etymology of *proboscis* is *pro*, 'forth, forward, before' and *bosko*, 'to feed, to nourish'.

Woodman unfeeds me with her glass tongue. I cannot feel any sweetness.

———

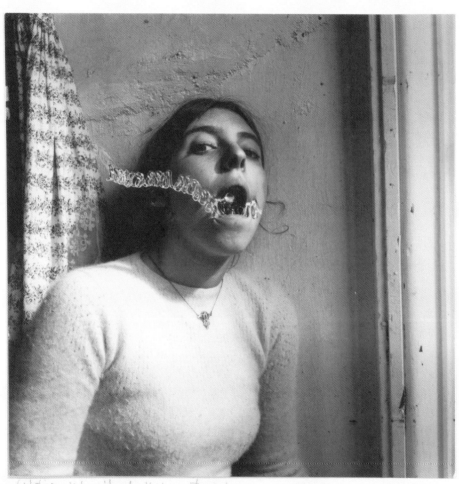

self portrait talking to vince

Magical coral
    is particularly fitting as a subject
            to be made out of glass.

6 Coral Castles

Changing from animal to stone and vice versa, coral, like the fairy tale itself, is possessed by the magic of animation. Hans Christian Andersen used it for a castle in the enchanting underwater world of 'The Little Mermaid'. The folk artist and amateur scientist Edward Leedskalnin made his own real, if landlocked, 'Coral Castle' (1923–51). Fairy-tale fantasies of living underwater (akin to the flight of Peter Pan or magic carpet rides in the Arabian Nights*) magically transfigure the limits of the body, like Briar Rose turning death into mere sleep. Both the princess and coral can be awakened into life.*

'Far out at sea the water is as blue as the petals of the loveliest cornflower and as clear as the purest *glass*, but it's very deep, deeper than any anchor line can reach . . . At the very deepest spot stands the sea king's castle. The walls are made of *coral* and the tall arched windows are of the clearest amber.' So begins the magical world of Hans Christian Andersen's 'The Little Mermaid'.[1] Andersen's fairy tale is an enchanted place, inhabited by mermen and mermaids who live for three hundred years, sing with unearthly beautiful voices, and have their dreams come true, like trading in your fish tail for legs, thanks to the Sea Witch's magical potion.

The Little Mermaid lives in a sea castle, where the walls are made of coral. Coral, like the fairy tale itself, is magical. Changing from animal to stone and vice versa, coral, like the fairy tale itself, is *possessed* by the magic of animation as was first touched upon in this book's introduction. Humans fly, before aeroplanes: Aladdin on his magic carpet; Peter Pan on his magic dust. Underwater, the Little Mermaid soars through the blue sea, wary of the 'polyps' (coral) that might grab her as she flies through the Sea Witch's forest.[2] Captain Nemo flies through the seven seas in an imagined, but not yet invented, magic-carpet submarine named the *Nautilus*, where the ship and its crew encounter barely imagined beings:[3] a gigantic sea monster (a narwhal); flowers that turn to stone (coral).

Jules Verne's 1870 fantasy story of mermen (*20,000 Leagues Under the Sea*) is science fiction. Yet it is like a fairy tale, in that it is dependent on imagination and magical thinking. Verne's narrative is akin to a scientific 'hypothesis' (which comes from the Greek 'to put under' or 'to suppose'). In her *Stranger Magic: Charmed States and the 'Arabian Nights'*, Marina Warner philosophically touches upon the usually opposing poles of the fairy tale and science.[4] On one pole, the magic of the fairy tale propels poetic truths; on the other, science (through its own imaginative inquiry and speculation) propels physical truths. Imagining science leads to real technical ingenuity and discovery. For example, Verne's fantasy of the submarine before its invention becomes prophecy.

Verne's sea is a magical place where Technicolor coral flourishes under the surreal, fairy-tale, Baudelaireish names 'Flower of Blood' and 'Froth of Blood'.[5] These 'living flowers' do not sing songs or dance, but they do perform *real* magical transformations, turning themselves into stone, as if their own tubular, snaky branches held the desire of Narcissus and the power of Medusa.[6] As Verne writes (of what must be *Corallium rubrum*),

I seemed to see the membranous and cylindrical tubes tremble beneath the undulation of the waters. I was tempted to gather their fresh petals, ornamented with delicate tentacles, some just blown, the others budding . . . But if my hand approached these living flowers, these *animated* sensitive plants, the whole colony took alarm. The white petals re-entered their red cases, the flowers faded as I looked and the bush changed into a block of stony knobs.[7]

Out of their famous glass, the Blaschkas made a colony of fiery *Corallium rubrum*, with the colour and texture of Italian oranges, speckled with icy snowflakes (its retractable white polyps). The fairy-tale quality of turning sand into glass is akin to coral's ability to metamorphose into a stony knob and reanimate back into life. Magical coral is particularly fitting as a subject to be made out of glass.

In the spirit of the Little Mermaid's coral palace, Verne's 'Coral Kingdom' and the Blaschkas' glass *Corallium rubrum*, the folk artist and amateur scientist Edward Leedskalnin made his own real, if landlocked, Coral Castle. The Latvian emigrant (who was obsessed with theories of magnetism) made his castle in Florida between the years of 1923 and 1951, after being spurned by a sixteen-year-old girl the night before he was to marry her. He made this castle, where everything is made from huge, massively heavy, pieces of coral (oolitic limestone), in honour of this unnamed girl whom the Latvian referred to always and only as 'Sweet Sixteen'. There is a throne room with a gigantic heart-shaped table with benches all around; beds with coral pillows; chairs, including a rocking chair for rocking into fairy-tale sleep; even a coral telescope. With your head on a coral pillow, you can look up to see a coral Mars, a coral Saturn, a single six-pointed Latvian star made of coral and a coral crescent moon held still by monolithic time, so that it never grows full. The castle is walled in but always open to the blue above. The most magical part of the Coral Castle is the mysterious gate that can be easily moved by the touch of a child's finger, even though it weighs nine tons.[8] It feels miraculous.

Leedskalnin worked secretly at night. How did this tiny, J. M. Barrie-sized man (five feet tall, a hundred pounds), single-handedly build his coral Stonehenge? We know that he borrowed a friend's truck to build his marvellous castle of heavy limestone, but that hardly solves the mystery. He claimed to have discovered the secret of levitation used when building the pyramids. 'He clearly used his brain to move the coral.'[9] The 'coral of eons ago' becomes a bed of limestone, which in the hands of Leedskalnin become literal beds.[10] In the words of the British art critic, modern painter and poet Adrian Stokes, although in a rather different context, we discover that 'ceaseless seas of experience construct the coral mind.'[11]

Leedsklalnin's monolithic castle carries the heft of deathbeds and tombstones, summoning Verne's 'coral cemetery', where Captain Nemo laid to rest the man who died on board the *Nautilus*. A cross of red coral, like 'petrified blood', could be found at the gravesite, where 'the polypi undertake to seal' the 'dead for eternity'.[12] If Verne's tale were a fairy tale and not science fiction, this man, who died on the *Nautilus* and was buried at the bottom of the ocean, might be magically awakened (like

How did this tiny,
J. M. Barrie-sized man

(five feet tall, a hundred pounds),

single-
handedly
build
his
coral
Stonehenge?

Briar Rose from her brambles and thickets), emerging from his own hundred-year sleep, out of the Coral Kingdom's 'real petrified thickets'.[13]

'Sweet Sixteen' was Leedskalnin's underwater Briar Rose. When they were both young, he might have dreamed of parting her thighs like the branches of coral, while sticky leaves of seaweed licked his cheeks like tongues: pleasingly rough, like a taste of sea-water molasses. Plunging deeper into the underwater coral thicket, beneath undulating waters, he would notice that the calyces are taking alarm, their petals re-entering their cases right before his eyes. They turn to stony knobs.

'Sweet Sixteen' is unreachable. She will always remain out of touch. Still, he waits for her in his Coral Castle.

———

7 Marvellous Middleness, in Seven Parts

In a fairy tale one thing can be in the middle of becoming so many things: like the frog becoming a prince, a piece of wood becoming Pinocchio, straw becoming gold, Alice becoming a long-necked serpent, an ugly duckling becoming a beautiful swan, a pumpkin becoming 'a beautiful golden coach', six live mice becoming 'a team of six horses, with prettily dappled mouse-grey coats' and six lizards becoming 'six footmen, their uniforms in gold braid'.[1] The fairy tale is a mise en scène of living and inanimate things, all of which hold marvellous middleness: the potential to transform. This chapter makes a carnival out of fairy-tale middleness in seven parts: from falling asleep into a world of dreams (where one thing can become so many things), to the paper cut-out shapes that fell from Matisse's scissors (where a pomegranate is also a bat), to falling into the stone forest of Lascaux ('by the flicker of a torchlight, the animals seem to surge from the walls, and move across . . . like figures in a magic lantern show').[2]

One: Falling Asleep

Let your lids drop, the fall is always worth it.

Esther Teichmann[3]

*A*lice in Wonderland begins with our little heroine feeling 'very sleepy'.[4] And then the great fall: 'Down, down, down. Would the fall *never* come to an end? "I wonder how many miles I've fallen by this time?" she said aloud.'[5]

'I'm falling asleep. I'm falling into sleep and I'm falling there by the power of sleep. Just as I fall asleep from exhaustion.'[6] This is how the first three lines of Jean-Luc Nancy's *The Fall of Sleep* (2007) fall into place, cascading, like a waterfall. The original French title of Nancy's book, *Tombe de sommeil*, insists on the multiple transformations of the word *tombe*. As Charlotte Mandell, the translator of the book into English, explains:

The slumberer softens into other worlds, within a shell of sleep.

161

The original French title of this book is *Tombe de Sommeil*, which means 'Tomb of Sleep.' Or 'tombstone of sleep' or 'monument of sleep.' 'Tomb,' however, and its relatives, does not have the same resonance for English-speaking readers as it does for French readers, who feel its connection to the verb *tomber*, 'to fall.'[7]

Nancy's book, like *Alice in Wonderland*, unbegins in the middle of *falling* asleep, falling between death and life. 'Like death, sleep, and like sleep, death – but without awakening.'[8] Likewise (as has already been touched upon), sleep is like death in two of the best-known Grimm fairy tales: 'Briar Rose' and 'Snow White'. In Philip Pullman's translation of the Grimms' 'Snow White', we get this: 'And slowly she woke up, and then she pushed open the lid of the coffin and sat up, fully alive once more. "Dear God, where am I?" she said.'[9]

Sleep is a fall into another world, in which the body loses itself and experiences an internal transformation. Sleep turns all of us into Morpheus,[10] the ancient god of dreams who appears in Ovid's *Metamorphoses*, the one who is 'the master mimic, the quickest of all to capture a person's walk, his facial expression and tone of voice.'[11] Yet sleep itself, according to Nancy, is not metamorphosis. The morphing is internal: there is no sign of the transformation on the external body. 'At the very most it could be understood as an endomorphosis.'[12] (An 'endomorph' is a person with a soft, round build.) The 'endomorphosis' (*endomorphose*[13]) takes place under eyelids shut closed. The slumberer softens into other worlds, within a shell of sleep. A mollusc buttoned.

Or, perhaps, with a Carrollinian nonsense-inflection, like the Dormouse stuffed into the teapot. The Latin *dormire* (meaning to sleep) is at the heart of the etymology of the dormouse, a squirrel-like creature who hibernates in winter and is also nocturnal. The latter explains why Carroll's Dormouse is in such a torpid state at the Mad Tea Party, even during the month of May (the month of Alice's adventure).[14] In the middle of sleeping and waking, the Dormouse is a night owl who could use a cup of tea.

Nancy, whose book entitled *Listening* opens up the *aural* (for 'the ears don't have eyelids'[15]), might have heard in *endomorphose* a bit of the

French *endormir* (to put or send to sleep) or even the fairy-taleish French *endormeur* (beguiler).

As Morpheus, the 'I' dissolves behind the closed eyes of sleep, transforming 'the pure matter of sleep into form'.[16] To dream is to be in a darkened movie theatre ('a veritable cinematographic cocoon'[17]). Vanished husbands, strangers, child-selves, mothers, fathers, friends, neighbours, even the famous, emerge on the screen of our mind's eye, like cinema. The sleeper, like Roland Barthes' movie spectator, adopts 'the silkworm's motto: *Inclusum labor illustrat*; it is because I am enclosed that I work and glow with my desire.'[18] Endless characters and things and places drop into the fall of sleep.

Like participants in one of those mysterious pagan festivals of the Lenten season (as photographed by the portrait and fashion photographer Axel Hoedt), when we fall into a slumber, we are creatures in a liminal state: not only between sleeping and waking, but often between people, places, animals, plants and things.[19] We become bear-man (our human eyes and shiny nose peek out from the beast's furry throat). A stork in white satin shorts, red tights and Hans Christian Andersen red shoes with rhinoceros-horned toes, whose *eatingmagination* has a penchant for little red-capped Punch. A tree-branch-bear-man taken for a walk, with a heavy rope fit for a horse. A puss-in-boots man, whose velveteen-rabbit dress is part nineteenth-century schoolboy and part twenty-first-century motorbike rider. His empty eye-sockets are black Os into the unconscious. Hoedt's in-the-middle-of-things animal-people (and even tree-people) hark back to the Duchess's sneezing baby as it is becoming a pig:

'Don't grunt,' said Alice; 'that's not at all a proper way of expressing yourself.'

The baby grunted again, and Alice looked very anxiously into its face to see what was the matter with it. There could be no doubt that it had a *very* turn-up nose, much more like a snout than a real nose; also its eyes were getting extremely small for a baby: altogether Alice did not like the look of the thing at all.[20]

our
human
eyes
and
shiny
nose
peek
out
from
the
beast's
furry
throat

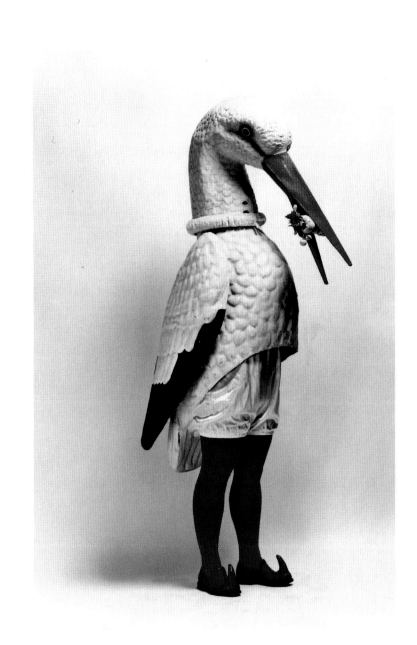

A tree-branch-bear-man
taken for a walk

the flower-garland-king

In a state of liminality: the I falls. The I sleeps. The I dreams. The eye watches the flower-garland-king riding his klopp-klopp-klopp horse: the top half of body is a sixty-pound beehive of fresh blossoms exploding with spring. (In waking life, the flower-garland-king is really a postman in a real English village with the fairy-tale name of Castleton.) When a human hand reaches out from between roses, carnations, foxgloves and daisies for a drink of whisky, the watcher/dreamer/viewer experiences a marvellous little shock.

To sleep is to nourish. He who sleeps does not feed on anything that comes to him from without. Like animals that practise hibernation, the sleeper feeds on his reserves. He digests himself in a way.[21] Perhaps this feeding on reserves is at the root of why Alice only nibbles, never really eats, while sleeping/dreaming in the underground of Wonderland.

Two: From the Middle of His Bed

Towards the end of life, Henri Matisse was often obliged to remain in bed, but he still created art all around himself by pinning cut-outs onto the interior walls of his home.[22] 'The cut-outs . . . developed during a time of great physical trial for Matisse when he underwent surgery, a difficult rehabilitation and finally, a sense of living on borrowed time.'[23] Like a snail, which begins its shell in the middle, Matisse exuded his marvellous cut-outs from within. As Gaston Bachelard notes in *The Poetics of Space*: 'the "mollusc exudes its shell," it lets the building material "seep through," so as to leak and "distil its marvellous covering as needed".'[24] (In the marginalia of a particularly magical late fifteenth-century Book of Hours, so small that is fits like an egg in the palm of the hand, a red-breasted, red-crested bird hatches from the shell of a snail. The marvellous miniature creature pecks on a blue forget-me-not flower from an aurelian field. So, too, bloom Matisse's cuttings.

In 1953, Matisse made *The Snail*. We see only the shell, made of gouache-painted squares, cut and torn. This snail is gargantuan. The snail's spiral-turning home has been writ large enough to embody the dynamically endomorphic Matisse.

Inside his shell, the physically restricted Matisse gardened with paper. As the artist explains, during an interview with the poet André Verdet, while in the process of making his famed *The Parakeet and the Mermaid* (1952):

'I have made a little garden all around me where I can walk . . . There are leaves, fruits, a bird'. As Matisse speaks, he points to 'a large mural composition of cut paper that takes up half the room'. Leaves in hues of green, red, blue, yellow and orange – heavy with finger-like tendrils or extended with limbs radiating outwards – and ultramarine pomegranates of varying sizes . . . the forms are pinned, some with multiple pins, but not too firmly or flatly . . . drooping, bending, relaxing, fluttering, reacting to a breath of air, making shadows.[25]

Matisse's *papereries* were pinned to the walls that surrounded him like butterflies not-yet dead or returning to life: quivering, wavering, trembling, awakening, sleeping, trying to go to sleep.[26]

snail's spiral—turning home

Before being pinned, Matisse's Rorschach-like cut-outs fell out of the artist's large seamstress-scissor-forceps into new life: restless forms, in which one thing can mean so many things, like an algae-seaweed-flower-star or a female-nude-parrot-propeller-swimming-shark or an unfurling-fern-frond-snail-shell-butterfly-proboscis-ribbon-candy-confetti or a pomegranate-bat-butterfly. ('"The question is," said Alice, "whether you *can* make words [or perhaps bubbles and cut paper] mean so many different things."'[27]) Matisse described his process of cutting out large sheets of gouache-painted paper as 'drawing with scissors'.[28]

Once cut, the *gouaches découpées* were carefully arranged, pinned, rearranged and repinned by Matisse's assistants (who wore pincushions on their wrists and were clothed in properly constructed dresses like seamstresses) onto the walls of his studio. 'For the sake of permanence and protection, once it was decided that a work was finished or when space was required in the studio, the composition was transferred from the wall through an elaborate tracing process, the pins were ultimately removed and the shapes were eventually glued into place.'[29] A close look at the cut-outs reveals tiny tear-duct holes, scars retained of an early life spent pinned. Matisse's assistant Lydia Delectorskaya 'expressed sorrow for the pinholes' "necessary evil".'[30]

Bed is where most of us were born and most of us will die. Bed is where most of us were conceived. Bed is a place where we are awakened by morning sunlight (Aurora and all of her goldenness) and close our eyes to sleep with the darkness of the night. In bed, Marcel Proust wrote most of his *In Search of Lost Time*. In bed, we are cushioned between dreams and waking life. Especially for Matisse, bed is an always-already-in-the-middle-of-things trope. Photographs of the period give way to Matisse's bedroom-cum-studio. Next to Matisse's bed, we spot the specially constructed 'cabinet with a roll-top desk, drawers labelled "pins" and slots for books and papers'.[31] In another we smile to see him drawing from his bed with a crayon attached to the end of an extraordinarily long stick: a Pinnochion pencil for drawing dreams (not lies). On the wall can be seen a smoking lamp and a 'feminine' oval shape with flowers, both

seamstress—scissor—forceps into new life

of which would become part of his fairy-tale masterpiece *The Thousand and One Nights* (1950), a piece that we will return to.

During his period of productively convalescing by lining the white walls around him with 'cut-paper leaves, flowers, fronds and fruit from imaginary forests . . . and . . . figures – acrobats, dancers, swimmers – looped and plunged into synthetic seas',[32] Matisse was a bit like Proust. Both sprouted their own interior paper gardens: Matisse from his studio-bed; Proust from his writing-bed. From their beds-as-boats, paper garden dreams unfolded in which one thing could become so many things.

Turning now to Matisse's *The Thousand and One Nights*, here his pair of scissors become an Orientalist magic bottle from the *Arabian Nights* and the paper cut-outs that emerge are akin to plumes of smoke, in the middle of becoming so many things. As in the story of 'Night 3' of my copy of the *Arabian Nights*, which features a magical brass bottle pulled up by a fisherman from the sea:[33] when the fisherman shakes it to pour out its contents, a tower of smoke emerges and becomes an *'ifrit*. The *'ifrit* 'had a mouth like a cave with teeth like rocks, while his nostrils were like jugs and his eyes like lamps'.[34] (An *'ifrit* is a powerful jinn, or demon in Arabian and Muslim mythology, which we have Anglicized as genie.)

Matisse was 81 when he made his *Thousand and One Nights*, confined to his wheelchair and unable to sleep. The horizontal scroll depicts the long collection of Arabic fairy and folk tales whose central theme is to ensure that the magical tales never stop being told. As readers familiar with the stories know, King Shahryar (in revenge for the infidelity of his wife) has gone mad: each and every night he marries a new virgin. After each of his wedding nights, the king orders his vizier to cut off the head of each new wife every morning.[35] 'This led to unrest among the citizens; they fled away with their daughters until there were no nubile girls left in the city.'[36] Left behind are the two daughters of the vizier: Shahrazad, the elder daughter, and Dunyazad, the younger. The clever and cunning Shahrazad has strategized a plan to put an end to the king's beheading of virgins (which would include herself and her sister). She volunteers as the next virgin to be deflowered and slaughtered, but

a Pinnochion pencil for drawing dreams (not lies)

H. matisse Juin 50

knows how she can outwit the king (and save her life, her sister's and others) through the power of storytelling. Before being decked out to be taken by her father the vizier to the evil Bluebeard-like king, she gives instructions to her younger sister, Dunyazad, explaining: 'When I go to the king, I shall send for you. You must come, and when you see that the king has done what he wants with me, you are to say "Tell me a story, sister, so as to pass the working part of the night." I shall then tell you a tale that, God willing, will save us.'[37] After the fated night of Shahrazad love-making with the king, Dunyazad asks her big sister to tell her a bedtime story. And, as Marina Warner explains:

Shahrazad will begin to her one, and will continue until dawn breaks, when 'speaking was no longer permitted' as the enigmatic refrain puts it. The Sultan [King Shahryar], who has been listening in, will want to know how that story ends, will want to hear more stories like it, and will give Shahrazad more time, sending away the vizier who arrives in the morning to take away the bride (his daughter) to the scaffold. In this way, she will be able to put off the day of her execution until the Sultan relents.[38]

King Shahriyar's yearning to know how the story ends and who wants to hear more stories is suggestive of the Grimms' 'The Golden Key'. Both are propelled by a desire to know, which results in generating further magical tales, without end.

In 1950, Matisse was stealing time, like Shahrazad herself. The 'game of the paper cut-outs' was 'an agreeable distraction' for his 'long hours of insomnia.'[39] Across this large horizontal work we are given clues to the imagery through the refrain from the *Arabian Nights*, which he has spelled out in cut-out black letters, separated into syllables, with beats of lime-green and kelly-green hearts in between: '*elle vit apparaitre le matin/ elle se tut discètement*' (as dawn approached, she fell discretely silent). The two smoking lamps in the cut-out, one white and the other back, suggest the movement from day to night. The words from the story appear over the black lamp, on a background of *Auroran* yellow, indicating night as the time of storytelling and the coming of dawn as the silencing of Shahrazad. The large red diamond shape in the last panel, next to the black lamp, has been read by some viewers as an image of female genitalia, suggesting the deflowering in the marriage bed before the bedtime stories began. (This iconographic reading becomes dynamic when Matisse's fruity-red lozenge shape is put into conversation with the similarly abstracted form *Labyrinth of Venus* (1985), painted in blood-red by the Cuban-American artist Ana Mendieta. *Labyrinth of Venus*, like *The Thousand and One Nights*, is a maze that turns on the sexualization of a woman's body like Russian nesting dolls one inside the other, like the bloody trail of Angela Carter's 'Wolf-Alice'.)

In Matisse's *The Snail*, the big squares of magenta, tree-green, tangerine-orange, tomato-red, iris-flower blue, buttercup yellow, lime green and night black slowly spin. So slow as to be nearly invisible to the naked eye, as slow as a real snail, whose slow movement is only visible by the gossamer trail it leaves behind. These unhurried squares, with their 'step by step unfolding . . . into a gold infinity round the edge' are in the middle of the 'whirlpool' of becoming other things, like the very tiny, clearly figurative, snail that playfully exudes its little shape atop the top-left, violet-orchid square.[40] The snail is crawling towards the black square. You have to look carefully.

It secretes its secret.

EL Laberinto de Venus   Ana Mendieta 1982

a maze that turns on the sexualization of a woman's body like Russian nesting dolls one inside

the other, like the bloody trail of Angela Carter's 'Wolf-Alice'

Three: A Visual Rhyme

'The closed outer shutters of Bosch's *Garden of Earthly Delights* [*c*. 1500–1505] form a huge closed eyeball,'[41] writes Marina Warner. To open *The Garden of Earthly Delights* is to unfasten the unconscious, like falling into sleep. Hidden inside are Bosch's hush-hush garden dreams found inside his surreal-botanical-dandelion-ball. The veined amniotic sac makes a glassine home for the little naked man and the little naked woman consumed in erotic play. Near their bubble, the touch of a toe, by a nearby upside-down man (his head and torso plunging like a duck diving after frogs, while he masturbates), threatens to puncture their fully inflated, perfectly round balloon.

Bosch's surreal-botanical-bubble lives within the large black, white and grey biosphere of the painting as it is experienced when the panel doors (the lids of the eyeball) are closed. A series of metonymic orbs/holes displace each other, in a 'visual rhyme',[42] with the inflection of Bataille's pornographic *Story of the Eye* (1928). For Bataille, the mouth becomes eye becomes egg becomes breast becomes nipple becomes testicle. For Bosch, the circular orbs and cavities create similar rhymes, although with less perfected assonance, owing to changes in scale, which make the miniature and the gigantic ambiguous. Nevertheless, in *The Garden of Earthly Delights*, the ear becomes eye becomes mouth becomes pond becomes the owl's hole in a tree becomes a pair of pink nipples becomes amniotic sac becomes strawberries becomes rectum becomes nest. However, the feasts of the earthly delights depicted are surprisingly bereft of flesh. As Warner notes: this is a 'fruitarians' bacchanal . . . involving neither roasted meats nor any kind of flesh at all, but only berries, cherries, strawberries, blackberries, flowers and sloes'.[43]

Both *The Garden of Earthly Delights* and *Story of the Eye* signify 'in the manner of a vibration which always produces the same sound'.[44] 'The visual rhyme – orb/world/eye – invites us to partake in its angle of view, to use it as an instrument, so that when the wings open to the spectacle of other worlds inside, it is as if they were revealed by a magnifying

hush—hush garden dreams found inside

bis surreal—botanical—dandelion—ball

lens, as were in use by jewellers and gem cutters and lens grinders in the Netherlands' at the time of its making.[45]

Four: *The Dictionary by the Brothers Grimm*

If the dictionary were a painting, it might look something like Bosch's *The Garden of Earthly Delights*. The writing of a dictionary is necessarily always *in medias res*. This Latin term translates as 'in the midst of things'. *In medias res* is the literary and artistic narrative technique of relating a story from the midpoint, rather than the beginning.

Like a plum becoming a prune, one word becomes something related but often quite different, just as in the telling and retelling of fairy tales, one story becomes another. Charles Perrault's 'Donkey-skin' becomes the Grimms' 'All Fur'; the Grimms' 'Bluebeard' becomes Angela Carter's 'The Bloody Chamber'. Just as Carter has noted that 'a fairy tale is a story where one king goes to another king to borrow a cup of sugar',[46] a dictionary is a story where a word goes next door to borrow letters and give others away.

The Brothers Grimm did more than collect and transcribe our most famous fairy tales: they were scholars with wide and varied interests, publishing many books together and individually. Among their publications are *Irish Elf Tales*, *Ancient German Law*, *German Grammar* and *The History of the German Language*. For over twenty years, they worked together on 'writing the *German Dictionary,* one of the most ambitious lexicographical undertakings of the nineteenth century'.[47] But before their *German Dictionary* was completed, Wilhelm died in 1859. Jacob continued working on it alone, until his own collapse in 1863. He had only got to letter F. The last word was fantastically fecund, with the berry-cherry-strawberry flavour of Bosch's *The Garden of Earthly Delights*: *Frucht* (fruit). *Frugal*. Stopped short in the middle, we are left waiting for what word will develop next: *Früh. Fuchs. Füchsin. Fuchtel. Fuder. Fug. Fuge . . .*

Five: Pregnant Pause

I dwell in the middle of a boy's stomach. A pregnant pause. In Anthony Goicolea's drawing entitled *Pregnant Pause* (2011), rendered like a scientific illustration, a boy is expecting. His stomach is a womb. He has swallowed a small animal. He is gravid with a puppy, perhaps a wolf. The foetal form sleeps peacefully inside the boy. Like a rabbit in an underground burrow. Like a fox in a den. Like a wolf in a small cave. On the tip of my tale-wagging tongue is the familiar folk rhyme:

What are little boys made of?
What are little boys made of?
Snips and snails
And puppy-dogs' tails

A *decrescendo* down, down, down the animal gullet. Goicolea's pencil practises fairy-tale midwifery and delivers mixed up stories. The boy does not cry 'Wolf!' – he has swallowed his bellow. Goicolea renders the inaudible, like the silence of an unborn wolf. An interloper. 'An enunciation without utterance.'[48]

The wolf-being is 'meaning in its nascent state.'[49] I place a stethoscope on the womb of the boy. I hear the rhythmic beat of the refrain of 'The Juniper Tree' cannibalism ('My father he ate me') – I hear the birthing cry of Little Red Riding Hood and her grandmother in the gut of the wolf.

Surprise. (Marvellous. Mirabilia.) The little child that I was, long dormant, presumed dead, dislodges – like that bite of apple stuck in Little Snow White's throat –and gets its voice back and sings to me Sergei Prokofiev's *Peter and the Wolf* (1936). The French horns (of the wolf) and the strings (of the boy) resound. I remember the grandfather's warning – 'Suppose a wolf came out of the forest' – my delight when a '"big grey wolf" does indeed come out of the forest' – the triumphant march with Peter, the bird, the hunters, the grandfather, the cat and the wolf – and being told that 'if you listen very carefully, you'd hear the duck quacking

Like a rabbit in an underground burrow. Like a fox in a den. Like a wolf in a small cave.

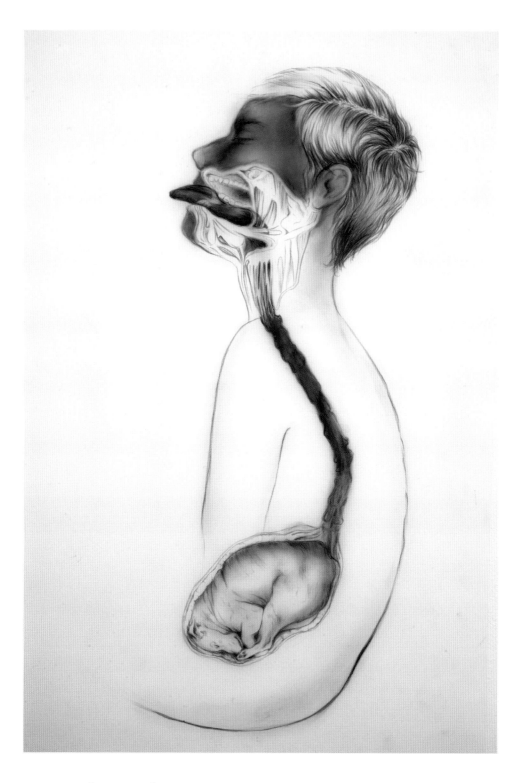

His stomach is a womb. He has swallowed a small animal.

inside the wolf's belly.'

'It is always in the belly that we – man or woman – end up listening or start listening. The ear opens onto the sonorous cave that we then become.'[50]

Six: *Robot after Rabbit*

On 12 September 1940, four adolescents, Jacques Marsal, George Agnel, Simon Coencas and Marcel Ravidat, under the leadership of the eldest (Ravidat), unblocked an Alice-in-Wonderland underground gullet to a marvellous cave: Lascaux. It was a plunge into an unknown world that had been asleep for 17,000 years.

By some accounts the discovery occurred when Ravidat's dog Robot chased a rabbit into the hole that led to the cave. (The rabbit seems to be a fairy-tale addition.[51]) Under the lightly fictionalized pen of the Kentucky writer Guy Davenport, the boys heard Robot's barks from below, 'vague and muted, as if down a well'.[52] Ravidat was the first through the hole, feet down to see if he could feel the bottom, while yelling '*Courage, Robot! Je viens!*'[53] Finding his foothold from ledge to ledge, he reached the bottom and was soon joined by the others. 'The hole through which they had entered was a dim wash of light above them.'[54]

Ravidat lit a match and fired the grease gun: the kind of torch with which he had gigged frogs at night . . . Everywhere they looked there were animals. The vaulted ceiling was painted, the crinkled walls lime white and pale sulphur were painted with horses and cows, with high-antlered elk and animals they did not know . . . The torch showed in its leaping flare a parade of Shetland ponies bounding like lamps. Above them jumped a dishevelled cow like the one in *Mère Oie* [Mother Goose] over the moon. Handsome plump horses trotted one after another, their tails arched like a cat's.[55]

Georges Bataille, whose lecture on Lascaux, given in Orléans on 18 January 1955 (three months before the publication of his famed book on

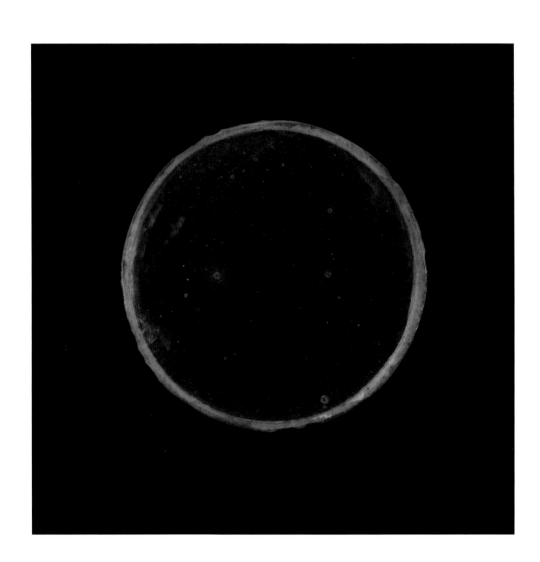

the topic[56]), gives a version of the boys-down-the-hole tale that is a fairy tale peppered with a strong Surrealist taste for the marvellous. Throughout the lecture, Bataille provides a sense of magic to the tale of Lascaux, which he names 'this marvellous cave'.[57] Etymologically, the word *marvellous* comes from *mirabilia*, which is Latin for a miraculous event. The marvellous, with its fairy-tale possibilities, brings surprise and shock: 'The marvellous is always beautiful, any marvellous is beautiful, there is no marvellous that is not beautiful', writes the Surrealist André Breton.[58]

According to Bataille, the hole that opened up Lascaux was a geographical fissure that had once been filled in with sticks to prevent local sheep from falling in. 'One day a woman removed the sticks so that she could put the dead donkey in the hole.' The donkey fell so far down the hole that the woman reasoned (if with a bit of enchantment) that there was an underground passage that 'led to a small château nearby'.[59] Later she would tell Marcel Ravidat about her discovery. Eventually, Ravidat and his three friends set out to 'explore the underground passage the lady had told them about . . . First Ravidat threw large rocks down the hole: the length of the fall and the echo shocked them all. Ravidat then stuck his head into the narrow orifice. All of a sudden he passed through and slipped and fell 7 meters.'[60] It was not long before the four boys 'found themselves next to the remains of the donkey' and soon 'for the first time, human beings from our time entered the most distant world.'[61]

Bataille asserts that 'the story rose from the simplest world of the fairy tale.'[62] And, indeed, the sensibility of enchantment gives a magical aura to the legend of Lascaux, especially through the mouth of Bataille. Of particular note is the fact that one of the boys, who scurried down the hole, told Bataille that upon finding the dazzling cave, the four of them 'immediately felt like someone discovering a treasure, a casket of diamonds or a cascade of precious gems'.[63] The discovery of Lascaux is also like the Grimms' 'The Golden Key', only in this case, the key is turned and we learn what 'wonderful things and precious things' the children found.[64]

'By the flicker of a torchlight, the animals seem to surge from the walls, and move across them like figures in a magic lantern show.'[65] Passed down as oral stories by local villagers, the legends of what drove the boys down the hole are folk narratives that retain the fairy-tale lure of the existence of marvellous kingdoms right below the surface of one's feet. ('We recognize our likenesses in the most distant past in the enchanted aspects of the subterranean,' writes Bataille of Lascaux.[66])

Before *Alice's Adventures in Wonderland*, the more traditional fairy tales are no stranger to the subterranean theme. Consider, for example, the three princesses that live underground in an enchanted world in the Grimms' 'The Worn-out Dancing Shoes':

They went all the way down, and when they were at the bottom, they stood in the middle of a marvellous avenue of trees whose leaves all made of silver and glittered and glimmered . . . Then they came to another avenue of trees, where all the leaves were made of gold, and finally to one where all the leaves were made of pure diamond.[67]

Italo Calvino has collected and written down traditional Italian folktales, including 'The Tale of Cats' (a story that I prefer to call 'Cats in the Hole'). The framework of the narrative is familiar: an evil mother treats her rude biological daughter as a princess and her well-mannered stepdaughter like a servant. But the opening is unusual for the non-Italian. The good stepdaughter tugs a cauliflower out of the ground, which leaves 'a hole the size of a well in the earth'.[68] The good stepdaughter then climbs down through the hole (by way of a ladder) and discovers a houseful of cats. Mamma Cat serves the good stepdaughter 'meat, macaroni, and roast chicken'.[69] She replaces her ragged clothes with 'the finest silk gown, a large and delicately worked handkerchief, and a pair of satin slippers'.[70]

In his introduction to the volume, Calvino notes that the 'prime motif of numerous and particularly southern folktales' is 'that of the *cavoliccidaru* (cabbage picker): the cupboard is bare, so father or mother, along with daughters, scour the countryside for plants with which to make soup; pulling up a cabbage larger than others, they come upon a passage into an underground world'.[71]

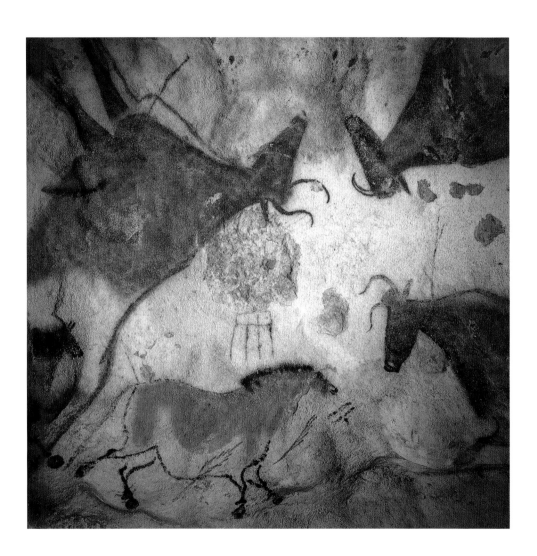

The good
stepdaughter tugs
a cauliflower out
of the ground,
which leaves
'a hole the size
of a well in
the earth'.

Secret worlds are the marvellous dreams of children and adults, looking to magically escape the realities of everyday life. Sometimes the dreams are erotic. In Esther Teichmann's photograph of a grotto patterned with shells, circles, diamonds and four-pointed stars, like a Turkish bath gone dry and pebble-grey (not a peacock-blue in sight), two girlish women, still in procession of their child-perfect skin, young and tender (like white spring carrots), are delicacies unpulled, *fruits de mer*, in an overgrown mollusc shell. As if peering through the aperture of that big shell that opened this chapter, also by Teichmann (writ, not large, but gigantic), we see that these *Alicious* girls (one, two, buckle no shoes) wear nothing at all, save for the Emperor's New Clothes.

Sometimes the dreams are nature. In Teichmann's photograph of beguiling stalagmites, like castle pillars, we find ourselves in an opalescent underground palace made by nature: the chasm appears as if loaded with emerald, opal, jade, turquoise, agate, amber, malachite, copper, silver and gold. We are, to quote Bataille on experiencing the beautiful wonders of the world (whether made by nature or by the work of the artist), 'dazzled' by a feeling of 'richness'.[72] We enter the cave, this otherworldly kingdom, as if dreamily following the Mistress of the Copper Mountain, like the young miner lad in Pavel Petrovich Bazhov's Russian magic tale:

Wherever she went, the way ahead opened to her . . . one large room after another . . . One was entirely green, the next was yellow with gold flecks, in another walls were covered with copper flowers. Other rooms were deep blue from lapis lazuli.[73]

Of note is the fact that Bazhov would write his greatest magic tales, 'The Stone Flower' and 'The Mountain Master', while *underground* during a time of self-imprisonment in order to avoid arrest during the height of the Purges around 1937–8. As Robert Chandler has noted: 'Bazhov seems to have achieved an extraordinary degree of creative freedom while in the eye of the storm, at the height of the Great Terror' (1936–8).[74] It turns out that 'Bazhov's own life story was as dramatic as any of his tales: after confinement within the magic kingdom of his own home, he awoke to

the chasm appears as if loaded with emerald, opal, jade, turquoise,

agate, amber, malachite, copper, silver and gold

sudden fame.'[75] In 1939, 'on his sixtieth birthday', a collection of his magic tales was published under the title *The Malachite Casket*.[76] 'And in 1943, Bazhov was awarded the Stalin Prize, in response to which he told a friend: "Hailed today, jailed tomorrow."'[77]

Fairy tales, folk tales and Russian magic tales give us the materials to dream of finding our own subterranean world of escape and enchantment, which sometimes, as in the astounding case of Bazhov, can come true.

For four French lads, the dream also came true: this time under the cloud of the Second World War. For six days, the 'Lascaux boys' kept their cave, their complete cosmogony, unplumbed – a secret. A secret within a secret. *Mise en abyme. In medias res.* But the boys knew that this secret was too spectacular, too important, to not be shared with the world. The boys invited their teacher Léon Laval to share their marvellous underworld, but the opening was too small. The next day, the passage was widened and he slipped through.[78] Days later, scientists would enter the cave. By 1941, Lascaux was classed as an historic monument and would be opened up to the public on 13 July 1948.

The orifice of the cave opened, like the closed panels of Bosch's *The Garden of Earthly Delights*, to marvellous pictures. Swimming stags. A spotted Chinese horse. An upside-down ochre horse, caught falling through the cave. A falling bird-man, imaged between a bison and a bird on a stick. 'Of the 1,963 representations counted, 915 are animal figures, 434 signs, 613 indeterminate figures and 1 is human.'[79]

In Lascaux's Hall of the Bulls, there is an enigmatic equid who has been named the Unicorn, because of its long straight horns, suggestive of the mythical animal. Enigmatically standing apart from other identifiable animals in the cave, the Lascaux beast, with rings of adornment loosely rendered like secret script on its flank, has been fancifully interpreted as 'a horse, bovine, feline or reindeer'. Nevertheless, its morphology does not 'correspond to any known species'.[80] Nor does this *dinicorn* have anything to do with the narwhal-like tusks of the imagined, yet once believed to be real, unicorn. Unimaginable as part of our visual repertoire, the beautiful beast is an imagined creature of Ice Age marvellousness.

In Lascaux's Axial Gallery, a large black stag wears its spectacular ant-lers like the oversized crown of a fairy-tale king, and with its 'head turned up, eyes rolled back and mouth open, suggests troating or bellowing'.[81] 'The open mouth is enveloped by a cloud of red.[82] Below the fantastic stag are stencilled liquorice-gumdrop shapes, each fuzzed by shadow, as they march up to or out of the simple enigmatic door, made of four straight black lines. The fuzzy gumdrops and the cloud of red were made by spraying pulverized pigment through the mouth.[83] Ice Age painters not only used brushes to paint, they spat dry or liquid paint directly from their mouths or blew it through a tube. Another *oralia* born from the mouths of Ice Age artists. Swallowed by the gullet of the cave, working from memory, animals (possibly in hopes of eating them) spewed out of the mouths of Ice Age artists onto the rock-walled belly of Lascaux.

Lascaux holds the meanings of her foetal frescoes, unborn, yet fully developed 'like a foal that can walk straight away'.[84] Do the frescoes, dubbed by Abbé Breuil as the 'Sistine Chapel of prehistory',[85] hold things to eat, to hurt, to worship, to make magic? Lascaux is the fist-sized never-to-be-truly-opened (understood) supra interior of the *Venus of Willendorf* writ large (writ gargantuan).

Sleep, 'a sign without signification',[86] universalizes the images of Lascaux, never to be roused: we can only dream stories behind these animals and one man. Their meaning poetically resists signification: it happened too long ago, long before the invention of writing as we know it.

Ravidat's initial opening up of the mouth of Lascaux offered the possibility of speaking: but we cannot read the signs. In a valiant effort to preserve what remains of its deteriorating voice, threatened by 'colonies of algae brought in by tourists' and other disruptions with heat and light,[87] the cave has been locked up by conservationists since 1963. I will never go through its mouth. Lascaux is locked and 'rocked to the rhythm of its [stone] heart and lungs'.[88]

antlers like the oversized crown of a fairy-tale king

Recently, with my middle son, I visited a cave in the Pacific Northwest. Wet nipples dripped on the ceiling of the cave. I thought I remembered being inside my mother's womb. Night was my food.[89] I became 'indistinct' from myself, from those around me, from the world, as if I had fallen into a cave of forgotten dreams.[90] I vanished as 'I'.[91] I walked through with my lantern and felt as if I could not find the end of the long journey through the night in the day.

People came through, their bodies barely visible. They laughed and spoke with a new freedom, like children on a sleepover. Like teenagers camping without adults. We were all free in the dark. We were free without light. As if we were asleep, we sleepwalked, delighted in an 'equality' suited by the cave's day-into-night 'darkness' and its 'silence'.[92]

When we came out of the big hole in the mountain that travelled underground, we laughed as though we had been on a rollercoaster – propelled by our own release into the darkness from which we began . . . in the middle of things.

Just as the fairy tale gives us the dream that we have a right to be happy and free, so does darkness.

———

8 De-windowing: Bernard Faucon's Land of Boys

The world plays at living behind a glass partition; the world is an aquarium; I see everything close up and yet cut off, made of some other substance.
Roland Barthes, *A Lover's Discourse*

Bernard Faucon dresses and photographs his manikin-boys on vacation, playing in the snow, departing on a train. Faucon's world is a 'Land of Boys' (empty, but much kinder than Pinocchio's 'Land of Toys'). Faucon see his boys as 'little men freed from their shop-windows'. Nevertheless, the boys are very still. They are waiting for enchantment (as in Snow White or Briar Rose). Faucon's photographs, like the fairy tale, are invested with hope for the little guy: a new life yet to come. And, in turn, the images startle the viewer with a strangeness almost real. A double take.

Bernard Faucon's grandmother offered him his first camera in 1967, a Semflex (France's post-war challenge to the Rolleiflex). He was seventeen.[1] His *oeuvre* focuses on childhood, most specifically a tender love of the adolescent, an *ephebophila* (*ephebe*, early manhood, + *philia*, love). Faucon is best known for his staged photographs of manikins: a big family of Pinocchios without the strings. ('I've got no strings/ To hold me down/ To make me fret, or make me frown . . . There are no strings on me' – so sings the wooden boy in Disney's 1940 animation.) Made not of pieces of wood but of plaster, Faucon's manikin-boys are modern French, not old world Italian. (As a life-size doll, the manikin is another *pupa* in this book's aurelian world.) After dressing his boys with care, Faucon (as master puppeteer) stages their birthdays, snowman building, First Communions, picnics and more, often with a dash of boyish pyromania, at times coupling the unreal boys with real boys, as in his *Diabolo menthe* (1980). The four little men (the word 'manikin' is from the Dutch *mannekijn*, meaning little man) hold a glass of the popular French soft drink of green mint syrup and lemonade. The colour of *Diabolo menthe* is 1939 *Wizard-of-Oz* Technicolor. Wicked-Witch-skin green. Emerald-City-candy green. The boy and his manikin friends show no interest in the raging fire behind them.

Neither-nor

Like Pinocchio, Faucon's life-size dolls with unblinking eyes ('even though their gestures could be "alive", their eyes remain fixed'[2]) are nei-ther dead nor alive, neither awake nor asleep, neither adult nor child. Like Pinocchio, they 'excite our imagination because we know they're impos-sible, requiring us to simulate belief, to play at make-believe'.[3] Faucon's teenage dolls (disturbing for their real size, like real adolescents) make a festival out of their neither-norness (which in French is constructed as 'ni-ni') so as to restore life back into our own static adulthood. The afterlife of looking at Faucon's picnics, holidays, snowball fights and other everyday activities enables us to break through our own lifelessness. The 'vocation' of Faucon's manikins, Roland Barthes notes, 'is having had resuscitated':[4] a dream that comes true in *Friends* (1978). Faucon's 'little men' hold the magic dust for breathing new life into their friends *and* the bodies of the viewers. Enchanting us with childhood, pleasure and erotics, they awaken us with a shock of the marvellous (the fairy-tale potential to transform[5]). They resuscitate us as if we were Briar Rose being awoken from our hundred-year sleep by the just-right kiss of the Prince Faucon:

They resuscitate us as if we were Briar Rose

Immediately after the kiss, she woke up, and the king and queen and the entire royal household and the horses and the dogs and the pigeons on the roof and the flies in the walls and the fire woke up. Indeed, the fire flared up and the cook gave the kitchen boy a box on the ear, while the maid finished plucking the chicken.[6]

In Faucon, as in Briar Rose, the fire flares up, so that we, too, are released from the shop window, the glass box, the snow-white coffin.

Barthes, who was smitten with the work of Faucon, not only wrote a little essay on the photographer, but offered him a little scrawled-out note that captured this 'marvellous' in Faucon's little men, writing: 'Your photos are marvellous; for me, it's ontological, if you'll allow this loaded word. The photo is in the limits of its own being: that is the fascination.' For André Breton in the 1920s, the 'marvellous' is stirred by the manikin.[7] For Barthes in the 1970s, the 'marvellous' is stirred by Faucon's ni-ni play with manikins.

Ni-ni is spiritedly tied to the famed 'fort-da' game theorized by Sigmund Freud and played by his toddler grandson Ernst. By symbolically turning his ma-ma into a toy, a wooden spool on a string, a yo-yo, a mama-Pinocchio,[8] Ernst imaginatively threw his jou-jou[9] ma-ma back and forth, controlling her comings and goings. When the wooden spool was away from him, he pretended that she was gone (saying 'fort'). When the spool was near him, he pretended that she was here (saying 'da'). But of course, she was *neither* here *nor* there. Ernst played fort-da with ma-ma. Faucon play ni-ni with boys. There is something that rings childish in ni-ni.

Just-ironed

In *First Communion* (1979), Faucon scatters his own catechisms by focusing on two boys in very, very clean sailor suits: one is a manikin-boy and the other a real boy. Their white shirts, with crisp blue ties, are typical of the fashion of Faucon's family of boys, who in the words of Guy Davenport, have a taste for 'leisure toggery suitable for summer and play' with that 'just-ironed, worn-for-the first-time look'.[10] Of note: 'Faucon grew up in a post-war France that embraced new ideas of hygiene, an "Americanization" of washing machines, modernized bathrooms, shampoo – a wave of consumerism boosted by fashion magazines such as *Marie-Claire* and *Elle*.'[11] On the lavender field clothesline in Faucon's *The Drying Line* (1982), we cannot see any boys, but we can see their 'sartorial egos'.[12] Between a blouse and a tea towel hangs a pair of boys' slip-on red and white underpants, which are part of the spirit of more minimal post-1945 underclothing. 'The *slip à poché*' or men's briefs (which are called

Y-fronts in the UK or tighty-whities in the U.S.) were 'introduced in 1945 according to *Marie-Claire* – wherein an illustration of a *slip minimum* has this caption: "Since he was 15 Michael's mother had inflected on him underwear such as his grandfather wore long-legged flannel drawers that fitted into his socks. Boys' underwear today has been reduced to a cotton or nylon pull-on [*slip*]."'[13]

Tight-fitting slip-on underpants are the feature of Ron Mueck's boyish *Pinocchio* (1996). Mueck, a child of toymakers, who started out his career as a window dresser, has made his own families of manikin-like babies, children, adolescents and adults. Mueck's beings are always hyper-realistic, save for scale, which ranges from the miniature to the gargantuan. *Pinocchio* is a medium-small, tidy, 33-inch young boy, proudly wearing his clean 'tighty whities'. His *slip à poche* is brand new, as if just pulled off of Faucon's clothesline in a field of lavender. The proud nose of the boy-child is pointed up, ready to grow. Pride is impossible to see in the empty stock figures of Faucon, collected and dressed in a Grimms' licked-clean tone.

In *First Communion*, the adolescent boy made of flesh eats not the body and blood of Christ, but blue and white sugared almonds (often called Jordan almonds), like painted Easter eggs (only small). This detail holds me, with adolescent madeleine memories of not only the disappointment of my first Communion wafer (at age fifteen), but the pleasure of eating sugared almonds in the darkness of the movie theatre. (As Barthes nostalgically writes: 'I look for *what is going to move me* [when we were children we used to look in the undergrowth for chocolate eggs which had been hidden there] . . . I wait for the . . . fragment which will concern me and establish *the meaning for me.*'[14]) In the background of this springtime picture, the viewer is blessed with flocks of manikin boys. I spot one overly grown adolescent manikin-man. But the traditional nuclear family is absent.

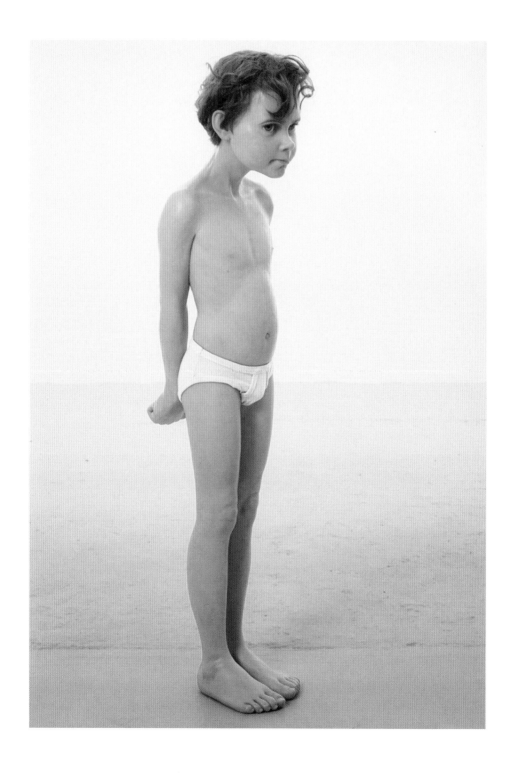

Faucon's Gastronomy

Faucon's photographs are printed with a secret technology known as the 'Fresson process', which gives the photographs an incredibly rich and intense colour, with the texture and colour of Jordan-almond 'matte porcelain'.[15] 'A Fresson print takes days to develop: each color has it its own template, and is oil pigment infused into *gelatin*.'[16] The Fresson recipe for making pictures is more on the level of the two-volume *Mastering the Art of French Cooking* (Simone Beck, Louisette Bertholle, Julia Child) than the *Better Homes and Gardens Cookbook* that I learned to cook with. Like lavish cuisine, Faucon's photographs suggest the appealing artifice of glazes and colours of the weekly prepared dishes of 1950s French cooking featured in the French women's magazine *Elle*. Such 'ornamental cookery' is a well-orchestrated gastronomy 'meant for the eye alone'.[17] If cuisine is food imagined as art, might we also see Faucon's photographs as art imagined as food?

Like the food in *Elle*, Faucon's Fresson eye-candy boys have a 'smooth coating' and 'a partiality for a pinkish colour'.[18] Note the colour of Faucon's baby-doll-skinned lads, both real and not real, in *Friends*. (Yet a closer look reveals the scratch and bruise on the live boy's upper

left thigh, the peeling liquorice-black hair on the manikin's head.) Faucon's 'Land of Boys' is 'dream-like cookery' and a 'fairy-land reality'.[19] Barthes commented that the consumers of the images and recipes for *Elle*'s extravagant 'fairy-land' cookery were 'genuinely working-class . . . Compare with *L'Express*, whose exclusively middle-class public enjoys a comfortable purchasing power: its cookery is real, not magical'.[20] The readers of *Elle* have neither the time nor the money to make the classic *salade niçoise* of *L'Express*. The *eatingmagination* of *Elle* provides page-licking pictures for an entire pink meal (*Le Souper rose*).[21] Pink is the shiny smooth coating on the cold chicken. Pink are the ladles of prawn soup. Pink is paprika salad. Pink is the champagne. Pink is the magical pudding. Pink is a fairy-tale *oralia*.

De-shop-windowed

Faucon's models' clothes carry the history of the development of department stores, iconic holders of shopping history, like La Samaritaine and their big glass windows of dressed manikins; but what they actually wear hails the presentness of the discount department store Prisunic.[22] The department store window is neither inside nor outside. It transgresses inside and outside. The etymology of transgress is to 'step across' and that is what Faucon's manikins do. They step through the glass without breaking it. As Faucon writes:

I would hurriedly set up the dummies, and after the shot, pack up and set off again. As they invested those places that bore the mark of my childhood I imagined that those little men freed from their shop-windows [*dévitrinés*], released unknown forces, brought to light sublime, masterful evidence.[23]

For this release of his little men from their shop windows, Faucon uses the made-up term *dévitrinés*, which literally translates as de-shop-windowed. (A *vitrine* is a display case or a shop window.) Faucon's manikins find themselves de-windowed in sugar snow, wearing shorts, eating cake, drinking sweet, green concoctions, sailing away, making films, building a giant cat's cradle, having a picnic, having their clothes dried in fields of lavender.

Window-shopping began with the development of the new French department stores like Le Bon Marché (founded in 1852) and the Louvre (founded in 1855). The 'department stores offered a kind of Arabian Nights world of limitless gratification of time and space' and things.[24] Appetites were intensified by delicious displays behind the big plate windows, which had grown out of the new 'iron and glass technology', with improvements in artificial lighting magically enhancing the 'theatricality' of the *mise en scène*.[25]

'Curiouser and curiouser!', as Alice proclaims as she is 'opening out like the largest telescope that ever was!',[26] for the new concept of adolescence rose hand in hand at the end of nineteenth century with the development of the French department store. By the end of the twentieth century, we find that the adolescent is most at home cruising the mall, manikins everywhere whetting their desire. The term 'window-shopping' in French is, of course, suggestively sensual: *lèche-vitrines* – literally 'licking windows'.[27]

Somewhere between fairy tale and department store display, Faucon de-windows in the spirit of Frank Baum's animated straw Scarecrow, velvety Cowardly Lion and clanking Tin Woodman who inhabit the world of Oz. Baum, who was also an amateur photographer, and who wrote a play entitled *The Maid of Arran*, composing all of the songs and even performing the male lead, was no stranger to window dressing. From 1880 to 1890, he briefly ran Baum's Bazaar in Aberdeen, South Dakota. By 1900, 'when ... [Baum] sat down to write *The Wizard of Oz*', he was *also* writing 'a treatise entitled "The Art of Decorating Dry Good Windows", a ... [handbook] for would-be window dressers that culminated Baum's brief career as the editor of *The Shop Window*.'[28] Fascinated with the power of manikins in a shop window, one can find among his collection of twelve *American Fairy Tales* (1901) his own de-windowing story entitled, 'The Dummy that Lived'. Baum's son, Harry Neal Baum, claimed that the Tin Woodman came directly out of a store window.

Sometime before he began writing children's stories, Baum was asked to set up a hardware-store-window. 'He wanted to create something eye-catching . . . so he made a torso out of a washboiler, bolted stovepipe arms and legs to it and used the underside of a saucepan for a face. He stopped with a funnel hat and what would become the inspiration for the Tin Woodman was born.'[29]

Likewise, I smile like a post-war manikin (apparently before the war they were more solemn-faced) at the fact that the famous window-decorator Gene Moore was appointed as the display director for Bonwit Teller in 1945. As queen of the New York window world, he hired his fellow queer friends as his window-dressing pages, including Robert Rauschenberg, Andy Warhol and Jasper Johns.[30] Moore came up with the idea of giving manikins a belly button, bringing them that much closer to being alive, de-windowed. According to Moore, who has been photographed dancing with a manikin: 'People recognized the manikins in my windows. Some of the manikins even acquired fans . . . I admit I once kissed one of the manikins, but I won't tell which. I just wanted to see what it would be like. It was like kissing a desk.' [31]

Sugar Babies

Faucon not only has an appetite for sweet boys, he also has a penchant, if a fearful one, as we shall see, for sugar. *The Birth of Caramel* (1996) features a delicious tree festooned with gooey caramel cocoons, tinselled in translucent sugary filament. In his own cookbook, *Tables d'amis: vingt-et-un menus de Bernard Faucon*, Faucon tells the reader that as an adolescent he used to thread grapes, which were soaked in caramel, on wooden skewers; he christened his creation Viennese Brochettes and would sell them on the street.[32] (On the front of the cookbook is one of Faucon's most reproduced photographs, *The Banquet*, 1978).

In *Gulliver* (1979), a boyish manikin with infinitely sad and sweet velvet eyes, even if made of plaster, wears shorts, mauve socks, school-boy shoes and a creamy, velvety jumper. His 'normal' height appears

tinselled in translucent
sugary filament

Tables d'amis

Vingt-et-un menus
de Bernard Faucon
légers, mais consistants, faciles à préparer
pour nourrir ses amis

Photographies de Jean-Claude Larrieu

Préface
par
Hervé Guibert

WILLIAM BLAKE & CO. / A & A EDIT.
LE TEMPS QU'IL FAIT

Aliciously-grown, Gulliver-big, thanks to the scale of the red-roofed Tudor-inspired plastic doll's house behind him and the Los Angeles swimming pool between his legs. Of particular interest is the fact that the winding driveway that leads to his little home (and perhaps to lost childhood itself) is made of Hansel-and-Gretel sugar.

In *The Fourteenth Room of Love: The Snowstorm* (1985), a robin's-egg blue room is windswept with its own snow drift of sugar. In *Ring de Jour* (1978), there is no sugar, but the snow has the sparkle of a sugary, Disneyish Winter Wonderland. Here, snow never melts and the frozen (unmoving, unblinking) manikin-boys wear funny blue raincoats with their hoods tied up (save for the one boy in shiny, London-double-decker-bus red, with matching rain hat). These boys wear shorts in the snow, with short socks and shoes: they are frozen, but seem to never get cold. They are forever young, thanks to the mechanics of the photograph. (As a small child, in search of his own Alicious bottle tagged 'DRINK ME', Faucon asked if there were a medicine that could prevent his growing up.)

Sugar: you don't need it, but you desire it. Sugar is neither food, nor not food. Sweet sugar makes jam, biscuits and sweets taste nice, but it is also at the root of tooth decay. In keeping with the paradoxes of sugar, Faucon links sugar to a kind of Lady Godiva punishing sight. (According to the legend, when Lady Godiva rode naked on her horse through the streets of Coventry, with only her hair to cover her, a certain tailor peeped through his window to steal a look and was struck blind in consequence. He became known as 'Peeping Tom of Coventry'.) In the photographer's own guilt-ridden, retributive words, cast in sugar:

Eating candy and cakes is surely above all to devour with one's eyes . . . However, as time goes by I am increasingly worried about something. Why is it that sugar makes dogs go blind? Could there be a mysterious relationship between sugar and sight? Could the punishment be designed to fit the sin?[33]

Barthes also finds a violence in sugar by connecting it to sight, specifically photography. In his *Camera Lucida*, both sugar and photography overfill by force. In Barthes' words:

The Photograph is violent: not because it shows violent things, but because on each occasion *it fills the sight by force*, and because in it nothing can be refused or transformed (that we can sometimes call it mild does not contradict its violence: many say that sugar is mild, but to me sugar is violent, and I call it so).[34]

Waiting for Enchantment

Like Pinocchio, we expect enchantment. We wait for the little manikin-men to come to life. We wait for ourselves to come to life. We adolescently wait for love. Again I repeat the words of Barthes: 'Waiting is an enchantment.'[35] Likewise, and still immersed in *A Lover's Discourse*, Barthes asks of himself, and answers himself: 'Am I in love? – Yes, since I am waiting.'[36]

As if an adolescent pupa, as if nestled inside, I wait for the moving, the Faucon movie, to take place. Again I return to Barthes' scene of the movie theatre as a cocoon for developing desire: 'Invisible work of possible affects emerges from a veritable cinematographic cocoon . . . I appropriate the silkworm's motto *Inclusum labor illustrat*; it is because I am enclosed that I work and glow with all my desire.'[37]

The situation is not unlike Faucon's *The Departure* (1978): here the manikins are caught as they are leaving for their summer holiday (a time when butterflies will emerge from their cocoons). A few of the 'little men' on board the train cast butterfly nets out the windows. Cerulean blue, buttercup yellow and turquoise blue: these butterfly catchers are party flags in anticipation of monarch and swallowtail days.

The fluttery theme of *The Departure* is repeated in *Butterfly Catching* (1978). In both, images of butterfly nets hail the metamorphosis of all children, who move from caterpillar to pupa to butterfly. Flight (though of a birdly, not butterfly nature) is even in the photographer's own name,

a robin's-egg blue room is windswept
    with its own snow drift of sugar

which in French means falcon. All of these winged metaphors merge with the recurrent images of soaring to be found in Faucon's work: as in *Flight* (1977) which pictures a boyish fascination with flight; or *The Child who Flies* (1979), which turns on the magical, childish wish to transgress, to fly like Peter Pan. Nabokov tells of his own adolescent waiting: 'I remember as a boy keeping a hawk-moth's pupa in a box for something like seven years, so that I actually finished high school while the thing was asleep – and then finally it hatched . . . during a journey on a train.'[38] (I see the young Nabokov in Faucon's *Le Départ*.)

To play with Faucon is to seek the butterfly, to seek that which is *missed*. As the French fiction writer Marie Darrieussecq, author of her own fairy-tale dystopia *Pig Tales*, writes in one of her Faucon 'poems':

L'EFFET PAPILLON
Jeu: cherchez le papillon chez Faucon.
Cherchez qui manqué dans les chambres.
J'ai compté.

THE BUTTERFLY EFFECT
Play: seek the butterfly in Faucon.
Seek who is missed in the rooms.
I counted.[39]

I think of the work of the reclusive Morton Bartlett, who made his own realistic half-size family for almost three decades from 1936 to 1963. Bartlett's 'Once-upon-a-time' began (in 1936) when he was absent-mindedly fiddling with a ball of clay and the first doll was born. Likewise, Carlo Collodi's *The Adventures of Pinocchio* (1883) begins with 'Once upon a time there was a piece of wood.'[40] (And, it was a piece of wood that laughed and cried like a child, exclaiming: 'Don't hit me too hard' or 'Stop it! You're tickling me all over!'[41]) When Geppetto makes a 'wooden head' out of this talking block of wood, Pinocchio is born.

Bartlett was a magical Surrealist (without membership to the avant-garde group), whose world took hold from an ecstatic encounter with a ball of clay. He lived his entire life alone. His perfectly proportioned fifteen children (from the ages of eight to sixteen), with all the right clothes, mostly girls, were a long time in the making, about one year for each child. He strove for perfection; 'we know that his source material included anatomy and costume books as well as popular magazine growth charts . . . he knitted hats, cardigans and sweaters, embroidered jackets and bags, and meticulously sewed skirts.'[42] After dressing them in their handmade clothes and setting them up with props, he photographed them for his own family album. (See, for example, *Sitting Boy*, *c.* 1943–63.) Bartlett made his own family of Pinocchios. No one, save for Bartlett, was over the age of sixteen. It was his own 'Land of Toys'.

Bartlett's dolls, so finely dressed and cared for, were his secret family, not unlike D. W. Winnicott's patient, a young boy who was obsessed with string, and made his own closeted family of bears. The boy, carefully sewing trousers for his family of bears, treated them like, if not a mother, a wonderful aunt. As Winnicott writes:

He has a number of teddy bears, which to him are children.
No one dares to say that they are toys. He is loyal to them,
expends a great deal of affection over them, and makes trousers
for them, which involves careful sewing. His father says that
he seems to get a sense of security from his family, which he
mothers in this way.[43]

As Shakespeare writes in his fairyish *A Midsummer Night's Dream*:

Love takes the meaning in love's conference.
I mean that my heart unto yours is knit.
So that but one heart we can make of it. (II.2.52–4)

Bartlett's 'family without familialism'[44] was found in 1992, after the artist's death: each 'child' wrapped carefully in newspaper and stored in boxes.

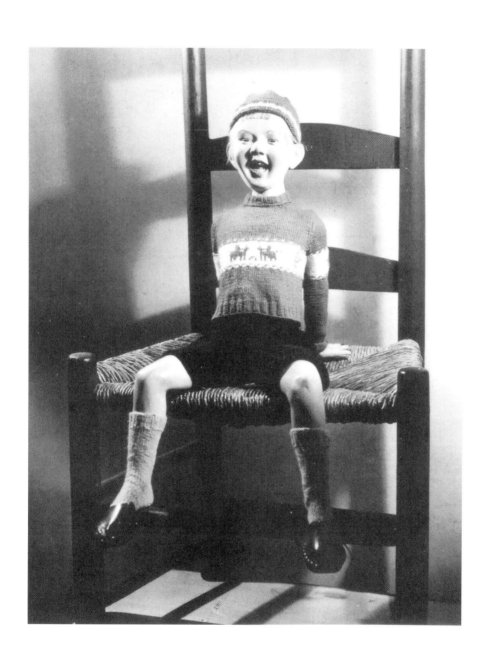

handmade clothes

Bartlett's family stayed in the closet; they never went on holiday, as Faucon's manikins did.

Winnicott and Bartlett tell stories of knitting love, as does Faucon in his *Threads of Wool* (1979), which features an elaborate cat's cradle of strings in trees and on the ground, built by two little men (here the naked *manikins* are 'real'). In an exquisite play on the French word *fils*, which translates as threads or son/male child, Faucon here and through his whole body of photographs has knitted his own boys-only, close-knit family.[45] As a boy, Faucon 'tied such a geometry of strings in a tree, with some hope that he might be able to walk among them'.[46] Faucon's boyish gesture was a way of knitting writ large, a way of making trees into home, into family: a neither-inside-nor-outside place for *manikins* to be resuscitated.

For Barthes, scandal moves from great subjects to small ones, with the perverse desire afforded by the ni-ni. In a passage from his published interview 'Dare to be Lazy', knitting, specifically knitting by a male, not unlike Bartlett's own knitting for his secret family, appears as a public, obscene act of open homosexuality. As you listen, keep in mind that 'laziness' is perhaps the trope of boyish adolescence:

Perhaps the most unconventional and thus the most literally scandalous thing I ever saw in my life – scandalous for the people watching, not for me – was a young man seated in a subway car in Paris who pulled some knitting out of his bag and openly began to knit. Everyone felt scandalized, but no one said anything.

Now, knitting is the perfect example of a manual activity that is minimal, gratuitous, without finality, but that still represents a beautiful and successful idleness.[47]

For Barthes, both the adolescent and knitting are examples of successful idleness, are ni-ni performances.

Adolescent knitting needles come to the fore in Oz as well. In the second Oz book, *The Marvellous Land of Oz* (1904), Tip, who has already constructed his own manikin (Jack Pumpkinhead), meets an adolescent

girl named Jinjur who is tired of her life of scrubbing floors, churning
butter and milking cows. She has assembled a group of like-minded
girls armed with knitting needles. This adolescent 'Army of Revolt' have
their eyes on consumerism. As if raiding shop windows, they take over
Oz, turning the gems of the Emerald City wall into rings, bracelets and
necklaces. Even the royal treasury is robbed to buy every knitting-needle-
carrying girl twelve new gowns.[48]

Japan

Faucon often took his manikins to Japan for exhibitions. When he stopped
photographing manikins in 1981, he sold them to a museum in Japan.
Today the manikins are retired (on permanent holiday) in Kyoto, Japan.

Faucon's ni-ni approach is a fierce emptiness, which is akin to the
same empty–full gastronomy that feeds Barthes' *Empire of Signs* (1970). In
the latter, Barthes feeds his ni-ni fantasy of a country that he calls 'Japan':
a place neither fictional nor real, neither empty nor full ('which might be
more properly called *The Empire of Empty Signs*'[49]). As Edmund White
has written:

If Japan did not exist, Barthes would have had to invent it – not that
Japan does exist in *Empire of Signs*, for Barthes is careful to point
out that he is not analyzing the real Japan but rather one of his own
devising. In this fictive Japan, there is no terrible innerness as in the
West, no soul, no God, no father, no ego, no grandeur, no meta-
physics, no 'pro-motional fever' and finally no meaning . . .
In Barthes' Japan, Zen is all-important, especially for 'that loss of
meaning Zen calls a satori.'[50]

Empty but full is the light of photography in *Camera Lucida* and
the light of Japan in *Empire of Signs*. Likewise, Barthes finds satori in
Faucon's empty, but full, manikins, made doubly full and doubly empty
by photography itself. ('Un mot oriental (japonais) conviendrait mieux:
le *satori*.'[51])

cat's cradle of strings in trees and on the ground

As a gay man who did not speak Japanese, Barthes felt protected by the emptiness of signs he experienced in Japan, where there was 'nothing to grasp'. Barthes' love of his empty (but full) Japan, then, is a mirroring of Faucon's empty (but full) manikins, both of which mirror Barthes' love of the empty (but full) sign of the androgyne. Japan, manikin, adolescent, boy all are part of Barthes' ni-ni nesting-doll sign play. In the spirit of Stendhal Syndrome (a love-sick swooning for Italy), Barthes Syndrome is a love-sick swooning for Japan: a kind of ephebophilia for a country.

I can only smile at the fact that Faucon, with his empty but full manikins, is a star in Japan. I smile again at the fact that the Japanese television comedy programme *The Fuccons*, about a stereotyped Kennedy-era American family who comes to live in Japan, was inspired by Bernard Faucon. The television programme features still photographs of manikins, who have been de-windowed.

Fin

Faucon's career as an artist-photographer began in the mid 1970s and was stopped voluntarily in 1997.[52] Faucon's suspension of doing photographic works coincided with his insistence that no longer is anyone allowed to photograph him. Nevertheless, when I visited his Paris apartment, not only did he feed me a sweet cornmeal cake, cantaloupe and chocolate drink (he ate nothing), he also permitted me to photograph some of the enchantment around me. I took a picture of the white orchids that we brought for him, aglow with coloured patches of light (blue-green, turquoise, yellow, yellow-orange and coral-pink), which were magically projected from the kind of rainbow lamp that one often finds in a child's bedroom. I also took a picture of a gallery poster of his work, which was casually taped over a large mirror, obscuring the reflection. An aversion to mirrors. In *sa chambre*, Count Faucon reflects no image, exists Draculaish, only sunny and clean with all of his pretty things.

Faucon's final photograph was part of a series entitled *The End of the Image* (1993–5). These small-format colour photographs feature fragments of poetic text, written in thick white 'ink', like sugar icing, on the skin of

magically projected

from the kind

of rainbow lamp

that one

often finds

in a child's

bedroom

boyish youth, offering itself to be licked off. The culinary script is infused with the philosophy (Faucon studied at the Sorbonne). On the skin of the boys, as flesh made word, Faucon writes fairy-tale lines. There is an echo of Alice's EAT-ME phrase spelled out in currants on a little cake in 'Tu es l'alphabet en pain d'épices qui cache les mots' (You are the ginger-cake alphabet hiding the words). There is a bit of Pinocchio bad boy in the 'Land of Toys' in 'Comme une effraction dans une construction de sucre d'orge' (Like breaking into a shop window of toys). There is a tender morsel of 'Juniper Tree' stew (the terrifying tale in which the mother of a little boy cuts off her son's head, cooks it in a stew, salts it with the tears of his sister and serves it to the poor boy's father) in 'Tendre cannibalisme' (Sweet Cannibalism). There is the reality of J. M. Barrie's children who are 'gay and innocent and heartless'[53] little monsters in 'Ni ange, ni ogre, mais le malheur veut . . .' (Neither angel nor ogre, but as ill fortune will have it . . .).

As Faucon has remarked: 'The skins and bodies are no longer the skin and body of any particular child, they are the skins and bodies of our lost childhoods. A big, unique body unfolding infinitely. The very childhood of life, the source of all nostalgia.'[54] Faucon's sweet adolescence, preternaturally harboured for a long time through the bodies of boys that infused his work and his own boyish looks. And then, it departed, like a butterfly escaping its chrysalis-skin.

The End of the Image is the end of Faucon's boyishness and photography. One bit of flesh from the series simply reads 'fin' (the end). Only in fairy tales can a boy live 'happily ever after'.

———

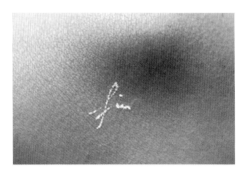

9 Tragic Candyland: Minou Drouet

It is never a good thing to speak against a little girl.
Roland Barthes, 'Myth Today'

la petite princesse des mots

Once upon a time there was born a real little girl named Minou Drouet (1947). For a long time Minou (whose name means 'kitten' in French) did not speak. She was silent until she was six years old. And then she awakened to become France's 'little princess of words': a child genius poet. She wrote of surreal fairy-tale trees and a 'tragic candyland'. Eaten by the very culture that produced her, she ended up feeling like 'a little rabbit who once turned its fur inside out for fear of moths'.

Wonderland is in the Air

It is 1957, the year Roland Barthes published *Mythologies*. Audrey Hepburn has charmed her audiences with *Funny Face*. In *Mythologies* Barthes has described the film star as 'woman as child, woman as kitten'.[1]

In France and America, a girl sensation is erupting. The public has fallen in love with girls who are roughly 4,562.5 days old (twelve and a half years). And, for those less Humbert Humbertish, there are child-women who are older, but somehow not. (Was Brigitte Bardot really so naive as to believe at the age of eighteen that mice laid eggs?)

'A breeze from Wonderland is in the air.'[2] Girls are everywhere, not only in films, but as authors. Just three years before, in 1954, the aggressive publisher René Julliard scored an international triumph with Françoise Sagan's *Bonjour tristesse*. Sagan was eighteen years old. (By 1957, the childish, boyish, sexy Jean Seberg would star in the film adaptation of *Bonjour tristesse*.)

Just a year earlier, in 1956, Vladimir Nabokov had published *Lolita* and B.B. (Brigitte Bardot) found herself to be an American sensation for her role in *And God Created Woman*, where she ate childishly and made love with the 'same unceremonious simplicity'.[3] While the always-barefoot B.B. was preserving the 'limpidity' of childhood and its 'mystery',[4] the aggressive Julliard scored again. After the success of *Bonjour tristesse*, he snatched up the child-poet Minou Drouet and published her first book of poetry: *Arbre, mon ami* (Tree, My Friend). Drouet was only eight years old.

The familiar myth of the child (as innocent and as artistic genius) was ripened by Drouet. As James Kincaid has carefully schooled us, 'We construct an emptiness, a child, and set it to dreaming.'[5] Paradoxically, the empty childishness of Drouet (as the photographs proclaim) is sexual. Paradox, however, is not a contradiction: it is a rhetorical neither-nor strategy, an artistic treatment of a logical problem.[6] Myth itself, thereby, is a paradox: it cloaks truth in fiction and fiction in truth, as if it were a little girl. The child is a studied myth; the girl is its most pure form.

In 'Myth Today' (*Mythologies*'s concluding essay), Barthes claims with witty Saussurean irony that this Lottelita, this Lolitchen (think Werther and Nabokov), this poetess named Drouet, had her own system of signs. As Barthes explains with the clinical disinterest of a scholar-man who likes boys, not girls: 'A tree is a tree. Yes, of course. But a tree as expressed by Minou Drouet is no longer quite a tree, it is a tree which is decorated, adapted to a certain type of consumption, laden with literary self-indulgence, revolt, images, in short with a type of social usage which is added to pure matter.'[7] Barthes' 'semioclasm' is out to destroy the 'myth of Childhood-as-poet'.[8]

In the original French publication of *Mythologies*, the poetess gets an entire essay: 'Literature According to Minou Drouet'. There, Barthes further unveils Drouet's 'nymphancy' as inseparable from her poetry.[9] But the little treatise was axed in 1972, when the book was translated into English. The famed Drouet had already been forgotten.[10]

Today, as Robert Gottlieb notes, few people (especially those under a certain age) know much about Drouet, even in Paris. Was she a 'victim' of her publisher? Did Cocteau say something 'bitchy' about her?[11] Who is Minou Drouet?

Today, she is Mme Jean-Paul Le Canu. She is approaching seventy. She lives in hibernation in her childhood home, under the shadow of the big cedar tree that she has always loved. It seems that she, too, has chosen to forget 'la petite princesse des mots' (the little princess of words).[12]

The Story

Clock face,
crystal cage
. . .
siamese animal twin of my heart,
greedy eyes like children's eyes
who looking at pastries
undress the icing
from cakes all crackly with frost
mouth which nibbles with no respite
this tragic candy, time.
Minou Drouet, 'The Watch'

Once upon a time, in Brittany, Minou was born (1947). Minou means kitten (more accurately 'pussy') in French. Her father was a very poor field hand. Many said that her mother was a prostitute. As we all know, in real life and in fairy tales, 'daughters wander off into the woods, stumble into prostitution, fall in love with sailors, are eaten by wolves'.[13] It was not such a promising beginning. But when she was a year and a half old, a worrisome woman (and aspiring poetess) named Mme Drouet adopted quiet, barely mewing Minou.

By age six, little Minou still had not spoken a word. She was tight-lipped and silent, an *enfant* through and through. (As Richard Howard explains, the word for child in French, *enfant*, comes 'from the Latin *infans*; from *in* (not) and *fari* (to speak): the one who does not speak'.[14]) Minou was Briar Rose waiting to be awakened. (Here again, I echo that precisely spoken phrase by Roland Barthes: 'Waiting is an enchantment'.[15]) Again that chrysalis motif of the fairy tale, that charge of Bernard Faucon's little men, that Nabokovian love of the metaphor of metamorphosis. 'One day, her mother played a recording of a Brahms symphony for her. Minou swooned. When she was revived, she spoke perfect French in complex sentences. Shortly thereafter she began to write poetry.'[16]

Minou had become enchanted. Minou had become enchanting. As is the case in fairy tales, Maman was the wicked stepmother. Madame Drouet cracked the whip: ballet lessons, guitar lessons, hours of piano practice and gymnastics, 'every minute accounted for'.[17] Even though she could play Mozart while doing a backbend on the piano, Minou could never be perfect enough; one might even say 'empty' enough. (Remember another lesson that Kincaid taught us: 'innocence is . . . like air . . . there's not a lot you can do but lose it.'[18]) Madame Drouet beat the innocence (air) out of Minou for the most minuscule mistakes.

In a letter to the famous pianist Yves Nat, Minou complains:

Little girls' bottoms are really a wonderful gift from heaven for calming the nerves of mothers. I know perfectly well that's what they were invented for, for hands have hollows and bottoms have humps. It's because of you that I had my bottom spanked, because I didn't write Mr in the address and didn't put a capital letter.[19]

Minou's letter smacks of Eve Kosofksy Sedgwick's girlhood poetry under the rap of spanking. As Sedgwick writes in her 1987 startling re-telling of Freud's 'A Child is Being Beaten' as 'A Poem is Being Written': 'When I was a little child the two most rhythmic things that happened to me were spanking and poetry.'[20] Sedgwick confesses that, as a girl, she took sexual pleasure in writing poetry with plenty of enjambment to the eroticized beat of being spanked. (But for Sedgwick the results were very different.)

In the same letter, Minou speaks of 'angry trees which seem to be kicking at the sky, trees through which something so gentle was passing'.[21] Minou's words are strangely in accord with Hans Bellmer's 1935 photograph of Drouetish legs kicking their Mary Janes and bobby socks up into the trees.[22] The poupée legs (those standing and those kicking) are

angry trees which seem to be kicking at the sky

in bondage with, and/or in love with, these trees that grow in likeness with them. A shadowed figure lurks.

A strange and troubled child, Minou was odd. Minou did not fit in. As she writes in 'Photograph', 'I brought you nothing / but an ugly face, / a nose for telephoning / to the clouds'.[23] Minou found solace in the tree that she loved, her true friend, who lived (and still does) in her garden in la Guerche de Bretagne, 'a very big cedar of Lebanon'.[24]

Tree that I love,
tree in my likeness,
so heavy with music
under the wind's fingers
that turn your pages
like a fairy tale,
tree . . .[25]

Remember what Barthes says in 'Myth Today': 'A tree is a tree. Yes of course. But a tree as expressed by Minou Drouet is no longer quite a tree'.[26]

She is an Eighty-year-old Dwarf

If a bit overly sweet, this little kitten's Surrealist style was reminiscent of André Breton. But the public was suspicious of her 'genius', and claimed her mother was the true author of Minou's disturbing, delicious, wild poems. Jean Cocteau, who made his own fairy-tale film of *Beauty and the Beast* (1946), famously quipped: 'She's not an eight-year-old child, she's an 80-year-old dwarf'.[27] Cocteau saw her as Rumpelstiltskin, not Snow White.

It was in 1955, when some of Minou's poems and letters were privately circulated among French writers and publishers, that what Julliard called a 'minor Dreyfus Affair' began. Almost overnight, there were appearances on television and articles in magazines and newspapers. People took sides. Did she write the poems or not? Minou became a French and

American sensation. Minou was photographed by *Elle*, *Life*, *Time* and *Paris Match*: at her desk with her pen in hand, with her teddy bear, with her adoptive mother and cat, and almost always with that giant Drouet bow. (The bow is not only Bellmer's metonymy, it is also Minou's.)

On 20 January 1956, a test was organized by the Société des Auteurs, Compositeurs et Éditeurs de Musique (SACEM) to discover the truth: 'Minou was placed in a room behind one-way glass.'[28] She was told she could write on 'I am Eight Years Old' or 'Paris Sky'. Since, as she claimed, her 'eight years were already too sad', she chose 'Paris Sky'.[29] Within 28 minutes she had written 'Ciel de Paris'. It was written in the shape of Minou's beloved tree; like Apollinaire, she liked to make her poems into *calligrammes*, serpentine shapes, crystal cages of words.

Paris Sky,
weight,
secret,
flesh,
who by hiccups,
spits in our faces
through the open maw of rows of houses
a spurt of blood between its luminous stumps of bad teeth . . .[30]

Drouet is Shirley Temple on the good ship *Lollipop*, swallowed by the mouth that hiccups and 'spits in our faces' the myths of little girls as sugar and spice and everything nice. Drouet is Berenice trapped in Joseph Cornell's 1943 *The Crystal Cage*, like jelly in the sugary doughnuts that he childishly loved.

The SACEM test was a modern-day fairy tale: Drouet was Snow White in a glass box (coffin). Would she feel the pea under the pile of mattresses? Would her foot easily slip into the glass slipper? As Barthes notes: it was 'a detective story: did she do it or didn't she?'[31] (Fairy tales are always detective stories: they sort out real princesses from imposters.)

In the end, she won. She was awarded membership.

ird sen
malibran
fireworks
rainbow
high no
un dials
ightrope
ersian whe
e sunbursta
Berlioz rabb
himney sweeps
a Belle Cordia
ylights Baedoke
iero di Cosimo ea
parachutes emeralds
pageants Aerial atoll
strolling montgolfiers
camouflage colonnade
Madame Saqui Diana
Italian villas camel
fanfares La Fée Dra
ecny bushes Archimedes
ns Christian Anderson N
soirées de Vienne viole
covered Switzerland cele
Rosiphele snow bowls ph
ndigo Brigliadore green
daguerreotypes balloon
Edgar Allen Poe marvels
hooting stars Israfel a
winding staircases pan
World's Fair of 1940 as
Francesca Cerrito golden
Hotel de l'Ange lightning
soap bubbles solariums Kub
flower covered vallies fav
arold in Italy snow crys
ambler roses Kirscher ra
glint Mignon Gulliver
instrels canaries mirage
+ Citoyen Hauy moles Carpaccio
hases of the moon new coins ex
ss in Boots Taglioni ice cubes
ndigo orange star-lit fields phen
palaces of light Cendrillon asce
ghthouses constellation of Feu)
tropical plumage Bouguereau si
Liszt barometers owls siphons
Queen Mab ascensions high noon
agic lanterns Karl Maria von W
ber panoramas twilight bees f
usical instruments of glass a
olumbus aviaries illuminatior
ountains of the moon Kepler d
t. Elmo's fire skyscrapers hisl
adame Blanchard silk cord Milky Way
aerial flights of Carlotta Grisi homage
utomatons Benjamin Franklin Vermeer y
iracles of perspective Cygnus Gemini
Lac des Cygnes calliopes ladders ga
ather vanes roosters Caravaggio ufi
dioramas butterflies mines ropes han
leaning Tower of Pisa microscopic g
ountains rope dancers flutter wheels
La Dormeuse de Naples ceilings hydrograp
sanctuaries waterfalls Erik Satie kaleidosc
eflections Colossus of Rhodes bear market f
Couperin ropes of stars Rimbaud candol stre
white marble statues Neopolitan fisher boys
Persian wheels cupolas string quartets opti
recious stones birds of the Black Forest em
lue tints les nuages de Claude Achille wind
coral islands Mer de Glace lanterns Alice in
Fresnol's system camera obscura Leonardo da
Treyl Chinese gardens flights Seurat Napcli
lanetariums diadem of Marie Félicité steel
ugravings zootropes Chatterton castles cinematography
diamant au coeur cycloramas treasures Great Wall of China
stoor dust spires festivals marvels of motion swimming bir
dramas of light Raquel Meller Giorgione dawns wind bells r
mpases snow Paganini look-outs windows Gilles the golden city u
seraphim Albeniz aquariums Auriga trumpets crowns pet crows sextants u
Johann Strauss Montgolfier Mignon dovecotes toy merchants of Pekin hail k
eclipses transparencies Blue Grotto of Capri chrysalises botanical garde
earchlights Ingres Sunday afternoons flowers calliopes Giant's Causew
spectrums edelweiss Galna Ursa Major sunken cathedral of Ys chart
ose of the Winds birds' nests keys rivers hummingbirds artesian wel
skylights chains of glass distant hills Sleeping Gypsy of Rousseau
anga in the night hurdy-gurdies Penthesilea fauna strolling mounteba
firanda buoys Fingal's Cave Paul and Virginia rain snails verdant uh
Perdita radiance salamanders coral atolls Cockaigne Tyll Eulenspieg
till red yellow subterranean brooks J.J.Grandeville storks' nests er
Perrot mocking bird of Giulia Grisi circuses Lucille Grahn Mimi opti
abitat groups under glass voyages celestas Watteau irese velvet uge
velvet Phrigian caps Virgi   the Magi of Gozzoli entran
ope luminosities Euryanth   a Ondine serenades branche
ose tyrien tailor-birds r   pensions stalagmites dosit
iope Parizade cirro cumul   Blondin Novella d'Andrea
Speltarina pomegranites Ki   ond of Bavaria snow sleig
Corot distant music merma   ests Coppelia Niagara Fall
ists mirrors celestas Aur   gs Atlantis voyages circus
The Snow Image iridescent   shells Linnaeus Andromed
Wallendas sirens Neptunes   i animals ephemera Floring
eta Courier of St. Peters   shafts of light Rastelli
Lilian Leitzel Trixie Grin   Bois Dormant Fratellini
Fanny Elssler noctuelles D   irs chansonniers valses le
kests Zecca La Fontaine Th   go-rounds Hanlon efflores
leo de Merode shells la Perichole rocaille equestrians scenic railwa
Sontag Cordusn la fille au chevaux de lin Algeciras Garcia Offenbach
landas Baudelaire explorations crickets Baroque zoos galleons ladybu
pangolins La Belle au Bois Dormant 1900 Theresa Bird Millman ascensc

The Crystal Cage

Let's Eat Her

That young tender thing would be a delicious morsel.
Brothers Grimm, 'Little Red Cap'

My only grudge against nature was that I could not turn my Lolita inside
out and apply voracious lips to her young matrix, her unknown heart, her
nacreous liver, the sea-grapes of her lungs, her comely twin kidneys.
Vladimir Nabokov, *Lolita*

I must be a little rabbit who once turned its fur inside out for fear of moths.
Minou Drouet, extract from a notebook

As markers of lost time, photographs are always already tragic, deadly
murderers of life once lived, perhaps especially if they are picturing a
sweet little girl like Drouet. The camera is, to use the poetics of child-
Drouet, a killing 'mouth which nibbles with no respite / this tragic
candy, time'.[32] Likewise in *Camera Lucida* (as discussed with the work
of Bernard Faucon), Barthes glazes the photograph as sugar housed
in the violence that originally bespoke the fairy tale. I repeat the
quotation:

The Photograph is violent: not because it shows violent things,
but because on each occasion it fills the sight by force, and
because in it nothing can be refused or transformed (that we
can sometimes call it mild does not contradict its violence:
many say that sugar is mild, but to me sugar is violent, and I
call it so).

When Bellmer (in another doll photograph, this one from 1934) places a
headless poupée on a large letter O crowned with a bow, with her eye spat
back onto her footless ankle, the emptiness of the child is perversely set
to dreaming. It is the start of a surreal Once-upon-a-time tale that is not
so far from the (un)golden childhood that was lived by Minou.

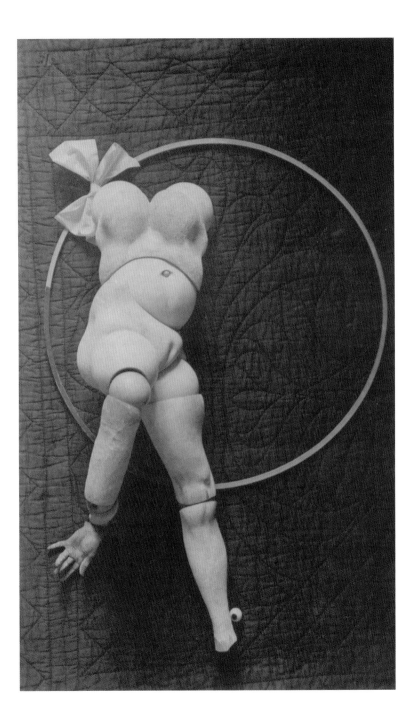

Barthes does not like 'Drouetist poetry'. It is 'docile, sugary poetry', 'stuffed' with 'formulas'.[33] According to Barthes, Drouet fulfills a cultural desire to demote and to tame literature into a sweet nothing.

As Richard Howard notes:

In the central range of French language, there is no word for child . . . If there have been children in French Literature, they are there as mere instances of acculturation; as victims (Hugo, Renard), as cult objects (Hugo again, Gide); either assimilated by Society as in infants (speechless) or transformed into members (remembered) or extruded as freaks (Minou Drouet).[34]

As Barthes writes: 'She is the kidnap victim of a conformist order which reduces freedom to prodigy status. She is the little girl the beggar pushes onto the sidewalk when back home the mattress is stuffed with money.' Through Minou's own delectably violent words, we look at her with 'greedy eyes like children's eyes / who looking at pastries / undress the icing / from cakes all crackly with frost / mouth which nibbles with no respite / this tragic candy, time.'[35]

Barthes is anorexic when it comes to eating Drouet. 'It may happen that I feel no hunger for the world,' claims Barthes in *The Neutral*, 'but the world will force me to love it, to eat it, to enter into intercourse with it.'[36] Barthes tells us that 'society is devouring Minou Drouet,'[37] but he remains tight-lipped, refusing to partake in 'this tragic candy'.

Completely sugar-coated and consumed by the time she was four-teen, Minou lost her passionate desire to write. As in the years before she was six, she was once again silent. She was back to sleep, forever held as the bowed, Bellmeresque little girl of 'tragic candy, time', with no hope of being de-windowed, of escaping her crystal cage, her glass coffin. For ever and ever, she is stuck as a little girl in the glass-covered daguerreotype of her eight-year-old self.

I look at a photograph of Minou at age eight and I 'shudder' at the loss of this little girl. As Barthes writes about the Winter Garden Photograph (which captured his mother as a little girl): 'I shudder [*je frémis*] like Winnicott's psychotic patient, over a catastrophe which has already occurred.'[38] (In English, *shudder* is a homonym for *shutter*.)

———

10 What is Black and White and Red All Over?
Answer: The Photographs of Ralph Eugene Meatyard

'I want a living baby, that's what I want.'

As dramatic replays of the Civil Rights Movement (including the murder of Emmett Till), the butchery of the Vietnam War and the hope that was shot down with the brutal killings of the Kennedys and Martin Luther King, the black-and-white photographs of Ralph Eugene Meatyard are not only mouthfuls of the Southern Gothic literary tradition, but the blood of the carnage in America during the time in which they were made. They are black-and-white pictures of the politics of the period, charged with the red voices of 'Snow White', 'Rumpelstiltskin', 'The Juniper Tree', 'Hansel and Gretel' and 'Little Red Riding Hood'. Perhaps Derek Jarman said it best: 'Red is a moment in time.'

In the fairy tale, red is the colour of the blood on the snow in 'Snow White'. Red is the colour of Bluebeard, who kills his wives and keeps them in a chamber, its floor awash with blood. Red is the colour of Little Red Riding Hood, who could only be red, who is cut out of the stomach of the wolf who has swallowed her and her grandmother. Red is the colour of Karen's shoes, which could only be red, and her chopped-off feet in Hans Christian Andersen's 'The Red Shoes'. As Andersen writes:

Dance she did, and dance she must, dance into the dark night. Her shoes carried her away over thickets and stumps, her feet were worn bloody. She danced across the heath to a lonely little house. She knew that this was where the executioner lived. She tapped her finger on the windowpane and said: 'Come out, come out! I cannot come inside, because I am dancing.'

And the executioner said: 'Don't you know who I am? I chop off the heads of the evil people and I can feel my axe trembling.'

'Don't chop off my head!' said Karen. 'Because then I won't be able to repent my sin. But chop off my feet with the red shoes!'

Then she confessed to her sin, and the executioner chopped off her feet with the red shoes. But the shoes kept dancing with the little feet across the fields and into the deep forest.[1]

In 1950, Ralph Eugene Meatyard (1925–1972),[2] the photographer with the fantastically bloody name, bought his first camera to take pictures of his newborn son. The camera was the Kentucky photographer's seemingly innocuous aperture (outwardly as harmless as the opening O of the fairy tale). He used his Rolleiflex to swallow and spit back his daughter Melissa, his sons Michael and Christopher, his wife Madelyn, and a few friends through the mouth of the fairy tales set in the American South, during the post-war period. His camera's mouth spoke the unspeakable (racism, Vietnam, American violence).

Meatyard's pictures are not in colour, yet they ooze with the same red that stains the colourless fairy tale. As Pullman writes of Grimm: 'As white as snow, as red as blood: that's about it.'[3]

Alive with Dolls

'Meatyard's photographs are alive with dolls . . . He scattered the broken little personas throughout the empty homesteads.'[4] In *Untitled* (child with dead leaves, mask and doll, 1959), a large-headed troll holds a pupa-girl-doll in his hand. The always-hungry monster-man-boy pauses before swallowing his prey. He faces the camera. He wears neat and tidy white socks, a clean pinstriped shirt and shorts. His knees are unscratched. His plastic doppelgänger wears shorts that match his own. 'I want a living baby, that's what I want,' demands Rumpelstiltskin.[5]

In many of Meatyard's pictures, the head of the doll has been severed (eaten?) and only the torso remains. In *Untitled* (two dolls, one headless, *c.* 1959), a decapitated naked black doll is placed atop a naked white doll. The white doll's kissy mouth is stuck open, a never-closing aperture awaiting a toy baby bottle. (She is a drink-and-wet baby doll.) Her smooth black curls, along with the thin-pencilled eyebrows above her open-and-close eyes under the weight of heavy black lashes, are the makings of a child beauty-pageant winner. The interracial overtone of the photograph is in black and white. One is reminded of John Cassavetes's 1959 film *Shadows*, the story of a light-skinned black woman and her romance with a white man, whose identity is exposed by the appearance of 'Lelia's' darker-skinned jazz-singing brother.[6] Meatyard's mixed-race beautiful and broken dolls are Lelia.

Foraging

With an oralian appetite, Meatyard's 'real' family of five foraged for good pictures and mystical foods: they were their own breed of Hansels and Gretels. They found violets and made 'violet jelly, an entirely new rosy-light filled potion, the stuff of fairy tales: from weeds came scented gems'.[7] Elderberries became a wine elixir. Enchanted food and the magic of photography went hand in hand for Meatyard and his family, a harkening back to the inception of the medium. (Readers will recall from this book's Chapter Two, 'An Alicious Appetite', that Charles Baudelaire noted that early photography was its culinary period – during which time images might be 'fixed', like cuisine, using sugar, caramel, treacle, malt, raspberry syrup, ginger, wine, sherry, beer and skimmed milk.[8] Likewise, albumen prints were made from egg whites.)

Mirror, Mirror

In Meatyard's *Untitled* (cranston Ritchie with mirror and dressmaker's manikin, *c.* 1958–9), we see the photographer's friend (who has a hook arm) standing rigidly next to the stiff black legless and armless *Venus de Milo,* who has been placed on a chair, so as to give her height.[9] Between them stands a tattered mirror, empty of reflection. ('Mirror, mirror, on the wall/ who in this realm is the fairest of all?'[10]) Meatyard's photograph

beautiful and broken dolls

marries the politics of the time: an injured white man and a damaged African woman. (In 1955, the Vietnam War began and Rosa Parks refused to give up her seat on the bus.) The mirror and the couple's stiff pose echo, if distantly, the man and woman on their 'Ring Day' in Jan van Eyck's famed *Arnolfini Portrait* (1434).[11] The Flemish painter's duo is pictured before an intense red bedchamber. In the back of the painting, we see that she has removed her precious pair of red shoes. The reds of the oil painting on oak would have been derived from the dried-up female bodies of the insect *Kermes vermilio*. In Meatyard's photograph of Ritchie with the dressmaker's dummy, the red is there: it is 'just too close to see'.[12] Unspeakable.

Wolf

In *Untitled* (Michael with 'RED' sign, 1960), the boy's grin becomes exaggerated and terrifying, due to the long exposure.[13] The boy is Little Red Riding Hood's wolf with big ears and terrifying Francis Bacon teeth. He is ready to eat up *Le Petit Chaperon rouge*, at the time of the Cold War. 'Red scare'.

Like the Seven Dwarfs

Meatyard's photographs are 'Southern Gothic': they inhabit the grotesqueries of American Southern writers such as Flannery O'Connor and Harper Lee. Most specifically, Meatyard's *The Family Album of Lucybelle Crater* (1974) was inspired by O'Connor's story 'The Life You Save May Be Your Own' (1953), an uneasy tale of intense, isolated dysfunctional loving between an old woman and her thirty-year-old daughter. The old woman's name is Lucynell Crater. The adult-daughter's name is Lucynell Crater. Meatyard's creation of a world where all boys and girls and all men and women are named Lucybelle Crater is a play on O'Connor's story with its creepy doubled Lucynells.

In the 64 images that make up the posthumously published photo-album book entitled *The Family Album of Lucybelle Crater*, not only does everyone have the same name but they all wear one of two rubber masks:

an ogre-woman mask, her hair in a rubber topknot, or an unpleasant, sagging-face, older-man mask. In one of the Lucybelle Crater photographs, a housewifey mother and a child in a long double-breasted jacket each wear one of these two masks. The caption for the family 'snap' of a bulging-eyed ogre and her Rumpelstiltskin son, written in white cursive on a black page (like a real family album), reads: 'Lucybelle Crater and 20 year old son's 3 year old son, also her 3 year old grandson Lucybelle Crater.' Apparently, they live on a shockingly vernacular suburban street.

In O'Connor's story, the daughter is a deaf-mute. She is so innocent that she looks to be fifteen. She has long pink-gold hair like a doll and eyes as blue as a peacock's neck. The old woman is toothless. When she opens her mouth, she reveals a toothless black hole.

Lucynell Crater and Lucynell Crater are doubled, like freaks in a Diane Arbus photograph, like inverted twins, like the subject and its photographic image. Like the infinite copies made possible through the process of photography. Like that 'tone-licked-clean' prose of the Grimms' tale, where characters come in multiples, like the seven dwarfs in Snow White.[14] 'The seven dwarfs all asleep in their beds side by side.'[15] (It was Disney who gave them individual names.) The dwarfs exist in another world, another realm, 'between the uncanny and the absurd'.[16]

Lucynell Crater loved her daughter past speech. Lucynell Crater loved her mother past speech. But, at age thirty, mute daughter Lucynell Crater will find speech. She will learn her first word from a loner named Mr Shiftlet who appears at the home of Lucynell Crater and Lucynell Crater and changes everything. A bit like Meatyard's friend Cranston Ritchie, the legs of Andersen's 'Karen', whose feet were cut off with an axe by the executioner – Mr Shiftlet has only a stump for an arm.

The first word of daughter Lucynell Crater was 'bird'. She got the bird out – which was swallowed and inside her.

Meatyard made his living as an optometrist, as a grinder of lenses. In 1967 he opened his own optician's shop in Lexington, Kentucky. He called

his shop 'Eyeglasses of Kentucky'. It is not hard to imagine Meatyard as a wicked Hoffmannian Sandman.

'Red is a Moment in Time'

It took me years to get the joke that turns on the homophone of 'red' as in the colour of 'Little Red Riding Hood' and 'read' as in I have 'read' 'Little Red Riding Hood' over and over. As a child of the 1960s in an America imbued by the assassination of John F. Kennedy (1963), Martin Luther King (1968) and Bobby Kennedy (1968) – coupled with the Vietnam War and the 1969 knife murder of Sharon Tate (Roman Polanski's pregnant wife) – violent images have bloodied my memories. So that, when I was a child and someone asked me, 'What is black and white and red/read all over?', I could see only a newspaper splattered in blood. I could not get the joke. Even today, if I hear the riddle, I remember watching my black-and-white television erupt with the announcement that Kennedy had been shot. I see myself with scissors making paper dolls in the light of the TV screen, caught in the never-ending funeral of Martin Luther King. I see myself in the night darkness of my bedroom as I listen to my mother running down the hall screaming to my father: 'Now, Bobby Kennedy has been shot!'

'Red is a moment in time,' writes Derek Jarman.[17]

Till . . .

On 28 August 1955, the African American boy Emmett Louis Till, who was only fourteen years old, was murdered in Mississippi by two white men. He was beaten, one of his eyes was gouged out and he was shot through the head. His disfigured body was disposed of in the Tallahatchie River. His neck was tied to a seventy-pound cotton-gin fan with barbed wire. He was lost in the river for three days.

When the poor boy's body was returned to his Chicago home, Till's heartsick mama insisted on a public funeral with a glass-covered casket – she wanted the world to see her son's unrecognizable, brutalized,

259

Red is a moment in time

disfigured, tortured, ruined, mutilated face. Tens of thousands went to see the black boy encased in his 'Little Snow White' glass casket. The image of the poor boy wearing a suit in his glass casket, turned monster by monstrous white men, was published in *Jet*, the nationwide black magazine, on 15 September 1995. As Barthes writes in his essay on 'The Great Family of Man' photography exhibition (curated by Edward Steichen and first shown at the Museum of Modern Art in New York in 1955, conceived as 'a mirror of the universal elements and emotions in the everydayness of life – as a mirror of the essential oneness of mankind throughout the world'): 'Why not ask the parents of Emmett Till, the young Negro assassinated by the Whites what *they* think of *The Great Family of Man*?'[18] Should I show you Till here?

The 1960s were hopeful and utopian flower-children hippie days. The 1960s were dystopian black-and-white-and-red-all-over days. After a lecture that I gave on Meatyard, the African American photographer Leslie Hewitt suggested that the monstrosities of the Kentucky photographer's pictures reflected Emmett Till. She asked me why I did not show the photographs of his butchered body in a glass coffin. I replied that I felt I could not show that image. To which she correctly replied, but his mother wanted us to see. His mother wants us to see her boy in his glass coffin framed in gold. Emmett Till's mother forces us to look at her son, to read the black and white and red all over. Emmett Till should be here.

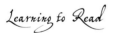

Learning to Read

I remember learning to read. I have a memory of a red dress when I was learning to read: its bodice was appliquéd with 'A' 'B' 'C'. I learned to read, like so many children in the 1960s, with the primer series of *Dick and Jane* books. Dick and Jane are as white as can be in their green and white house with its red door, as if in a fairy tale, along with a white dog with black spots named Spot. My memory is black and white and read/red all over.

Toni Morrison's 1970 novel *The Bluest Eye* tells the story of a young black girl named Pecola, whose name paradoxically sounds sweet like Coca-Cola and dirty like coal, who wishes for blue eyes like Shirley

Emmett Till should be here

Temple. This fine, troubling novel begins with a paragraph from *Dick and Jane*. The image is perfect. The punctuation and spacing of the letters are all in place, neat as a pin, neat as an American post-war white suburban street. The second paragraph of this book reduplicates the first *Dick and Jane* paragraph, but without any full stops to tell us that we are at the end of a sentence and without any capitalized letters to tell us that we are at the start of a new sentence. Where do sentences begin and end? I do not know where to breathe. I have trouble breathing. The third paragraph is a reduplication of the same paragraph again, but this time all the white spaces between the words are gone. It is all one long-running breathless sentence. It is segregated housing. It is cramped. It is dystopia. It is out of control.

There is no place for a black child in the *Dick and Jane* reader. No place to play. The words open up to reveal a black hole. A clean O of a mouth. No bite. Morrison gives us all rabbit hole, all darkness.

Fallen and inside, I begin to hear differently. As a child, my TV was in black-and-white. The newspaper was black-and-white. But my school primer called *Dick and Jane* was filled with blue storybook eyes. My fairy tales were coloured and Disneyfied.

The African American artist Carrie Mae Weems grew up in America like me, even went to university with me for a couple of years. She knows all about the colour of fairy tales, as can be seen in her series *Ain't Jokin'* (1987–8), in which she pictures the wicked queen as black (a twisted version of Cinder-ella). The accompanying text of Weems's photograph reads: 'Looking into the mirror, the black woman asked, "Mirror, Mirror on the wall, who's the finest of them all?" The mirror says, "Snow White, you black bitch, and don't you forget it!!!"' Weems, in the spirit of Meatyard and Toni Morrison, spits back the unspeakable.

Postscript

The Japanese photographer Miwa Yanagi has made a troubling photograph of *Little Red Riding Hood* (2004) in which we see the grandmother (who is actually a child wearing the mask of an old woman) finding

Here is the house. It is green and white. It has a red door.
It is very pretty. Here is the family. Mother, Father, Dick,
and Jane live in the green-and-white house. They are very
happy. See Jane. She has a red dress. She wants to play.
Who will play with Jane? See the cat. It goes meow-
meow. Come and play. Come play with Jane. The kitten
will not play. See Mother. Mother is very nice. Mother,
will you play with Jane? Mother laughs. Laugh, Mother,
laugh. See Father. He is big and strong. Father, will you
play with Jane? Father is smiling. Smile, Father, smile.
See the dog. Bowwow goes the dog. Do you want to play
with Jane? See the dog run. Run, dog, run. Look, look.
Here comes a friend. The friend will play with Jane. They
will play a good game. Play, Jane, play.

Morrison
gives us all
rabbit hole,
all darkness.

Here is the house it is green and white it has a red door it
is very pretty here is the family mother father dick and jane
live in the green-and-white house they are very happy see
jane she has a red dress she wants to play who will play with
jane see the cat it goes meow-meow come and play come
play with jane the kitten will not play see mother mother is
very nice mother will you play with jane mother laughs
laugh mother laugh see father he is big and strong father will
you play with jane father is smiling smile father smile see the
dog bowwow goes the dog do you want to play do you want
to play with jane see the dog run run dog run look look here
comes a friend the friend will play with jane they will play
a good game play jane play

Hereisthehouseitisgreenandwhiteithasareddooritisverypretty
hereisthefamilymotherfatherdickandjaneliveinthegreenandw
hitehousetheyareveryhappyseejaneshehasareddressshewants
toplaywhowillplaywithjaneseethecatitgoesmeowmeowcomea
ndplaycomeplaywithjanethekittenwillnotplayseemothermoth
erisverynicemotherwillyouplaywithjanemotherlaughslaughm
otherlaughseefatherheisbigandstrongfatherwillyouplaywithja
nefatherissmilingsmilefathersmileseethedogbowwowgoesthe
dogdoyouwanttoplaydoyouwanttoplaywithjaneseethedogrun
rundogrunlooklookherecomesafriendthefriendwillplaywithja
netheywillplayagoodgameplayjaneplay

we see the red

comfort in her granddaughter: a strikingly beautiful Asian girl. The two cuddle within the belly of a giant wolf: his fur is matted and mangled. Blood is all over the wolf, the grandmother and Little Red. Blood is inside the 'womb' of the beast and on the floor. Closer inspection reveals a big zip that has been unzipped to open up the wolf's belly. Only his feet and abdomen are visible: his beastly head is off-frame. A grotesque treatment of the grandmother's exposed arm and her masked face, coupled with the dry and oozing blood, is suggestive not only of Japanese horror movies, but of the photographs of the burned and bleeding victims of the bombing of Hiroshima, their clothes torn, their skin melted. The comic zip turns dark and becomes that of a body bag. The photograph is in black-and-white, like a documentary picture, but we see the red.

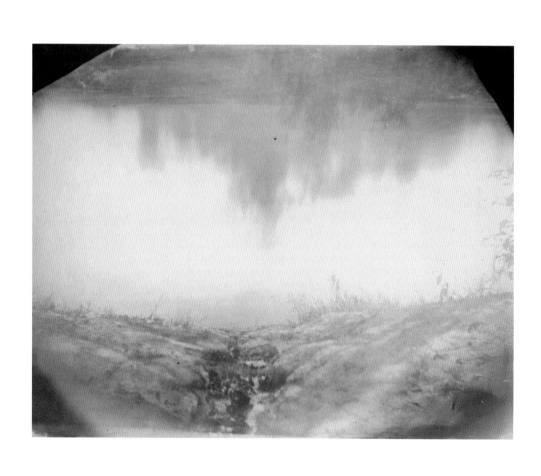

11 Dreaming Brown with Langston Hughes

The final chapter of Aurelia turns neither to fairy-tale red, nor fairy-tale gold – rather it embraces the warm and enchanting possibilities of dreaming brown. Paramount is the work of the visionary American poet Langston Hughes and his involvement with The Brownies' Book, *a monthly magazine for children founded by the writer and Civil Rights leader W.E.B. Du Bois. The aim of* The Brownies' Book *was to provide fairies 'of colour' to 'the Children of the Sun' – the editors' name for all African American children. The monthly* Brownies' Book *was short-lived (1920–21), but its legacy of dreaming brown lives on, if far, very far, from 'happily ever after'.*

Brown is the colour of sepia-tone photographs that capture time 'like flies in amber',[1] of birds and their nests, of fawns and owls and bears, of the furry skin of the kiwi fruit, of caramel, honey, chocolate, molasses and Pepsi-Cola, of the soil of the earth, a dead shoelace, the incense of death, an unseen bee's wing, a muddy river.

Brown is Sally Mann's wet-collodion photograph of a muddy river: 'the very spot from which the fourteen-year-old Emmett, naked and necklaced with a cotton-gin fan, was heaved into the Tallahatchie'.[2] Brown is also the 'humdrum, back-washy feeling of the place'.[3] Brown is hazelnut. Brown is the smell of musk and vanilla and the voice of the butterfly and the hush of a moth; the colour of the spots on a large tortoiseshell butterfly. A brown dwarf is a brown star too low in mass to burn hydrogen and shine. Toast is browned bread. Onions that are slowly browned are delicious.

Brown can be gloomy and serious, dusky dark, yet warm with wishful desire, hence José Esteban Muñoz's essay with its puerile sing-songy rhyming title of 'Feeling Brown, Feeling Down'. For Muñoz, feeling brown is a melancholic feeling: not necessarily miserable, at times reparative. 'Reparation is part of the depressive position; it signals a certain kind of hope.'[3] Brown is the colour of hope. Brown is the colour of the pupa of the hawkmoth that Nabokov waited for seven years to hatch.[4] Brown is tender, soft and boyish. 'I know a boy who is sky-soft brown . . . His smile is sorghum syrup drippin slow-sweet to the last', coos Toni Morrison.[5] Brown is Jacob van Oost the Elder's *Portrait of a Boy Aged Eleven* (1650): his furry hat and muff along with his jacket's puffed fabric-covered buttons chirp chestnut-brown-canary softness.

Brown is the colour of *The Sweet Flypaper of Life*, the book of photographs by Roy DeCarava with Langston Hughes's description of Harlem life. Sister Bradley refuses to be broken: 'I done got my feet caught in the sweet flypaper of life and I'll be dogged if I want to get loose.'[6]

Brown was once the colour of 'a patch of earth besides the front steps' of 20 East 127th Street in Harlem, where Langston Hughes lived. His backyard was dense and green, thanks to the flowering shrubs planted by a gardener named Mr Sacred Heart. And Boston ivy crept up the walls of the front of the house and luxuriated its way about. But that six-foot-square patch of earth remained nutty-brown barren from years of trampling by local children. In 1954, it was rescued by Hughes. Under the guidance of the poet, along with the aid of Mr Sacred Heart, neighbourhood children each picked a plant and were taught how to nurture it tenderly: nasturtiums, asters and marigolds. On a picket beside each plant was posted the child's name. The plot was christened by the *good* Pied-Piper poet, saviour of brown children, as 'Our Block's Children's Garden'.[7]

Brown is the colour of 'Beauty' – the full-lipped lover, the *Sleeping-Beauty* man of Isaac Julien's feeling-brown-feeling-down film *Looking for Langston* (1989). Langston's three-line poem entitled 'Suicide's Note' (1925) is decidedly brown and down, a haiku of giving up:

The calm,
Cool face of the river
Asked me for a kiss.[8]

The Scottish writer Andrew Lang wrote twelve 'coloured' fairy books: *The Blue Fairy Book*, *The Yellow Fairy Book*, *The Violet Fairy Book*, *The*

Brown was once the colour of
            'a patch of earth besides the front steps'
of 20 East 127th Street in Harlem,
      where Langston Hughes lived.

Crimson Fairy Book ... The Brown Fairy Book. A brownie is a benevolent sprite or goblin, a fairy. A Girl Guide. A point, as in a 'Brownie point'.

A brownie is a small square of rich, chewy chocolate cake, often containing nuts. Brownies were a favourite of the artist Joseph Cornell, who served them with cherry Coke at his 1972 'children-only' exhibit at New York's Cooper Union. The art was placed about three feet from the floor: the height of the consuming child who was allowed to eat the sweets while looking.

Oralia.

The Brownie was a magical snapshot camera invented by Kodak in 1900. Advertisements for the camera used illustrations of brownies (of the fairy type) crawling about. Kodak directed its advertisements towards children and the childlike, boasting that the Brownie was 'easily operated by any school boy or girl'.

With open hands reaching for the sky, *The Brownies' Book* was a monthly magazine for children founded by the writer and Civil Rights leader W.E.B. Du Bois.[9] Du Bois was the prince of black hope, 'an awakener',[10] not only of grown-ups but also of youth. *The Brownies' Book delivered fairies 'of colour' (real and imagined) to 'the Children of the Sun' – the editors' name for all African American children.*[11] Of equal importance was to instil black pride, including giving individual accolades to 'Little Brownies of the Month'. The pretty magazine was filled to the brim with stories, news, black history, letters from readers and photographs of black children, sometimes performing as fairies or brownies. Despite its short butterfly lifetime (January 1920–December 1921), the magazine was optimistic in its combined use of imagination and education.

In 1921, the year after he graduated from high school, Langston first poem, 'Fairies', in the magazine. Childlike and simple, written for the young, Langston's fairies weave their garments out of 'memories' *coloured* 'purple and rose'. Its purpose was reparative, to give the children of the sun delight, a garden for their minds. (Yet it was also in 1921 that the renowned Harlem Renaissance poet published his dark 'The Negro Speaks of Rivers'.)

Out of the dust of dreams
Fairies weave their garments
Out of the purple and rose of old memories
They make rainbow wings.
No wonder we find them such marvellous things![12]

The cover of the first issue of *The Brownies' Book* features a black girl standing high on her tippy-toes, with a crown on her head. She wears a pearl necklace, a white flowing Isadora Duncan dress, white tights and satin ballet shoes, with ribbons that tie at her ankles. This black fairy is adorned by a large circular trinket near her heart. She has large white wings of hope tied to her wrists. This butterfly-bat-moth is ready to fly. Her outstretched arms are unlocked, unsealed, receptive. Her unmuted hands touch me; they move me with 'something like a tender, open, possibility'.[13] A creature born from Hughes's 'The Dream Keeper', this girl's 'heart melodies' are wrapped in a 'blue cloud cloth/ Away from the two rough fingers of the world'.

Bring me all of your dreams,
You dreamer.
Bring me all of your
Heart melodies
That I may wrap them
In a blue cloud-cloth
Away from the too-rough fingers
Of the world.[14]

In the November 1921 issue of *The Brownies' Book*, Hughes published another little poem for children: a honeyed four-line verse entitled 'Winter Sweetness':

This little house is sugar.
   Its roof with snow is piled,
And from its tiny window
   Peeps a maple-sugar child.[15]

The Brownies' Book

JANUARY, 1920

454
1507

One Dollar and a Half a Year   Fifteen Cents a Copy

fairies 'of colour' to 'the
Children of the 'Sun'

The poem may seem 'benign', but there is radical strength in the sweet 'brownie' in the window. During an era when *The Story of Little Black Sambo* was one of the most popular books in the United States, Hughes changes the vocabulary of childhood. Under piles of snow-sugar-whiteness, from a tiny window peeps a maple-sugar child (a child of the sun).

The Brownies' Book gave the fairy tale a black mouth and toasted it brown: it celebrated, warned, swallowed, chewed and rebelled, awakening the fairy-tale realm in 'our children of the sun' lest they fall too deeply down the White Rabbit's hole.

Impossible

By the time of Emmett Till's death, the short life of *The Brownies' Book* was long over. It was a time when, perhaps, all children (but especially 'our children of the sun') needed its magic and hope.

Black Misery is the last book that Hughes would write: a book for children, seemingly without hope. It was published posthumously in 1969: the year after the assassination of Martin Luther King. 'The book is made up of black and white drawings (by Aurouni) with a caption accompanying each image. Hughes finished writing these captions just before his death in 1967.'[16] The book is a refrain of what misery is for a child in the United States. As Dianne Johnson writes:

A child is at the centre of each scenario, but if this is a children's book, it is the cruellest children's book. Whether or not adults would share it with young people is questionable. But it would have been impossible for *Black Misery* to have the same balance as some of the other books [by Hughes] without losing its integrity.[17]

Here are some choruses from *Black Misery*:

Misery is when you heard on the radio that the neighborhood you live in is a slum but you always though it was home.

Misery is when somebody meaning no harm called your little black dog 'Nigger' and he just wagged his tail.

Misery is when you first realize so many bad things have black in them, like black cats, black arts, blackball.

Misery is when your own mother won't let you play your new banjo in front of the <u>other</u> race.

Misery is when you start to help an old white lady across the street and she thinks you're trying to snatch her purse.

And the misery continues for every page of this short book. The last caption of the book reads:

Misery is when you see that it takes the whole National Guard to get you into the new integrated school.

No happy endings.
No sweetness.
No maple-sugar children in the window.

Jacqueline Rose's book *The Case of Peter Pan, or the Impossibility of Children's Literature* highlights the insurmountable impossibility of all children's literature. Rose's introduction lays down this sad fact:

There is, in one sense, no body of literature that rests so openly on an acknowledged difference, a rupture almost between writer and addressee. Children's fiction sets up the child as an outsider to its own process and then aims, unashamedly, to take the child *in*.[18]

By 1967, a fairy story for our 'children of the sun' was the *most* impossible.

———

275

No happy endings.

No sweetness.

Misery is when somebody meaning no harm called your little black dog "Nigger" and he just wagged his tail and wiggled.

No maple-sugar children in the window.

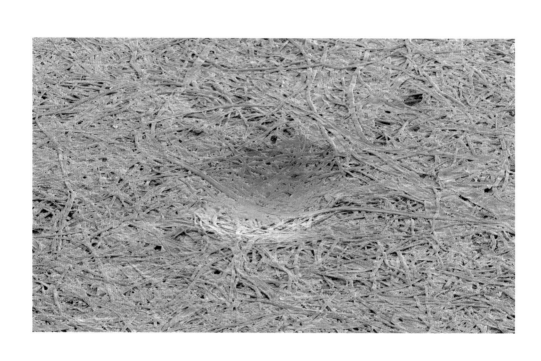

Conclusion: Full Stop

In our hearts, minds and memories (if not literally), the fairy tale begins with the big O of a golden 'Once upon a time'. And in our hearts, minds and memories, the fairy tale ends (if again, not always literally) with a golden full stop after 'and they lived happily ever after'. As Ernst Bloch simply put it: 'All fairy tales end in gold.'

The artist Jonny Briggs has magnified the indentation of a full stop from his late grandmother's notepad with an electron microscope and taken a photograph of it. At 2.5 metres across, it appears as a giant crater. Briggs's photograph of a full stop, entitled *The Other Side*, is writ extremely large. As well as suggesting a hole, whether it be that of a white rabbit or from pulling up a cauliflower in Italy or the letter O of Once upon a time, the title of Briggs's humongous full stop has an *Alice-through-the-Looking-Glass* sense of foreboding adventure. As the artist explains:

I was particularly interested in my Grandmother's notepad – you know when you get the ghost of writing indented from the previous page. I kept looking at the indentation of a full stop, which interested me, because there's a silence to it; it doesn't have words, and is somewhere between finishing and beginning.[1]

I close the doors to Bosch's *Garden of Earthly Delights*. I put the cauliflower back into the hole that led to the secret passageway. I emerge from my shell. I am awakened by the tiny pea below all of my mattresses. For, like the lovesick Elizabeth Smart, 'I am more vulnerable than the princess for whom seven mattresses could not conceal the pea.'[2] Not only writ large, but felt large, like Briggs's *The Other Side*, my aurelian full stop becomes a giant O. I am back at the beginning.

'The opening of a tale . . . All we need is the word "Once . . ." and we're off.'

my aurelian full stop becomes a giant O

REFERENCES

Preface: O

1 James Merrill, from the opening of 'The Book of Ephraim', from his long poem entitled *The Changing Light at Sandover* (New York, 2006), p. 3. The key lines from Merrill are as follows: 'I learned for the kind of unseasoned telling found/In legends, fairy tales, a tone licked clean.' As quoted in Philip Pullman, 'Introduction', in *Grimm Tales for Young and Old* (London, 2012), p. ix.
2 Ibid.
3 Pullman, *Grimm Tales for Young and Old*, p. xiii.
4 From Sylvia Plath's poem 'Morning Song', in *Sylvia Plath: Selected Poems* (London, 2003), p. 23.
5 In Latin, 'Once upon a time' retains the O: *Olim*. However, in French, German and Italian the O is not retained:

> French: *Il était une fois*
> Italian: *C'era una volta*
> German: *Es war einmal.*

6 Lewis Carroll, *Alice's Adventures in Wonderland*, in *The Annotated Alice: The Definitive Edition*, introduction and notes by Martin Gardner (New York, 2000), p. 67. The Cheshire Cat is not the only feline of the fairy-tale world: the Grimms gave us *tails* in 'Catskin', 'Cat and Mouse in Partnership' and 'The Fox and the Cat'. Charles Perrault gave us 'Puss in Boots'.
7 Javier Marías, *Heart So White*, trans. Margaret Jull Costa, with an introduction by Jonathan Coe (London, 2012), p. 131.
8 Michael Patrick Hearn, from his notes to L. Frank Baum's *The Wizard of Oz*. See *The Annotated Wizard of Oz*, ed. with an introduction and notes by Hearn (New York, 2000), p. 39, note 10.
9 Ibid., p. 43, note 17.

Introduction: I Am an Aurelian

1 From Vladimir Nabokov's Cornell Lectures, March 1951, on Gogol's *The Overcoat*, Stevenson's *The Strange Case of Dr Jekyll and Mr Hyde* and Kafka's *Metamorphosis*. Nabokov is explaining transformation with metamorphosis. See *Nabokov's Butterflies: Unpublished and Uncollected Writings*, ed. and annotated by Brian Boyd and Robert Michael Pyle, with new translations by Dmitri Nabokov (Boston, MA, 2000), p. 472.

2 Kurt Johnson and Steve Coates, *Nabokov's Blues: The Scientific Odyssey of a Literary Genius* (Cambridge, MA, 1999), p. 32.

3 Gérard de Nerval, 'Aurélia', in *Aurélia and Other Writings*, trans. Robert Duncan and Marc Lowenthal (Boston, MA, 1996), pp. 1–70.

4 Marina Warner, *Stranger Magic: Charmed States and the 'Arabian Nights'* (London, 2011), p. 9.

5 Marina Warner, *Once Upon a Time: A Short History of the Fairy Tale* (Oxford, 2014), p. 4.

6 Brothers Grimm, 'The Juniper Tree', in *Brothers Grimm: The Complete Fairy Tales*, trans., introduced and annotated by Jack Zipes (London, 1992), p. 211.

7 Alissa Nutting, 'The Brother and the Bird', in *My Mother She Killed Me, My Father He Ate Me: Forty New Fairy Tales*, ed. Kate Bernheimer (New York, 2010), p. 40.

8 Charles Perrault, 'The Sleeping Beauty in the Wood', in *Fairy Tales*, trans. with an introduction and notes by Christopher Betts (Oxford, 2009), p. 93.

9 Ibid.

10 Sometimes the original 'Sauce Robert' is translated into English simply as 'good sauce' or as 'mustard sauce'. In French, Perrault, *Contes de ma mère l'Oye* (Paris, 2003), p. 18.

11 In the translation by Christopher Betts, Aurore is simply the princess. Ibid., p. 17.

12 This term is Agnès Varda's, from her film *Ulysse* (1954).

13 Lewis Carroll, *Alice's Adventures in Wonderland*, as collected in *The Annotated Alice: The Definitive Edition*, with an introduction and notes by Martin Gardner (New York, 2000), p. 62.

14 Ibid., pp. 63, 64.

15 Richard Kelly, '"If You Don't Know What a Gryphon Is": Text and Illustration in *Alice's Adventures in Wonderland*', in *Lewis Carroll, A Celebration: Essays on the Occasion of the 150th Anniversary of the Birth of Charles Lutwidge Dodgson*, ed. Edward Guiliano (New York, 1982), p. 70.

16 Lewis Carroll, letter to C.H.O. Daniel, 23 November 1880, in Morton N. Cohen, ed., *Letters of Lewis Carroll*, vol. I (London, 1979), p. 392.

17 Joy Hinson, *Goat* (London, 2015), p. 16.

18 Agnès Varda, voiceover from *Ulysse* (1954).

19 Jack Zipes, 'Once There Were Two Brothers Named Grimm', in *Brothers Grimm: The Complete Tales*, trans. Zipes, p. xxxvii.

20 Jack Zipes, 'Introduction: Rediscovering the Original Tale of the Brothers Grimm', in *The Original Folk and Fairy Tales of the Brothers Grimm: The Complete First Edition*, trans. and ed. Jack Zipes (Princeton, NJ, and Oxford, 2014), p. xix.

21 Ibid., p. xx.

22 Ibid.

23 Ibid.

24 Scholars Maria Tatar and Jack Zipes have provided excellent histories of the fairy tales and their variations.

25 Angela Carter, *The Second Virago Book of Fairy Tales* (London, 1992), p. xi.

26 Maria Tatar, *The Classic Fairy Tales* (New York, 1999), p. 107.

27 Angela Carter, *Angela Carter's Book of Fairy Tales* (London, 2011), p. xii.

28 Ibid.

29 Ibid.

30 Carroll, *Alice's Adventures in Wonderland*, p. 17.

31 Michael Moon, *A Small Boy and Others: Imitation and Initiation in American Culture from Henry James to Andy Warhol* (Durham, NC, 1998), p. 138.

32 Jean-Luc Nancy, *Listening*, trans. Charlotte Mandell (New York, 2007), p. 31.

33 The *Oxford English Dictionary* defines 'gold-bug' as follows: 'a plutocrat, millionaire; also "a political nickname for an advocate of a single (gold) standard"'.

34 Vladimir Nabokov, 'The Aurelian', in *Vladimir Nabokov: Collected Stories* (London, 2010), p. 284.

35 Ibid., pp. 289, 281.

36 Ibid., p. 282.

37 Nymphalidae is the largest family of butterflies; it contains around 6,000 species, including well-known species such as the monarch and the red admiral.

38 Michael A. Salmon, *The Aurelian Legacy: British Butterflies and their Collectors* (Berkeley and Los Angeles, CA, 2000), p. 31.

39 Brothers Grimm, 'Snow White', from Philip Pullman, *Grimm Tales for Young and Old* (London, 2012), p. 217.

40 Vladimir Nabokov, *Speak, Memory: An Autobiography Revisited* (London, 1998), pp. 86–7.

41 Ibid., p. 87.

42 Ibid.

43 Vladimir Nabokov, 'Good Readers and Good Writers', from *Lectures on Literature* (San Diego, New York and London, 1980), p. 2.

44 Vladimir Nabokov, *Lolita: The Annotated Lolita*, ed. Alfred Appel Jr (New York, 1970), p. 54.

45 Kurt Johnson and Steve Coates, *Nabokov's Blues: The Scientific Odyssey of a Literary Genius* (Cambridge, MA, 1999), p. 132.

46 Nabokov, *The Annotated Lolita*, p. 168.

47 Ibid., p. 356.

48 Ibid., p. 340.

49 Ibid.

50 Ibid., p. 125.

51 Ibid., p. 11.

52 Ibid., p. 127.

53 Ibid., p. 141.

1 Eating Gold

1 Laura Mulvey, 'Visual Pleasure and Narrative Cinema', in her *Visual and Other Pleasures* (Bloomington, IN, 1989), p. 22.

2 Ovid, *Metamorphoses: A New Verse Translation*, trans. David Raeburn (London, 2004), p. 428.

3 Ernst Bloch, 'Better Castles in the Sky at the Country Fair and Circus, in Fairy Tales and Colportage', in *The Utopian Function of Art and Literature: Selected Essays*, trans. Jack Zipes and Frank Mecklenburg (Boston, MA, 1988), p. 168.

4 As Jack Zipes notes: 'It should be pointed out that the Grimms tales are not strictly speaking "fairy tales", and they never used that term, which, in German, would be *Feenmärchen*. Their collection is much more diverse and includes animal tales, legends, tall tales, nonsense stories, fables, anecdotes, and, of course, magic tales (*Zaubermärchen*), which are clearly related to the great European tradition of fairy tales that can be traced back to ancient Greece and Rome.' Jack Zipes, 'Introduction: Rediscovering the Original Tales of the Brothers Grimm', in *The Original Folk and Fairy Tales of the Brothers Grimm: The Complete First Edition*, trans. and ed. Jack Zipes (Princeton, NJ, and Oxford, 2014), p. xxx.

5 Ibid., p. xlii.

6 Brothers Grimm, 'The Golden Key', in *The Complete Fairy Tales*, trans., introduced and annotated by Jack Zipes (London, 2007), p. 780.

7 Roland Barthes differentiates the *writerly*, in which the reader *writes* along with the author, from the *readerly*, a 'classic text', in which the reader 'is plunged into a kind of idleness', in *s/z: An Essay*, trans. Richard Miller (New York, 1974), p. 4.

8 Ibid.

9 Roland Barthes, *A Lover's Discourse*, trans. Richard Howard (New York, 1978), p. 73.

10 Ibid., pp. 54–61.

11 Ibid., p. 54.

12 See Teresa de Lauretis, 'Desire in Narrative', in her *Alice Doesn't: Feminism, Semiotics, Cinema* (Bloomington, IN, 1984), pp. 103–57.

13 Ibid., p. 103.

14 Roland Barthes, 'An Introduction to the Structural Analysis of Narrative', trans. Lionel Duisit, *New Literary History*, VI/2 (Winter 1975), p. 272.

15 Sophocles, *Oedipus the King*, trans. Stephen Berg and Diskin Clay (Oxford, 1978), p. 77.

16 Ibid., pp. 81–2.

17 Marquis de Sade, *Philosophy in the Bedroom*, trans. Joachim Neugroschel (London, 2006), p. 171.

18 Definition of 'sadism' in the *Oxford English Dictionary*.

19 Feeding the baby whenever hungered is as signalled – usually by crying or sucking on his hands – rather than according to a set schedule.

20 Adam Phillips, *On Kissing, Tickling and Being Bored* (Cambridge, MA, 1993), p. 94. Kisses as non-nutritive eating is picked up again in Chapter Two, 'An Alicious Appetite'.

21 Robert Burton, *The Anatomy of Melancholy*, ed. Holbrook Jackson (New York, 2001), p. 247.

22 Edward Eggleston, 'Some Curious Colonial Remedies', *American Historical Review*, v/2 (December 1899), pp. 200–201.

23 Ibid., p. 202.

24 Hannele Klemettilä, *The Medieval Kitchen: A Social History with Recipes* (London, 2012), p. 123.

25 Ibid., p. 129.

26 James Franco, 'A Star, a Soap and the Meaning of Art: Why an Appearance on *General Hospital* Qualifies as Performance Art', *Wall Street Journal*, 4 December 2009.

27 'The Palmerston Gold Chocolate Cups', www.britishmuseum.org, accessed 18 July 2016.

28 Roland Barthes, *Mourning Diary*, trans. Richard Howard (New York, 2010), p. 3.

29 This version is quoted from a treasured book from my own childhood, with images by the terrific husband-and-wife illustrators Alice and Martin Provensen. *Aesop's Fables*, selected and adapted by Louis Untermeyer (New York, 1965), p. 33.

30 Marina Warner, *From the Beast to the Blonde: On Fairy Tales and Their Tellers* (London, 1995), p. 322.

31 Charles Perrault, *The Complete Fairy Tales*, trans. Christopher Betts (Oxford, 2009), p. 53.

32 Christian Boltanski, as quoted in *Christian Boltanski: Lessons of Darkness*, catalogue published on the occasion of the exhibition by the same name, curated by Lynn Gumpert and Mary Jane Jacob (Chicago, Los Angeles and New York, 1988), p. 81.

33 Tim Krabbé, *The Vanishing*, trans. Sam Garrett (London, 2003), p. 108.

34 Ibid., pp. 109–10.

35 Ibid., p. 11.

2 An Alicous Appetite: *Alice's Adventures in Wonderland* and *Through the Looking-Glass*

1 Lewis Carroll, *The Annotated Alice: The Definitive Edition*, introduction and notes by Martin Gardner (New York and London, 2000) p. 177. Hereafter, page numbers for citations to both *Alice's Adventures in Wonderland* and *Through the Looking-Glass* will be parenthetically noted, referring to this edition.

2 See Marina Warner's brilliant work on eating, the fairy tale and Lewis Carroll, especially the chapter 'Now . . . We Can Begin to Feed', in her *No Go the Bogeyman: Scaring, Lulling, and Making Mock* (New York, 1998), pp. 136–59.

3 For her discovery of various useful quotations on Alice and hunger, I am indebted to Kate Arpen, a postgraduate student in my seminar on 'Forgetting' – now so many years ago, I have almost forgotten it! (Spring 2006, University of North Carolina, Chapel Hill).

4 Recall that for his schooling the Mock Turtle could only afford the 'regular course', which began with 'Reeling and Writhing' (98). Alice does, however, seem to miss home (if only a little bit) when she says, after so much growing and shrinking, 'It was much pleasanter at home' (39).

5 Marina Warner, *Fantastic Metamorphoses, Other Worlds* (Oxford, 2002), p. 201.

6 Hélène Cixous, 'Introduction' to Lewis Carroll's *Through the Looking-Glass* and *The Hunting of the Snark*, trans. Marie Maclean, *New Literary History*, XIII/2 (1982), p. 247.

7 In his famous essay on the fetish, Freud famously supplies objects like a tube of lipstick or a pair of women's shoes as objects to fetishize. For Freud, such stand-ins for the penis represent both an acknowledgement of and protection against castration. In Freud's hands, the fetish object is always sexual and shielding. Similarly, Oppenheim's high-heeled pumps are erotic, yet chaste in their whiteness. Furthermore, by the tying up of the pumps, the threat is held down by string, kept in check. Also of note, Freud unsettles the goodness of the child's governess, or nurse (the second mother) by noting that it is she who most often exposes us to the outside world and teaches us about sexuality. See Jane Gallop, 'Keys to Dora', in her book *Feminism and Psychoanalysis: The Daughter's Seduction* (New York, 1983), pp. 132–50.

8 As Martin Gardener writes: 'The phrases "mad as a hatter" and "mad as a March Hare" were common at the time Carroll wrote.' See *The Annotated Alice*, pp. 66–7, note 8.

9 Cixous, 'Introduction', p. 240.

10 Jacques Lacan, 'The Agency of the Letter in the Unconscious, or Reason Since Freud', in *Écrits: A Selection*, trans. Alan Sheridan (New York, 1977), p. 167.

11 As Lacan writes: 'In the case of *Verschiebung*, "displacement", the German term is closer to the idea of that veering off of signification that we see in metonymy,' ibid., pp. 160, 175.

12 Ibid., p. 165.

13 It was the Uruguayan poet Lautréamont who first wrote this famed line that was late adopted by the Surrealists, who treated him as a prophet.

14 *The Wordsworth Dictionary of Phrase and Fable*, based on the original book by E. C. Brewer (London, 2006), p. 538.

15 Marcel Proust, *In Search of Lost Time*, vol. VI: *Time Regained*, trans. C. K. Scott Moncrieff and Terence Kilmartin (New York, 1992), p. 257.

16 This may be true of many anorexics, who look into ordering and controlling their world through withholding from themselves – a subject further touched upon later in this essay.

17 For an illuminating discussion of the impossibility of 'the art of forgetting', see Umberto Eco's 'An Ars *Oblivionalis*? Forget It', PMLA, CIII (1988), pp. 254–61.

18 Gaston Bachelard, *The Poetics of Space*, trans. Maria Jolas (Boston, MA, 1994), p. 19.

19 Ibid., p. 20.

20 Harald Weinrich, *Lethe: The Art and Critique of Forgetting*, trans. Steven Rendall (Ithaca, NY, and London, 1997), p. 4.

21 Milan Kundera, *The Book of Laughter and Forgetting*, trans. Michael Henry Heim (New York, 1981), pp. 234–5.

22 Lewis Carroll is, of course, Charles Dodgson's pen name. He had a problem with stuttering, sometimes resulting (perhaps only mythically) in the pronouncing of his name as 'Do-do Dodgson' – hence the fascination of the Dodo as yet another alter ego in Wonderland. It is

said (again, perhaps only mythically) that Carroll lost his stutter in the presence of little girls; this would make Alice Liddell part of the cure.

23 J. M. Barrie, '*Peter Pan in Kensington Gardens*' and '*Peter and Wendy*', ed. Peter Hollindale (Oxford, 1999), p. 135; emphasis mine.

24 Adam Phillips, 'On Eating, and Preferring Not To', in *Promises, Promises: Essays on Literature and Psychoanalysis* (New York, 2001), p. 134.

25 Connecting Melville's story 'Bartleby, the Scrivener: A Story of Wall Street' (1853) to the plight of the anorexic is at the heart of Phillips's essay 'On Eating, and Preferring Not To'. As he writes, 'At first the boss takes it for granted, in a commonsensical way, that Bartleby will do the work demanded of him; just as, in a commonsensical way, one might assume that people will eat, simply in order to live, or feel well; as though food only has a use-value, and not an exchange value as well,' ibid., p. 283.

26 Carroll's photographs are delicious confections made of little girls (and little boys): we can safely eat them with our eyes, without using our mouths. See my *Pleasures Taken: Performances of Sexuality and Loss in Victorian Photographs* (Durham, NC, 1995). On the concept of photography's relationship to the real and to personal desire, see Roland Barthes, *Camera Lucida: Reflections on Photography*, trans. Richard Howard (New York, 1981), p. 75.

27 Angela Carter, 'Wolf-Alice', in *The Bloody Chamber and Other Stories* (London, 2007), p. 148.

28 Ibid., p. 140.

29 Nina Auerbach, *Romantic Imprisonment: Women and Other Glorified Outcasts* (New York, 1986), p. 167.

30 *Lewis Carroll's Alice: The Photographs, Books, Papers and Personal Effects of Alice Liddell and Her Family*, Sotheby's Catalogue (London, Sotheby's Catalogue, 6 June 2001), p. 49.

31 Lewis Carroll, 'Eight or Nine Wise Words about Letter-writing', in *Lewis Carroll: The Complete Works* (London, 2005), p. 450.

32 This is how Carroll must have felt in the presence of little girls who had grown up. In a letter to Florence Balfour, he likens himself, with the shock of finding her, the once tiny 'microcosm[,] suddenly expanded into a tall young person' to 'the old lady who, after feeding her canary and going for a walk, finds the cage entirely filled, on her return, with a live turkey', or 'the old gentleman who, after chaining up a small terrier overnight, finds a hippopotamus raging around the kennel in the morning'. See Lewis Carroll, *The Selected Letters of Lewis Carroll*, ed. Morton N. Cohen (New York, 1982), p. 117.

33 See elin o'Hara slavick's evocative full-to-the-brim description of Gowin's photograph of girlhood, eggs, eyes and snaky charm, 'One Picture, One Paragraph', http://saint-lucy.com/one-picture-one-paragraph/elin-ohara-slavick, accessed 16 May 2016.

34 Maria Tatar, *Off with Their Heads! Fairy Tales and the Culture of Childhood* (Princeton, NJ, 1992), p. 194.

35 Nancy Armstrong, 'The Occidental Alice', *Differences: A Journal of Feminist Cultural Studies*, II/2 (1990), p. 16.

36 Adam Phillips, *On Kissing, Tickling and Being Bored* (Cambridge, MA, 1993), p. 94.

37 Carroll, *Selected Letters of Lewis Carroll*, p. 96.

38 It is feasible that Carroll, a man of God and of mathematics, made all of these associations. As Robert Hendrickson has written in *The Facts on File: Encyclopedia of Word and Phrase Origins* (New York, 1987), p. 571: 'The Romans used *X* to denote the number ten and *x* in mathematics generally means "an unknown quantity." One theory holds that the *X* stands for a kiss because it originally represented a highly stylized picture of two mouths touching – *x*. Furthermore in early times illiterates often signed documents with a St Andrew's cross of *X* and kissed that *X* to show their good faith (as they did with any cross or Bible), which reinforced the association. But these explanations may be folk etymology, as may the story that mathematically the *X* is a "multiplier" – in this case of love and delight.'

39 I thank the art historian Mark Crinson for alerting me to this fascinating idea.

40 Lindsay Smith, 'Lewis Carroll: Stammering, Photography and the Voice of Infancy', *Journal of Visual Culture*, III/1 (2004), p. 99.

41 Ibid., p. 104.

42 Colin Gordon, *Beyond the Looking Glass: Reflections of Alice and her Family* (San Diego, CA, 1982), p. 84.

43 This photograph was first seen in this book's preface. It is unclear whether the glass negative for *'Open Your Mouth and Shut Your Eyes'* was among those found in the chocolate box in Alice Liddell's granddaughter's house.

44 Warner, *No Go the Bogeyman*, p. 139.

45 Phillips, *On Kissing, Tickling and Being Bored*, p. 97. The relationship between kissing and eating, as described by Phillips, was first brought up in Chapter One, 'Eating Gold'.

46 Ibid.

47 Ibid.

48 Alison and Helmut Gernsheim, *The History of Photography* (Oxford, 1955), p. 258. For an excellent analysis of the concept of the devouring eye and the culinary aspects of photography, see Olivier Richon, *Allegories* (London, 2000), pp. 8–14.

49 Lewis Carroll, 'Novelty and Romancement', in *Lewis Carroll: The Complete Works* (London, 2005), p. 404.

50 Ibid.

3 A Raindrop Unfallen: Innocence and Jacques-Henri Bernardin de Saint-Pierre's *Paul and Virginia*

1 James Kincaid, *Erotic Innocence: The Culture of Child Molesting* (Durham, NC, 1998), p. 53.

2 Roland Barthes, *Camera Lucida: Reflections on Photography*, trans. Richard Howard (New York, 1981), p. 53. Barthes is discussing the 1926 family portrait photograph by James Van Der Zee, where he found 'punctum': a trace of his beloved aunt.

3 Ibid., p. 45. In the original French, *La Chambre claire: note sur la photographie* (Paris, 1980), p. 77.

4 I first learned of the 'Loneliest Palm' from the Mauritian-born British artist Gayle Ching Kwa.

5 Ian Parker, 'Digging for Dodos: The 2006 Mauritius Dodo Expedition', *The New Yorker Magazine*, www.newyorker.com/magazine, 22 January 2007.

6 Jacques-Henri Bernardin de Saint-Pierre, *Paul and Virginia*, trans. John Donovan (London, 2005), p. 47.

7 Ibid., p. 64.

8 Ibid., p. 45.

9 Ibid., p. 46.

10 See Carol Mavor, *Pleasures Taken: Performances of Sexuality and Loss in Victorian Photographs* (Durham, NC, and London, 1995), pp. 43–69.

11 Bernardin, *Paul and Virginia*, p. 46.

12 In 1863, Charles Kingsley published *The Water-Babies: A Fairy Tale for a Land Baby*. In 1864, Cameron took several photographs of Elizabeth and Alice Keown under the title of *Water Babies*.

13 *At Freshwater: A Comedy* is Virginia Woolf's play (meant only for a private audience), which featured her great Aunt Julia.

14 Parker, 'Digging for Dodos'.

15 Bernardin, *Paul and Virginia*, p. 63.

16 Emily Brontë, *Wuthering Heights*, ed. V. S. Pritchett (Boston, MA, 1956), p. 68.

17 Bernardin, *Paul and Virginia*, p. 47.

18 Ibid., p. 72.

19 Ibid.

20 Ibid., p. 74.

21 U-chronia is the no-time of u-topia (no-place). Uchronia is a neologism coined by Charles Renouvier in his 1876 novel *Uchronie (l'utopie dans l'histoire): esquisse historique apocryphe du développement de la civilisation européenne tel qu'il n'a pas été, tel qu'il aurait pu être.*

22 Bernardin, *Paul and Virginia*, p. 70.

23 Ibid., pp. 120–21.

24 Hans Christian Andersen, 'The Little Mermaid', as collected in *Hans Christian Andersen: Fairy Tales*, trans. Tiina Nunnally, ed. Jackie Wullschlager (New York, 2005), p. 85.

25 *Le Petit Chaperon rouge* was published anonymously and has been attributed, if shakily, to Charles Perrault. See Christopher Betts, introduction to *Charles Perrault: The Complete Fairy Tales*, trans. Christopher Betts (Oxford, 2009), pp. ix–xv.

26 Derek Jarman, *Chroma: A Book of Colour – June '93* (London, 2000), p. 33.

27 Bernardin, *Paul and Virginia*, p. 67.

28 Ibid., p. 63.

29 While the painting is believed to be inspired by Bernardin, the connection is a firm

conjecture, if not a fact. The Metropolitan Museum owns the painting and writes this on their website: 'When Cot exhibited this painting at the Salon of 1880, critics speculated about the source of the subject. Some proposed the French novel *Paul et Virginie* by Bernardin de Saint-Pierre (1737–1814), in which the teenage protagonists run for shelter in a rainstorm, using the heroine's overskirt as an impromptu umbrella; others suggested the romance *Daphnis and Chloe* by the ancient Greek writer Longus'; www.metmuseum.org/collection/the-collection-online/search/435997. The art historian James Henry Rubin sees *Paul and Virginia* in Cot's painting but favours the narrative of *Daphnis and Chloë*. See Rubin, 'Pierre-Auguste Cot's *The Storm*', in *Metropolitan Museum Journal*, xiv (1979), pp. 191–200.

30 Bernardin, *Paul and Virginia*, p. 64.
31 Ibid., p. 52.
32 Ibid., p. 64.
33 Ibid., p. 48.
34 Thomas More, *Utopia*, ed. George M. Logan and Robert M. Adams (Cambridge, 2002), pp. 77, 78.
35 Nelson George, 'Black-and-white Struggle with a Rosy Glow', *New York Times*, www.nytimes.com, 9 August 2011. *The Help* is based on the best-selling 2009 novel by Kathryn Stockett.
36 Bernardin, *Paul and Virginia*, p. 44.
37 Ibid., p. 42.
38 Ibid., p. 44.
39 Ibid., pp. 44–5.
40 See 'Who Resisted and Campaigned for Abolition?', http://revealinghistories.org.uk, accessed 16 May 2016.
41 Bernardin, *Paul and Virginia*, p. 78.
42 As Barthes writes in 'The Great Family of Man', in *Mythologies*, selected and trans. Annette Lavers (London, 1972), p. 101: 'Any classic humanism postulates that in scratching the history of men a little, the relativity of their institutions or the superficial diversity of their skins . . . one very quickly reaches the solid rock of a universal human nature. Progressive humanism, on the contrary, must always remember to reverse the terms of the very old imposture, constantly to scour nature, its "laws" and its "limits" in order to discover History there, and at last to establish Nature itself as historical.'
43 Bernardin, *Paul and Virginia*, p. 67; emphasis mine.
44 Ibid., p. 86.
45 Ibid., p. 8.
46 Ibid.
47 Ibid., p. 15.
48 Ibid., p. 86.
49 Ibid.

50 Ibid.
51 Ibid., p. 9.
52 Emily Dickinson, 'Grief is a Mouse – ', 1863 (J. 793/Fr. 753).

4 Poto and Cabengo

1 In Chapter Nine, 'Tragic Candyland', we will encounter the original 'Princess of Words': Minou Drouet, a child poet living in France who came to fame in the 1950s.
2 From the voiceover of the documentary film about the two girls narrated and produced by Jean-Pierre Gorin, entitled *Poto and Cabengo* (1980), 73 minutes, distributed as a DVD by Criterion, in Series 31: *Three Popular Films by Jean-Pierre Gorin* (2012).
3 Jon Lackman, 'Dugon, Haus You Dinikin, Du-Ah: The Secrets of Twin Speak', www.slate.com, 24 August 2011.
4 For example Chris Marker's *La Jetée* (1962) and his *Chats perchés* (2004) or Jean-Luc Godard's *Histoire(s) du cinema* (1998).
5 Voiceover of Gorin's *Poto and Cabengo*.
6 See Lucien Malson, *Wolf Children and the Problem of Human Nature*, with the complete text of Jean-Marc-Gaspard Itard's *The Wild Boy of Aveyron* (New York, 1972), pp. 91–179. Of further interest here is the fact that the word *enfant* comes from the Latin *infans*: from *in* (not) and *fari* (to speak). See Chapter Nine, 'Tragic Candyland'.
7 François Truffaut, as quoted in Vicky Lebeau, *Childhood and Cinema* (London, 2008), p. 76.
8 The film deal never came through. The promise of economic salvation for Christine and Tom remained an empty one.
9 Lewis Carroll, *The Annotated Alice: The Definitive Edition*, introduction and notes by Martin Gardner (New York and London, 2000), p. 148.
10 The portmanteau words of the Jabberwocky poem, in particular 'slithy', were first discussed in this book's Chapter Two, 'An Alicious Appetite'.
11 The subject of empty words, mirrors and glass is at the heart of the work of Jacques Lacan, as is taken up in Chapter Five, 'Speaking in Glass'.
12 Carroll, *The Annotated Alice*, p. 220.
13 Ibid., p. 13.
14 Voiceover, *Poto and Cabengo*.
15 Vladimir Nabokov, *Lolita: The Annotated Lolita*, edited, with preface, introduction and notes by Alfred Appel Jr (New York, 1970), pp. 78, 192.
16 Voiceover, *Poto and Cabengo*, 1980.
17 Lackman, 'Dugon, Haus You Dinikin, Du-Ah'.
18 Brothers Grimm, 'Hansel and Gretel', in *The Original Folk and Fairy Tales of the Brothers Grimm: The Complete First Edition*, trans. and ed. Jack Zipes (Princeton, NJ, and Oxford, 2014), p. 44.
19 Ibid., p. 48.

20 Ernst Bloch, *The Utopian Function of Art and Literature*, trans. Jack Zipes and Frank Mecklenburg (Cambridge, MA, and London, 1988), p. 168.

21 Ibid., pp. 176–7.

22 Hope Kingsley, with contributions by Christopher Riopelle, *Seduced by Art: Photography Past and Present* (London, 2012), p. 202.

23 Brothers Grimm, 'Little Snow White', in *The Original Folk and Fairy Tales*, p. 177.

24 Ibid.

25 Ibid.

26 Ibid.

27 Ian McEwan, *The Cement Garden* (Stuttgart, 2000), pp. 38–9.

28 From a follow-up story that appeared on American television on the Learning Channel, 6 June 2002. Further information on the outcome of the twins is scant. Gorin is no longer in contact with them.

29 Lucie Dolène speaking of her singing in the French version of Disney's *Snow White* in artist Pierre Huyghe's short film, *Blanche-Neige Lucie* (1997).

30 Ibid.

5 Speaking in Glass

1 Brian Dillon, 'A Dry Black Veil', *Cabinet*, 35 (Fall 2009).

2 Walter Benjamin, *The Arcades Project*, ed. Rolf Tiedemann, trans. Howard Eiland and Kevin McLaughlin (Cambridge, MA, London, 1999), p. 103.

3 J. M. Barrie, *Peter and Wendy*, in *'Peter Pan in Kensington Gardens'* and 'Peter and Wendy', ed. Peter Hollindale (Oxford, 1999), p. 100.

4 Georges Bataille, 'Dust', in *Encyclopaedia Acephalica*, ed. Alastair Brotchie, trans. Iain White (London, 1995), as cited in Dillon, 'A Dry Black Veil'.

5 Jacques Lacan, 'The Agency of the Letter in the Unconscious, or Reason Since Freud', in *Écrits: A Selection*, trans. Alan Sheridan (New York, 1977), p. 167. See Chapter Two, 'An Alicious Appetite'.

6 Ibid.

7 Roland Barthes, 'An Introduction to the Structural Analysis of Narrative', trans. Lionel Duisit, *New Literary History*, VI/2 (Winter 1975), p. 272. Barthes' observation was first discussed in Chapter One, 'Eating Gold'.

8 Günter Grass, *The Tin Drum*, trans. Ralph Manheim (New York, 1989), p. 63.

9 From personal email correspondence with Briggs, 28 February 2013.

10 Grass, *The Tin Drum*, p. 65.

11 David Whitehouse, 'Models of Invertebrate Animals (1863–1890)', in Susan M. Rossi-Wilcox and David Whitehouse, *Drawing Upon Nature: Studies for the Blaschkas' Glass Models* (Corning, NY, 2007), p. 16.

12 Charles Perrault, 'Cinderella, or The Little Slipper Made of Glass', in *The Complete Fairy Tales*, trans. Christopher Betts (Oxford, 2009), p. 134.

13 Susan M. Rossi-Wilcox and David Whitehouse, 'Preface', in *Drawing Upon Nature*, p. 5.

14 Richard Evans Schultes and William A. Davis with Hillel Burger, *The Glass Flowers at Harvard* (Cambridge, MA, 1992), p. 14.

15 Consider David Constantine's fine story, 'In Another Country', in which 'Katya' is discovered 'fresh' some sixty years later, frozen in the ice, just as she was before when she fell off the steep rocky mountain. 'Still there apparently, just the way she was. Twenty, in the dress of that day and age.' David Constantine, 'In Another Country', in *In Another Country: Selected Stories* (Windsor, Ontario, 2015), p. 14.

16 Hans Christian Andersen, *The Snow Queen*, trans. Tiina Nunnally, ed. Jackie Wullschlager (New York, 2004), p. 177.

17 Ibid., p. 180.

18 See Elizabeth Howie, 'Dogs, Domesticity, and Deviance in the "Storyville Portraits of E. J. Bellocq"', MA thesis, University of North Carolina, Chapel Hill, 2000. Howie accessed this intriguing fact through 'Lee Friedlander, unpublished interview with Joe Sanarens, New Orleans, 1969', Museum of Modern Art (New York), Photography Study Room.

19 Ibid.

20 Lewis Carroll, *Through the Looking-Glass*, in *The Annotated Alice: The Definitive Edition*, introduction and notes by Martin Gardner (New York, 2000), p. 204.

21 Ibid.

22 Ibid.

23 Ibid.

24 Schultes et al., *The Glass Flowers at Harvard*, p. 48.

25 Ibid.

26 Wilhelm Hauff, 'The Tale of Little Mook', in *Little Mook and Dwarf Longnose*, trans. Thomas S. Hansen and Abby Hansen (Boston, MA, 2004), pp. 1–32.

27 Marina Warner, *Stranger Magic: Charmed States and the 'Arabian Nights'* (London, 2011), p. 334.

28 Ibid.

29 Ibid.

30 John Berger, 'Why Look at Animals?', in *About Looking* (New York, 1980), p. 5.

31 Pliny the Elder, *Natural History*, trans. John F. Healey (London, 1991), p. 362.

32 Walter Benjamin, *Berlin Childhood around 1900*, trans. Howard Eiland (Boston, MA, 2006), p. 65.

33 Ibid.

34 Julius Lessing, as quoted in Walter Benjamin, *The Arcades Project*, ed. Rolf Tiedemann, trans. Howard Eiland and Kevin McLaughlin (Cambridge, MA, 1999), p. 184.

35 Isobel Armstrong, *Victorian Glassworlds: Glass Culture and the Imagination, 1830–1880* (Oxford, 2008), p. 207.

36 Perrault, 'Cinderella', trans. Betts, p. 132.

37 Brothers Grimm, 'Cinderella', in *The Original Folk and Fairy Tales of the Brothers Grimm: The Complete First Edition*, trans. and ed. Jack Zipes (Princeton, NJ, and Oxford, 2014), p. 74.

38 Brothers Grimm, 'All Fur', ibid., p. 216.

39 Marcel Proust, *In Search of Lost Time*, vol. VI: *Time Regained*, trans. Andreas Mayor and Terence Kilmartin, revd D. J. Enright (London, 2000), p. 432.

40 Brothers Grimm, 'The Frog King, or Iron Heinrich', in Philip Pullman's *Grimm Tales for Young and Old* (London, 2012), p. 4.

41 Perrault, 'Cinderella', trans. Betts, p. 130.

42 Brothers Grimm, 'Little Snow White', in *The Original Folk and Fairy Tales of the Brothers Grimm*, p. 171.

43 Ibid.

44 Jacques Lacan, 'The Mirror Stage as Formative of the Function of the I as Revealed in Psychoanalytic Experience', in *Écrits: A Selection*, trans. Alan Sheridan (New York, 1977), p. 2.

45 E.T.A. Hoffmann, 'The Sandman', in *The Golden Pot and Other Tales*, trans. Ritchie Robertson (Oxford, 2008), p. 86.

46 Ibid., p. 87

47 Ibid., p. 108.

48 Manuel Rivas, 'Butterfly's Tongue', in *Vermeer's Milkmaid and Other Stories*, trans. Jonathan Dunne (London, 2002), p. 7. The story's ending is disturbing with keen simplicity. The Spanish Civil War is ready to disrupt and the kind teacher is accused of being a criminal and a traitor. As he is carried off with other prisoners in lorries, even the children throw stones at him.

6 Coral Castles

1 Hans Christian Andersen, 'The Littler Mermaid', in *Hans Christian Andersen, Fairy Tales*, trans. Tiina Nunnally, ed. Jackie Wullschlager (New York, 2005), p. 67; emphasis mine.

2 Ibid., p. 80.

3 See Caspar Henderson's fine book *The Book of Barely Imagined Beings: A 21st Century Bestiary* (London, 2012). As Henderson writes: 'I woke with the thought that many real animals are stranger than imaginary ones, and it is our knowledge and understanding that are too cramped and fragmentary to accommodate them: we have *barely imagined* them' (p. x).

4 Marina Warner, *Stranger Magic: Charmed States and the 'Arabian Nights'* (London, 2011), p. 23.

5 Jules Verne, *20,000 Leagues Under the Sea* (New York, 2006), p. 148.

6 *Corallium rubrum* was once called *Gorgonia nobilis* in reference to Medusa, the most famous of the gorgons. In Ovid's *Metamorphoses*, her head turns seaweed into coral. 'The fronds which were fresh and still abundant in spongy pith/ absorbed the force of the Gorgon and hardened under her touch', Ovid, *Metamorphoses*, trans. David Raeburn (London, 2004), p. 168.

7 Ibid., p. 148; emphasis mine.

8 The description of Edward Leedskalnin's Coral Castle (1923–51), which still exists in Florida today, is based on the work of Kristin G. Congdon and Kara Kelley Hallmark, *American Folk Art: A Regional Reference* (Santa Barbara, CA, 2012), p. 227.

9 Ibid., p. 228.

10 As Daniel Moore writes in his review of Stephen Bann's *The Coral Mind*: 'Coral is the best symbol for a method of study based on the organic accretion of material which contributes to a flowering whole, and the corals of eons ago turn into those beds of limestone that Stokes spends so much time discussing in *The Stones of Rimini*'; *Birmingham Journal of Literature and Language*, I/2 (2008), p. 59.

11 Adrian Stokes, *Smooth and Rough* (1951), as quoted in Stephen Bann's 'Introduction' to *The Coral Mind: Adrian Stokes's Engagement with Architecture, Art History, Criticism, and Psychoanalysis*, ed. Bann (University Park, PA, 2007), pp. 1, 11.

12 Verne, *20,000 Leagues Under the Sea*, p. 150.

13 Ibid., p. 149.

7 Marvellous Middleness, in Seven Parts

1 Charles Perrault, 'Cinderella, or The Little Slipper Made of Glass', in *The Complete Fairy Tales*, trans. Christopher Betts (Oxford, 2009), p. 132.

2 Judith Thurman, 'First Impressions: What Does the World's Oldest Art Say about Us?', *New Yorker*, www.newyorker.com, 23 June 2008. Thurman's fine essay was the inspiration for Werner Herzog's 2013 film *Cave of Forgotten Dreams*.

3 My long-time engagement with the work of Esther Teichmann has been especially influential on *Aurelia*, most especially this chapter. See Teichmann's *Falling into Photography: On Loss, Desire, and the Photographic* (London, forthcoming), a two-volume edition of writing and images, which cascade into sleep, shells and darkrooms.

4 Lewis Carroll, *The Annotated Alice: The Definitive Edition*, introduction and notes by Martin Gardner (New York, 2000), p. 11.

5 Ibid., p. 13.

6 Jean-Luc Nancy, *The Fall of Sleep*, trans. Charlotte Mandell (New York, 2007), p. 1.

7 Charlotte Mandell, 'Translator's Note', ibid., p. ix.

8 Nancy, *The Fall of Sleep*, p. 41.

9 Brothers Grimm, 'Snow White', in Philip Pullman, *Grimm Tales for Young and Old* (London, 2012), p. 217.

10 Nancy, *The Fall of Sleep*, pp. 4, 8–9.

11 Ovid, *Metamorphoses*, trans. David Raeburn (London, 2004), p. 453.

12 Nancy, *The Fall of Sleep*, p. 4.

13 Jean-Luc Nancy, *Tombe de sommeil* (Paris, 2007), p. 4.

14 Of interest: the word 'dormouse' is used as an attribute of sleepiness, as in Shakespeare's *Twelfth Night* when Fabian says: 'To awake your dormouse valour'.

15 Pascal Quignard, *La Haine de la musique* (Paris, 1996), p. 107, as quoted by Jean-Luc Nancy, *Listening*, trans. Charlotte Mandell (New York, 2007), p. 14.

16 Nancy, *The Fall of Sleep*, p. 9.

17 Roland Barthes, 'Leaving the Movie Theater', in *The Rustle of Language*, trans. Richard Howard (New York, 1986), p. 346.

18 Ibid.

19 See Axel Hoedt, *Once a Year* (Göttingen, 2013).

20 Carroll, *The Annotated Alice*, p. 63.

21 Nancy, *The Fall of Sleep*, p. 6.

22 Matisse made the cutouts during the final fifteen years of his life.

23 Karl Buchberg, Nicholas Cullinan, Jodi Hauptman and Nicholas Serota, 'The Studio as Site and Subject', in *Henri Matisse: The Cut-outs* (London, 2014), p. 15.

24 Gaston Bachelard, quoting Valéry, *The Poetics of Space*, trans. Maria Jolas (Boston, MA, 1994), p. 106.

25 Buchberg et al., 'The Studio as Site and Subject', p. 11.

26 Proust called the glued-in extensions added to the manuscript of *In Search of Lost Time*, which were folded accordion-style into the pages of the book, reaching up to four feet in length, his *paperies*.

27 Carroll, *The Annotated Alice*, p. 213.

28 Buchberg et al., 'The Studio as Site and Subject', p. 12.

29 Ibid.

30 Jodi Hauptman, 'Inventing a New Operation', in *Henri Matisse: The Cut-outs*, p. 267, note 14.

31 Buchberg et al., 'The Studio as Site and Subject', p. 14.

32 Ibid., p. 266, note 14. The description is a quote from Matisse's studio assistant Hilary Spurling.

33 The various translation and additions to the *Arabian Nights* are a tangled affair, far beyond my education and scope. An excellent study and introduction to the tales has been painstakingly researched and provided by Marina Warner in *Stranger Magic: Charmed States and the 'Arabian Nights'* (London, 2011). As she writes of the *Arabian Nights*: 'From its first appearance in print, between 1704 and 1721, in the French translation of Antoine Galland, the tales mirrored Arab civilisation and *mentalité* for the West, but at the same time communicated a fantastic dream of Araby', p. 20.

34 *The Arabian Nights: Tales of 1001 Nights*, vol. 1: *Nights 1 to 294*, trans. Malcolm C. Lyons with Ursula Lyons (London, 2010), p. 22.

35 A vizier is a high state official in the Turkish empire, Persia and certain other Muslim countries.

36 *The Arabian Nights*, the story told before the stories of the 'Nights' begin, p. 7.

37 Ibid., p. 10.

38 Marina Warner, *Stranger Magic*, p. 2.

39 Nicholas Cullinan, '"An Agreeable Distraction": The Early Reception of Matisse's Cut-outs', in *Henri Matisse: The Cut-outs*, p. 25.

40 T. J. Clark, 'The Urge to Strangle', review of *Henri Matisse: The Cut-outs*, *London Review of Books*, XXXVI/11 (15 June 2014), accessed online, www.lrb.co.uk, 13 March 2015.

41 Marina Warner, *Fantastic Metamorphoses, Other Worlds* (Oxford, 2002), p. 50.

42 Marina Warner's term for Bosch's play with orb/world/eye, ibid., p. 50.

43 Ibid., p. 44.

44 Roland Barthes, 'The Metaphor of the Eye', in *Roland Barthes: Critical Essays*, trans. Richard Howard (Evanston, IL, 1972), p. 245.

45 Ibid.

46 Angela Carter, *The Second Virago Book of Fairy Tales* (London, 1992), p. xi, as discussed in this book's Introduction.

47 Jack Zipes, 'Once there were Two Brothers Named Grimm', in *Brothers Grimm: The Complete Fairy Tales*, trans., introduced and annotated by Zipes (London, 2007), p. xxxv.

48 Nancy, *Listening*, quoting Bernard Baas, p. 28.

49 Ibid., p. 27.

50 Ibid., p. 37.

51 The discovery of the hole leading to the beguiling frescoes of Lascaux, as is recounted by Norbert Aujoulat, a renowned expert on Lascaux, turns on the four boys unblocking a fox's earth. After enlarging the passage, they throw a stone into the narrow hole they have made. It rolls for quite a long time, indicating that the hole is very deep. After much discussion and hesitation, it is Ravidat who decides to cross this first obstruction. See Aujoulat's *The Splendour of Lascaux: Rediscovering the Greatest Treasure of Prehistoric Art*, trans. Martin Street (London, 2005), p. 266.

52 Guy Davenport, 'Robot', in *The Guy Davenport Reader* (Berkeley, CA, 2013), p. 8.

53 Ibid., p. 9.

54 Ibid., p. 11.

55 Ibid., p. 14.

56 Georges Bataille, *Prehistoric Painting: Lascaux; or The Birth of Art*, trans. Austryn Wainhouse (Geneva, 1955).

57 Georges Bataille, 'Lecture, January 18, 1955', in *The Cradle of Humanity: Prehistoric Art and Culture*, ed. Stuart Kendell, trans Michelle Kendell and Stuart Kendell (New York, 2005), p. 93.

58 André Breton, 'First Manifesto of Surrealism' [1924], in *Manifestoes of Surrealism,* trans. H. R. Lane and R. Seaven (Ann Arbor, MI, 1972), p. 14.

59 Bataille, 'Lecture', p. 95.

60 Ibid., p. 96.

61 Ibid.

62 Ibid., p. 95.

63 Ibid., p. 96.

64 Brothers Grimm, 'The Golden Key', in *The Original Folk and Fairy Tales of the Brothers Grimm: The Complete First Edition*, trans. and ed. Jack Zipes (Princeton, NJ, and Oxford, 2014), p. 473.

65 Judith Thurman, 'First Impressions: What does the World's Oldest Art Say about Us?', *New Yorker*, 23 June 2008.

66 Bataille, 'Lecture', p. 102.

67 Brothers Grimm, 'The Worn-out Dancing Shoes', in *The Original Folk and Fairy Tales of the Brothers Grimm*, p. 433.

68 Italo Calvino, *Italian Folktales*, trans. George Martin (London, 2000), p. 446.

69 Ibid., p. 447.

70 Ibid.

71 Calvino, introduction to *Italian Folktales*, p. xxxi.

72 Bataille, 'Lecture', p. 101.

73 Pavel Petrovich Bazhov, 'The Mistress of the Copper Mountain', trans. Anna Gunin, in *Russian Magic Tales from Pushkin to Platonov*, ed. Robert Chandler (London, 2012), p. 231. I am indebted to the poet Rebecca Hurst for opening up the work of Bazhov and his use of the underground as a place of both magic and refuge.

74 Robert Chandler, 'Pavel Petrovich Bazhov (1879–1950)', in *Russian Magic Tales from Pushkin to Platonov*, p. 222.

75 Ibid.

76 Ibid.

77 This is what Bazhov reportedly said to a friend according to Chandler, ibid.

78 Aujoulat, *The Splendour of Lascaux*, p. 267.

79 Ibid., p. 257.

80 Jean Clottes, *Cave Art* (London, 2008), p. 106.

81 Jean Clottes working from the observations of Norbert Aujoulat, in *Cave Art*, p. 109; see Aujoulat, *The Splendour of Lascaux*, p. 90.

82 Aujoulat, *The Splendour of Lascaux*, p. 90.

83 As is the case in other caves, like Chauvet, the artist used his or her mouth to paint: Clottes, *Cave Art*, p. 17.

84 John Berger, 'Past and Present', *The Guardian*, 12 October 2002.

85 Abbé Breuil, as quoted in Clottes, *Cave Art*, p. 106.

86 Nancy, *The Fall of Sleep*, p. 45.

87 Ajoulat, *The Splendour of Lascaux*, p. 268.

88 Nancy, *The Fall of Sleep*, p. 30.

89 Ibid., p. 6.

90 Ibid., p. 7 and throughout.

91 Ibid., p. 11.

92 Ibid., pp. 17–18.

8 De-windowing: Bernard Faucon's Land of Boys

1 Jean-Luc Monterosso, 'Bernard Faucon', in *Encyclopedia of Twentieth Century Photography*, ed. Lynne Warren (New York and London, 2006).

2 Roland Barthes, 'Bernard Faucon', in *Oeuvres complètes*, vol. v: *1977–80*, ed. Éric Marty (Paris, 2002), p. 472.

3 Guy Davenport, 'Robot', in *The Guy Davenport Reader* (Berkeley, CA, 2013), p. 963.

4 Barthes, 'Bernard Faucon', p. 474.

5 For a closer look at the 'marvellous', as embraced by both Surrealism and the fairy tales, see Chapter Seven, 'Marvellous Middleness'.

6 Brothers Grimm, 'Briar Rose', in *The Original Folk and Fairy Tales of the Brothers Grimm: The Complete First Edition*, trans. and ed. Jack Zipes (Princeton, NJ, and Oxford, 2014), p. 164.

7 André Breton, 'First Manifesto of Surrealism' [1924], in *Manifestoes of Surrealism*, trans. H. R. Lane and R. Seaver (Ann Arbor, MI, 1972), p. 16.

8 See Rosalind E. Krauss, 'Yo-yo', in Yve-Alain Bois and Rosalind E. Krauss, *Formless: A User's Guide* (New York, 1999), pp. 219–23.

9 Baudelaire's 1853 essay 'La Morale du joujou' (The Philosophy of Toys) chooses 'not *jouet*, the usual words for toy', but rather an 'almost pet name with a nursery ring . . . its repetition hints at baby talk and hence at playing'. Marina Warner, 'Out of an Old Toy Chest', *Journal of Aesthetic Education*, XLIII/2 (Summer 2009), p. 3. In other words *joujou*, like 'mama' and 'papa', grows out of reduplicating sounds.

10 Guy Davenport, 'The Illuminations of Bernard Faucon and Anthony Goicolea', *Georgia Review*, LVI/4 (Winter 2002), p. 973. Davenport notes that his perspective is supported by Kristen Ross's study of the new, clean, post-war, Structuralist France. See her fine book *Fast Cars, Clean Bodies: Decolonization and the Reordering of French Culture* (Cambridge, MA, 1996).

11 Davenport, 'The Illuminations of Bernard Faucon and Anthony Goicolea', p. 973.

12 The notion of the 'sartorial ego' comes from Joan Copjec. See her chapter on the photographs of G. G. de Clérambault entitled 'The Sartorial Superego', in *Read My Desire: Lacan Against the Historicists* (Cambridge, MA, 1994), pp. 65–116.

13 Davenport, 'The Illuminations of Bernard Faucon and Anthony Goicolea', p. 973.

14 Roland Barthes, *Sollers Writer*, trans. and introduced by Philip Thody (London, 1987), p. 77.

15 Davenport, 'The Illuminations of Bernard Faucon and Anthony Goicolea', p. 961.

16 Ibid., p. 961; emphasis mine.

17 Roland Barthes, 'Ornamental Cookery', in *Mythologies*, selected and trans. Annette Lavers (London, 1972), p. 78. In *Mythologies*, Barthes has a field day with post-war culture. His book features essays that centre on 1950s consumerist myths, with titles such as 'Soap-powders and Detergents', 'Operation Margarine', 'The Jet-man', 'Toys', 'Plastic', 'The New Citroën' and 'Ornamental Cookery'.

18   Ibid.

19   Readers will recall that Pinocchio goes to the 'Land of Toys', where he ends up sprouting donkey ears. Barthes, 'Ornamental Cookery', p. 79.

20   Ibid., pp. 79–80

21   The term *eatingmagination* is discussed in this book's Introduction, 'I Am An Aurelian'.

22   Davenport, 'The Illuminations of Bernard Faucon and Anthony Goicolea', p. 973.

23   The story is told on Faucon's website, in French and English. In the English translation of Faucon's setting up of the manikins, the term *dévitrinés* is not used or translated. In the original French he writes: 'Je fixais en hâte les poses, après le déclic, je remballais tout, je repartais. Je devinais que ces petits hommes «dévitrinés», en investissant ces lieux marqués par mon enfance libéraient des forces inconnues, mettaient à jour de sublimes, de magistrales évidences.'

24   Brian Nelson, 'Introduction', in Émile Zola, *The Ladies Paradise* (Oxford, 2012), p. xii.

25   Kristen Ross, 'Introduction: Shopping', in Émile Zola, *The Ladies' Paradise* (Berkeley, CA, 1992), pp. vi–vii.

26   Lewis Carroll, *Through the Looking-Glass,* in *The Annotated Alice: The Definitive Edition,* introduction and notes by Martin Gardner (New York, 2000), p. 20.

27   Nelson, 'Introduction', p. xii.

28   Stuart Culver, 'What Manikins Want: *The Wonderful Wizard of Oz* and *The Art of Decorating Dry Goods Windows*', *Representations*, 21 (Winter 1988), p. 97.

29   Frank L. Baum, *The Annotated Wizard of Oz*, ed. with an introduction and notes by Michael Patrick Hearn (London, 2000), p. 88, note 2.

30   Gene Moore and Jay Hyams, *My Time at Tiffany's* (New York, 1990), p. 40.

31   Ibid.

32   Bernard Faucon, *Table d'amis: vingt-et-un menus de Bernard Faucon* (Paris, 1991), p. 62.

33   Faucon, as quoted by Adam D. Weinberg in his essay 'Bernard Faucon', in *Cross-references: Sculpture into Photography* (Minneapolis, MN, 1987), p. 18.

34   Roland Barthes, *Camera Lucida: Reflections on Photography*, trans. Richard Howard (New York, 1981), p. 91.

35   Roland Barthes, *A Lover's Discourse: Fragments*, trans. Richard Howard (New York, 1978), p. 38.

36   Ibid., p. 39.

37   Barthes, 'On Leaving the Movie Theatre', in *The Rustle of Language*, trans. Richard Howard (New York, 1987), p. 346. This passage from Barthes was first discussed in Chapter Seven, 'Marvellous Middleness'.

38   Vladimir Nabokov, 'From Nabokov's Cornell Lectures, March 1951', in *Nabokov's Butterflies: Unpublished and Uncollected Writings*, ed. and annotated by Brian Boyd and Robert Michael Pyle, with new translations by Dmitri Nabokov (Boston, MA, 2000), p. 473.

39   From the untitled and very poetic series of fragments that begins Bernard Faucon's *Bernard Faucon* (Paris, 2005), p. 23. Translation is the author's.

40   Carlo Collodi, *The Adventures of Pinocchio*, trans. Ann Lawson Lucas (Oxford, 1996), p. 2.

41 Ibid., pp. 2, 3.

42 Lee Kogan, 'Folk Art Viewpoint', in *Family Found: The Lifetime Obsession of Morton Bartlett*, ed. Marion Harris (New York, 2002), p. 34.

43 D. W. Winnicott, 'Transitional Objects and Transitional Phenomena', in *Playing and Reality* (New York, 1989), p. 18.

44 Roland Barthes, *Roland Barthes by Roland Barthes*, trans. Richard Howard (New York, 2010); this phrase is the caption that Barthes gives to a photograph of himself (as an adolescent), his mother and his younger brother at the start of the book. The opening images to the book are without page numbers.

45 Davenport, 'The Illuminations of Bernard Fancon and Antohny Goicolea', p. 971.

46 Ibid.

47 Roland Barthes, 'Dare to Be Lazy', in *The Grain of the Voice: Interviews, 1962–1980*, trans. Linda Coverdale (Berkeley and Los Angeles, CA, 1991), pp. 340–41.

48 Frank Baum, *The Land of Oz* (New York, 1979). See also Stuart Culver, 'Growing Up in Oz', *American Literary History*, IV/4 (Winter 1992), p. 609.

49 Edmund White, 'From Albert Camus to Roland Barthes', *New York Times*, 12 September 1982, Book Review, sec. 7, p. 1.

50 Ibid.

51 Barthes, 'Bernard Faucon', p. 471.

52 After stopping photography, Faucon turned to other projects, such as *The Happiest Day of My Youth* (1997–2003), where he organized one-day celebrations around the world in which young people were given their own disposable cameras to take their own festive photographs.

53 J. M. Barrie, *Peter and Wendy*, intro. and notes by Peter Hollindale (Oxford, 1991), p. 226.

54 This story of skin is on Bernard Faucon's official and very beautiful website: www.bernardfaucon.net, accessed 18 May 2016.

9 Tragic Candyland: Minou Drouet

1 Roland Barthes, 'Myth Today', in *Mythologies*, selected and trans. Annette Lavers (London, 1972), p. 57.

2 Vladimir Nabokov, *Lolita: The Annotated Lolita*, ed. Alfred Appel Jr (New York, 1977), p. 133.

3 Simone de Beauvoir, 'Brigitte Bardot and the Lolita Syndrome' [1959], in *Rosemarie Trockel*, ed. Elizabeth Sussman and Sidra Stich (New York, 1991), p. 55.

4 Ibid., p. 54.

5 James Kincaid, 'Dreaming the Past', paper presented at the University of North Carolina, Chapel Hill, 24 April 1993.

6 Barthes' attachment to the concept of neither-norness is was introduced in this book's Chapter Eight, 'De-windowing: Bernard Faucon's Land of Boys'.

7 Barthes, 'Myth Today', p. 109.

8 Roland Barthes, 'Preface to the 1970 edition', in *Mythologies*, p. 9; Barthes, 'Myth Today', p. 149.

9 The term 'nymphancy' is Nabokov's, as used in *Lolita*, p. 224.

10 In the more recent 2012 English translation, *Mythologies: The Complete Edition*, trans. Richard Howard and Annette Lavers, Barthes' essay 'Literature According to Minou Drouet' is now included (New York, 2012), pp. 172–80. The essay first appeared in English in *Roland Barthes: The Eiffel Tower and Other Mythologies*, trans. Richard Howard (New York, 1979), pp. 111–18.

11 Robert Gottlieb, 'A Lost Child: The Strange Case of Minou Drouet', *New Yorker*, 6 November 2006, p. 70.

12 Jean-Max Tixier, 'Notes', in *Minou Drouet: Ma vérité* (Paris, 1993), p. 14.

13 Sarah Shun-Lien Bynum, *Madeleine is Sleeping* (New York, 2004), p. 72.

14 Richard Howard, 'Childhood Amnesia', *Yale French Studies*, 43 (1969), p. 165.

15 Roland Barthes, *A Lover's Discourse: Fragments*, trans. Richard Howard (New York, 1978), p. 38.

16 Charles Templeton, *An Anecdotal Memoir* (Toronto, 1983), p. 111.

17 Gottlieb, 'A Lost Child', p. 73.

18 This proclamation of Kincaid's was first discussed in Chapter Three, 'A Raindrop Unfallen'.

19 Minou Drouet to Yves Nat, letter in *First Poems*, trans. Margaret Crossland (London, 1956), p. 67.

20 Eve Kosofsky Sedgwick, 'A Poem is Being Written', in *Tendencies* (Durham, NC, 1993), p. 182.

21 Drouet to Nat, letter in *First Poems*, p. 67.

22 Bellmer took the picture in 1935 and then had it hand-coloured in 1949. See Sue Taylor, *The Anatomy of Anxiety* (Cambridge, MA, 2002), pp. 78, 204.

23 Minou Drouet, 'Photographie', in *Le Pêcheur de lune* (Paris, 1959), p. 79 ('Je ne vous avais apporté / qu'un si laid visage, / un nez pour téléphoner / aux nuages'). Translation mine.

24 Gottlieb, 'A Lost Child', p. 76.

25 Minou Drouet, 'Tree that I Love', in *First Poems*, p. 3.

26 Barthes, 'Myth Today', p. 109.

27 'Books: Kitten on the Keys', *Time*, 28 January 1957.

28 Templeton, *An Anecdotal Memoir*, p. 112.

29 Gottlieb, 'A Lost Child', p. 72.

30 Minou Drouet, 'Ciel de Paris', in *Le Pêcheur de lune*, p. 27 ('Ciel de Paris, / poids, / secret, / chair, / qui, par hoquets, / crache à nos faces / par la gueule ouverte des rangées de maisons / un jet de sang entre ses chicots lumineux . . .'). Translation mine.

31 Roland Barthes, 'Literature According to Minou Drouet', in *Mythologies: The Complete Edition*, p. 172. As stated earlier, the essay was cut from the first English translation of *Mythologies*, but it does reappear here in the 2012 translation.

32 Minou Drouet, 'The Watch', in *Le Pêcheur de lune*, 32.

33 Roland Barthes, 'Literature According to Minou Drouet', pp. 173, 175, 177.

34 Howard, 'Childhood Amnesia', p. 166.

35 Minou Drouet, 'The Watch', in *Then There Was Fire: Further Poems by Minou Drouet* (London, 1957), p. 32.

36 Roland Barthes, *The Neutral: Lecture Course at the Collège de France* [1977–8], trans. Rosalind Krauss and Denis Hollier (New York, 2005), p. 153.

37 Barthes, 'Literature According to Minou Drouet', p. 179.

38 Roland Barthes, *Camera Lucida: Reflections on Photography*, trans. Richard Howard (New York, 1981), p. 96.

10 What is Black and White and Red All Over? Answer: The Photographs of Ralph Eugene Meatyard

 1 Hans Christian Andersen, *Fairy Tales*, trans. Tiina Nunnally, ed. Jackie Wullschlager (New York, 2004), pp. 210–11.

 2 Years ago, Amy Ruth Buchanan was an undergraduate student of mine and wrote a first-rate dissertation on Meatyard. The photographer was unknown to me at that time. Buchanan's writing and analyses had a profound effect on me that can still be felt in this chapter. I am indebted to her scholarship and insights.

 3 Philip Pullman, 'Introduction' to *Grimm Tales for Young and Old* (London, 2012), p. xvi.

 4 Eugenia Parry, 'Forager', in *Ralph Eugene Meatyard: Dolls and Masks* (Santa Fe, CA, 2011), p. 14.

 5 Brothers Grimm, 'Rumpelstiltskin', as collected in Pullman, *Grimm Tales for Young and Old*, p. 223.

 6 The comparison between Meatyard's photograph and Cassavetes's film is suggested by Judith Kellner in her *Ralph Eugene Meatyard* (London and New York, 2002), p. 48.

 7 Parry, 'Forager', p. 10.

 8 Alison and Helmut Gernsheim, *The History of Photography* (Oxford, 1955), p. 258. For an excellent analysis of the concept of the culinary appetite of the photographing eye, see Olivier Richon's 'A Devouring Eye', in *Olivier Richon: Fotografie 1989–2004* (Milan, 2004), pp. 25–33.

 9 Ibid., p. 48.

10 Grimm, 'Snow White', as collected in *Brothers Grimm: The Complete Fairy Tales*, trans., introduced and annotated by Jack Zipes (London, 1992), p. 238.

11 See Linda Siede, 'Jan van Eyck's *Arnolfini Portrait*: Business as Usual?', *Critical Inquiry*, CLXI/1 (Autumn 1989), pp. 54–86. The comparison between Meatyard's photograph and the *Arnolfini Portrait* is suggested by Kellner, *Ralph Eugene Meatyard*, p. 28.

12 This is Mary Kelly's phrase that she uses to speak of the unseen presence of woman in her work, in an interview with Hal Foster entitled 'That Obscure Subject of Desire', *Interim*, exh. cat., New Museum of Contemporary Art, New York (New York, 1980), p. 55.

13 Kellner, *Ralph Eugene Meatyard*, p. 52.

14 Pullman, 'Introduction', in *Grimm Tales*, p. iv.

15 Ibid.

16 Ibid.

17 Derek Jarman, *Chroma: A Book of Colour – June '93* (London, 2000), p. 37.

18 Edward Steichen, *The Family of Man* (New York, 1955), p. 3; Roland Barthes, *Mythologies*, selected and trans. Annette Lavers (London, 1972), p. 101.

11 Dreaming Brown with Langston Hughes

1 This phrase belongs to the photography theorist Peter Wollen.

2 Sally Mann, *Deep South* (New York, Boston and London, 2005), pp. 50–52.

3 José Esteban Muñoz, 'Feeling Brown, Feeling Down: Latina Affect, the Performativity of Race and the Depressive Position', *Signs*, XXXI/3 (Spring 2006), p. 687.

4 *Nabokov's Butterflies: Unpublished and Uncollected Writings*, ed. and annotated by Brian Boyd and Robert Michael Pyle, with new translations by Dmitri Nabokov (Boston, MA, 2000), p. 473.

5 Toni Morrison, *The Bluest Eye* (New York, 1993), p. 58.

6 Roy De Carava and Langston Hughes, *The Sweet Flypaper of Life* (Washington, DC, 1984), p. 106. The book was originally published in 1955.

7 See Arnold Rampersad's vivid description of the garden in his *The Life of Langston Hughes*, vol. II: *1941–1967, I Dream a World* (Oxford and New York, 2002), p. 242.

8 Langston Hughes, 'Suicide's Note', in *The Collected Poems of Langston Hughes*, ed. Arnold Rampersad (New York, 1995), p. 55.

9 Along with Augustus Granville Dill as business manager and Jessie Fauset as literary editor.

10 Michael Schmidt, *The Novel: A Biography* (Cambridge, MA, and London, 2014), p. 950.

11 The idea for the magazine was 'expressed first in the pages of *The Crisis*, the official magazine of the National Association for the Advancement of Colored People, which W.E.B. Du Bois edited from 1910–1936'. See Dianne Johnson-Feelings, ed., *The Best of the Brownies' Book* (Oxford, 1996), p. 12.

12 Langston Hughes, 'Fairies', in *The Collected Poems*, p. 597.

13 Roland Barthes, 'Myth Today', in *Mythologies*, selected and trans. Annette Lavers (London, 1972), n. 29, p. 157. Here Barthes is speaking about the child-poet Minou Drouet (see Chapter Nine, 'Tragic Candyland'), who was both idealized and victimized by French culture and the media. Under the 'myth' of Drouet lies 'something like a tender open possibility'; Barthes is providing here the utopian hope of 'the child'.

14 Langston Hughes, 'The Dream Keeper', in *The Collected Poems*, p. 45.

15 Langston Hughes, 'Winter Sweetness', in *The Collected Poems*, p. 597.

16 Dianne Johnson, 'Introduction', in *The Collected Works of Langston Hughes: Works for Children and Young Adults: Poetry, Fiction, and Other Writing*, ed. Dianne Johnson (Columbia, NY, and London, 2003), p. 6.

17 Ibid.

18 Jacqueline Rose, *The Case of Peter Pan, or The Impossibility of Children's Fiction* (Philadelphia, PA, 1993), p. 2.

Conclusion: Full Stop

1   From a conversation between the author and the artist.
2   Elizabeth Smart, *By Grand Central Station I Sat Down and Wept* (London, 2015), p. ix.

ACKNOWLEDGEMENTS

Special thanks to Jane Blocker, Jonny Briggs, Alison Connolly, Alison Criddle, Teresa de Lauretis, Annabel Dover, Page duBois, Susannah Farrell, Bernard Faucon, Vona Groarke, Stella Halkyard, Elizabeth Howie, Rebecca Hurst, Sarah Jones, Wendy Ligon-Smith, John McAuliffe, Ambrose Mavor-Parker, Augustine Mavor-Parker, Oliver Mavor-Parker, Helene Moglen, Megan Powell, Sophie Preston, Olivier Richon, Michael Schmidt, Hazel Shaw, Hayden White, Ken Wissoker and all of my lovely students in 'Fairy Tales and Other Utopias' over the years. And another 'ta' to Ali Criddle: she has nourished this book with so many golden helpings that one thank you is simply not enough. Seedcorn funding from The John Rylands Library, University of Manchester, provided access to golden books of hours and glass-plate photographs. This book began when Ranji Khanna and I were in a tight-knit writing group of just two. Brian Dillon has long enabled me to see the magic in things as mundane as dust. Sina Najafi has enabled my enchantments with glass and bubbles and much more. For his tender-biting work on Joseph Cornell, Michael Moon invented the word 'oralia', which has kept me thinking for years. I thank elin o'Hara slavick for showing me so many enchanted images over the years (many of which are her own) and for arranging our special visit to Bernard Faucon's house in Paris, where he showered us with gifts, edible and non-edible. José Esteban Muñoz – the brown dream is for you. Amy Ruth Buchanan is my constant companion with every word I write, even if she lives very far away from my island: I aim to please her. I eat up art through the streets of London, guided by one of the most marvellous artists I know: Esther Teichmann. Marina Warner, the great mythographer of our time, has taught me more than I can remember. Furthermore, she has genially believed in me for many, many years: this has left me feeling no less than magical. Very special thanks to Michael Leaman, who planted the golden seed. I am very grateful to Aimee Selby, the sensitive copyeditor who corrected and polished the text with help from the managing editor, Martha Jay. I shared a butterfly net with Susannah Jayes for capturing many of the images. The gifted designer of this book is Simon McFadden and I thank him for the fairy dust that made *Aurelia* fly. A very belated thanks to Allan Kaprow, who informed me (so many years ago) that I wanted to write a book about Alice and fairy tales, and he was right (even if I did not know it then). And to my father, who taught me to read and patiently listened while I read *Alice's Adventures in Wonderland* aloud to him. (And, who also let me bring home a little black rabbit given to me by a magician by the name of the Great Toussaint.) And most of all thanks to Kevin Parker and our fairy-tale time at Rose Cottage, under the reign of Romeo, next to the cave with the big mouth and under the shadow of the castle.

LIST OF ILLUSTRATIONS

Repertory Theater stage production of *Alice in Wonderland*, 1947.

p. 114 Postcard to advertise *Alice Malice*, performance by Carol Mavor, San Diego, California, 8 June 1984. Author's private collection.

p. 116 (top and bottom) Jean-Pierre Gorin, stills from the film *Poto and Cabengo* (1980). Zweites Deutsches Fernsehen (ZDF) and Jean-Pierre Gorin.

p. 119 Bernard Faucon, *Untitled*, 2009, soap bubble photograph, from the book *Eté 2550* (Arles, 2009). Courtesy of the artist.

p. 120 Carl Durheim, *Untitled* (post-mortem photograph of a child), *c.* 1852, hand-coloured daguerreotype. Getty Center, Los Angeles.

p. 125 Jean-Pierre Gorin, from the film *Poto and Cabengo* (1980). Zweites Deutsches Fernsehen (ZDF) and Jean-Pierre Gorin.

p. 126 Jonny Briggs, *First Shoe*, 2011, object made of glass. Courtesy of the artist.

p. 129 Kiki Smith, *Glass Stomach*, 1985, glass. Photo Ellen Labenski. © Kiki Smith, courtesy Pace Gallery.

p. 130 Kiki Smith, *Untitled*, 1988-90 (detail), 230 cast-glass pieces (sperm), each 6–8" long, on three rubber sheets; The Museum of Contemporary Art, Los Angeles. © Kiki Smith, courtesy Pace Gallery.

p. 132 Robert Gober, *Untitled*, 1992, child's shoe made of beeswax and human hair. Digital Image © The Museum of Modern Art, New York/Scala, Florence, 2016.

p. 134 Sean Graff, *Untitled* (boy under glass), 1997, photograph. Courtesy of the artist.

p. 136 Leopold and Rudolf Blaschka, *Athecate Hydroid*, *c.* 1886–1936, glass. Photo Zeke Smith, 2016. Harvard Museum of Natural History.

p. 137 Leopold and Rudolf Blaschka, *Hepatica trilbola*, *c.* 1886–1936, glass. Harvard Museum of Natural History.

p. 138 Loading the glass flowers into two hearses in front of the Botanical Museum for the 1976 Steuben Glass exhibition.

p. 140 Unknown photographer, from Langford Brooke's collection of family photographs,

c. 1900, glass plate negative. John Rylands Special Collections, University of Manchester.

p. 141 *Amorphophallus titanium*, 'corpse flower', photographic documentation of a bloom. Huntington Botanical Gardens, San Marino.

p. 142 Leopold and Rudolf Blaschka, *Pitcher Plants (Nepenthes sanguinea)*, *c.* 1886–1936, glass. Harvard Museum of Natural History.

p. 143 Mojaris, India, 1790–1890, leather, embroidered with gold thread and encrusted with emeralds, rubies, sapphires and diamonds. Courtesy of the Bata Shoe Museum, Toronto.

p. 147 Studio Van Eijk and Van der Lubbe, *Moulded Mole*, 2004, size 32 shoes made from moles. Courtesy of the artists.

p. 148 Francesca Woodman, *Untitled*, 1979, photograph. Courtesy of George and Betty Woodman.

p. 150 Megan Powell, 'Untitled (number 11)', from the series *Portals*, 2014, photograph. Courtesy of the artist.

p. 153 Francesca Woodman, *Talking to Vince* (self-portrait), 1975–8, photograph. Courtesy of George and Betty Woodman.

p. 154 Leopold and Rudolf Blaschka, *Corallium rubrum*, 1879, glass. Harvard Museum of Natural History.

p. 158 Esther Teichmann, *Coral Castle*, 2014 (built by Edward Leedskalnin, 1923–51), fibre-based silver gelatin print Courtesy of the artist.

p. 160 Esther Teichmann, 'Untitled', from the series *Fractal Scars, Salt Water and Tears*, 2014, fibre-based silver gelatin print. Courtesy of the artist.

p. 164 Axel Hoedt, 'Bear', Sachsenheim, Germany, 2013, photograph, from the series *Once A Year*. Courtesy of the artist.

p. 165 Axel Hoedt, 'Stork', Endingen, Germany, 2013, photograph, from the series *Once A Year*. Courtesy of the artist.

p. 166 Axel Hoedt, 'Leading a Branch Bear', Empfingen, Germany, 2013, photograph, from the series *Once A Year*. Courtesy of the artist.

pp. 167–8 Axel Hoedt, *Cat*, Messkirch, Germany, 2013, photograph, from the series *Once A Year*. Courtesy of the artist.

(The Fourteenth Room of Love: The Snowstorm), 1985, photograph. Courtesy of the artist.

p. 223 Bernard Faucon, *Ronde de jour* (Ring de jour), 1978, photograph. Courtesy of the artist.

p. 224 Bernard Faucon, *Le Depart* (The Departure), 1978, photograph. Courtesy of the artist.

p. 227 Morton Bartlett, *Sitting Boy*, *c.* 1943-63, photograph of doll made by Bartlett sitting in a chair. Marion Harris, New York.

p. 228 Morton Bartlett, *Handmade Clothes*, *c.* 1943–63, fabric, thread, yarn and buttons. Marion Harris, New York.

p. 231 Bernard Faucon, *Les Fils de laine* (Threads of Wool), 1979, photograph. Courtesy of the artist.

p. 233 Carol Mavor, *Untitled* (at Faucon's House), 2014, photograph. Author's private collection.

p. 235 Bernard Faucon, *Fin* (The End), 1994, photograph. Courtesy of the artist.

p. 236 Minou Drouet, *c.* 1956, photograph by Roger Hauert.

p. 241 Hans Bellmer, *La Poupée* (The Doll), 1935, hand-coloured black-and-white photograph. © ADAGP, Paris, and DACS, London, 2016.

p. 244 Minou Drouet, *c.* 1956, photograph by Roger Hauert.

p. 245 Joseph Cornell, *The Crystal Cage* (*Portrait of Berenice*) (detail), 1943, calligram: photomontage and text as published in the magazine View, January 1943. © The Joseph and Robert Cornell Memorial Foundation/ VAGA, NY/DACS, London, 2016.

p. 247 Hans Bellmer, *La Poupée* (The Doll), 1934, photograph. © ADAGP, Paris, and DACS, London, 2016.

p. 250 Ralph Eugene Meatyard, *Untitled* (child with dead leaves, mask and doll), 1959, photograph. Fraenkel Gallery, San Francisco.

p. 254 Ralph Eugene Meatyard, *Untitled* (two dolls, one headless), *c.* 1959, photograph. Fraenkel Gallery, San Francisco.

p. 255 Ralph Eugene Meatyard, *Untitled* (Cranston Ritchie with mirror and dress-maker's manikin), *c.* 1958–9, photograph. Fraenkel Gallery, San Francisco.

p. 258 Ralph Eugene Meatyard, *Lucybelle Crater*, 1970–72, photograph. Fraenkel Gallery, San Francisco.

p. 260 Ralph Eugene Meatyard, *Untitled* (Michael with 'red' sign), 1960, photograph. Fraenkel Gallery, San Francisco.

p. 264 Toni Morrison, *The Bluest Eye* (New York, 1970).

p. 265 Miwa Yanagi, 'Little Red Riding Hood', 2004, photograph, from the series *Fairy Tales*. Courtesy of the artist.

p. 266 Sally Mann, *Untitled* (#34 Emmett Till Riverbank), 1998, photograph. © Sally Mann.

p. 269 Jacob van Oost the Elder, *Portrait of a Boy Aged Eleven*, 1650, oil on canvas. National Gallery, London.

p. 270 Langston Hughes photographed in front of 'Our Block's Children's Garden', 20 East 127th Street, New York, 1955.

p. 273 Cover of the first issue of *The Brownies' Book*, edited by W.E.B. Du Bois, January 1920. The New York Public Library.

pp. 276–7 Langston Hughes, text and illustration by Arouni, from *Black Misery* (New York, 1969).

p. 278 Jonny Briggs, *The Other Side* (electron micrograph of the indentation of a full stop on my late Grandmother's note pad), 2013, photograph. Courtesy of the artist.